Guess Who's Coming to Dinner *Now*?

American History and Culture

Neil Foley, Kevin Gaines, Martha Hodes, and Scott Sandage
GENERAL EDITORS

Guess Who's Coming to Dinner Now? *Multicultural Conservatism in America*
Angela D. Dillard

Guess Who's Coming to Dinner *Now?*

Multicultural Conservatism in America

ANGELA D. DILLARD

 New York University Press

NEW YORK AND LONDON

NEW YORK UNIVERSITY PRESS
New York and London

Library of Congress Cataloging-in-Publication Data
Dillard, Angela D., 1965–
Guess who's coming to dinner now? : multicultural conservatism
in America / Angela D. Dillard.
p.   cm. — (American history and culture)
Includes bibliographical references and index.
ISBN 0-8147-1939-2 (acid-free paper)
1. Minorities—United States—Political activity. 2. Conservatism—
United States. 3. Pluralism (Social sciences)—United States.
4. United States—Race relations—Political aspects. 5. United
States—Ethnic relations—Political aspects. 6. Politcal culture—
United States. 7. Group identity—Political aspects—United States.
8. United States—Politics and government—1989– 9. United
States—Social conditions—1980–   I. Title. II. American history
and culture (New York University Press)
E184.A1 D46 2001
305.8'00973—dc21   00-011346

New York University Press books are printed on acid-free paper,
and their binding materials are chosen for strength and durability.

Manufactured in the United States of America

10 9 8 7 6 5 4 3 2 1

*To My Mother and Father for Teaching Me
about Life, Love, and Politics*

Contents

Conservative, *n.* A statesman who is enamored of existing evils, as distinguished from the Liberal, who
wishes to replace them with others.

—*Ambrose Bierce,* Devil's Dictionary

The Problem of Definition

A conservative Latino man, a black conser-
vative woman, and a gay Christian conservative . . . this may sound like a
set-up for an off-color joke, but members of such a diverse contingent
could easily pass one another on Capitol Hill, gather for a roundtable
discussion at a public policy think tank, or be seated together at a dinner
gala sponsored by the Republican National Committee. Such occur-
rences happen frequently among the individuals I have labeled "multicultural conservatives." I admit that even this tag began as something of a
joke during a dinner party given by a close friend. I was regaling the
company with stories and anecdotes uncovered while doing preliminary
research for this book and was delighted by their confused and often
horrified expressions. Seeking to get off another zinger at the expense of
my erstwhile companions, I hit upon the idea of describing the existence
of African American, Latino, homosexual, and women conservatives as
"multicultural"—a term generally reserved by common affirmation for
leftists and liberals. This does not mean that women and minority conservatives embrace multiculturalism as an ethic and a philosophy. They
do not. The phrase seemed, however, a perfect (if controversial) way to

designate what they have brought to the post–World War II conservative movement.

The other segment of this book's title is derived, of course, from the 1967 film *Guess Who's Coming to Dinner*, starring Sidney Poitier. Poitier's character, John Prentice, is a distinguished and accomplished doctor specializing in the treatment of tropical diseases who falls in love with the young, white daughter of a crusading liberal newspaper publisher. Released in the same year as the Supreme Court's *Loving* decision, which barred states from prohibiting interracial marriages, the film chronicles the attempts by both families to accept the impending union. While notable for its depiction of interracial love and intimacy, *Guess Who's Coming to Dinner* nonetheless fails to address the dynamics of entrenched racial prejudice and foregrounds class (his prominence, her wealth) to make the possibility of marriage palatable. As the producer Stanley Kramer asserted, Dr. Prentice's status was essential, since neither the woman nor her parents would have been interested in a garage attendant.[1] Hence, the standards it erects for peaceful integration and interracial marriage are deep and wide. Such standards also reflect, at least in part, the positions currently adopted by those women and minority conservatives who believe in the redemptive possibilities of assimilation, individualism, and character—a topic to which I devote a good deal of attention in the following pages.

Having settled on a playful but hopefully thought-provoking title, as I began to write this book I was immediately confronted with the problem of definition. Exactly what, after all, is a conservative in the context of a nation that lacks the basic ingredients of an organic conservative tradition? As Louis Hartz insisted, there is only one definitive political tradition in the United States, and it is decidedly liberal. In his seminal analysis of the connections between social structure and ideology, Hartz maintained that the absence of a feudal heritage and an anti-industrial Right led naturally to the triumph of bourgeois Lockean liberalism that equated the acquisition of private property with the pursuit of happiness. Without a landed aristocracy to overthrow or a landless mob to silence, liberalism reigned supreme and formed the foundation of American political culture.[2] Many self-proclaimed conservatives, however, remain undaunted by such critiques. According to Russell Kirk, to cite just one prominent example, this lack of historical foundation is unimportant, since conservatism is neither a political system nor an ideology. Instead, it is a worldview and a style of thought about society and human nature. In an attempt to circumvent Hartz, Kirk claims that American conservatism is rooted not so much in distinct social and economic structures of the nation as in the realm of ideas.

In his introduction to *The Portable Conservative Reader*, Kirk ventures a basic outline of six foundational principles. The first principle is a belief in a transcendent moral order, be it God or natural law, through which "we ought to try and conform the ways of society"; the second, closely related, is the principle of social continuity, that is, the vision of the "body social" as a "kind of spiritual corporation." Third is the principle of prescription, or the willingness to cherish "the wisdom of our ancestors." The individual is foolish, as Edmund Burke once famously asserted, but the species is wise. Prudence is the fourth guiding principle of conservatism. It encourages the consideration of the probable, long-term consequences that lurk behind any public measure. Thus are conservatives ever on guard against the doctrine of unintended consequences.

Variety comes in fifth on Kirk's list. As distinguished from the artificial egalitarianism of radical systems, variety seeks "the preservation of a healthy diversity" by accepting the necessity of "orders and classes, differences in material conditions, and many sorts of inequalities." And, last but not least, there is imperfectability: the knowledge that human nature suffers from certain innate faults. These deep flaws in our nature ensure that the radical dream of a perfectly just and completely equal social order is hopelessly utopian and doomed to failure. "All that we reasonably can expect," Kirk summarizes, "is a tolerably ordered, just, and free society, in which some evils, maladjustments, and suffering continue to lurk." Which is all well and fine as long as you are not the long-suffering party.[3]

While some may dispute aspects of Kirk's definition—religious conservatives might make additions, libertarians subtractions—it nonetheless suffices as a good basis for discussion. For my part, I find Kirk's description a little too rosy. It skirts first and foremost the embrace of liberal individualism and unfettered capitalism so common to American political thought overall and among the majority of contemporary conservatives. Kirk also obscures the ways in which the American conservative tradition, especially its southern branch, was historically structured by the defense of slavery as an organic social institution, which positioned the male slave owner as paternalistically in charge of his extended household. In the process, white women and enslaved men and women were reduced to the status of children and property.[4] The right to own slaves as property, moreover, was premised, among other things, on the doctrine of States' Rights, which accelerated the fall of Reconstruction and which would become particularly pernicious during the battles over federal civil rights legislation.

In 1956, for instance, one hundred senators and congressional representatives from eleven southern states signed the "Southern Manifesto," proclaiming the landmark *Brown v. Board of Education* ruling an abuse of federal judicial power. "This unwarranted exercise of power by the Court, contrary to the Constitution,

> is creating chaos and confusion in the States principally affected. It is destroying the amicable relations between the white and Negro races that have been created through 90 years of patient effort by the good people of both races. It has planted hatred and suspicion where there has been heretofore friendship and understanding. Without regard to the consent of the governed, outside agitators are threatening immediate and revolutionary changes.[5]

The species is not always wise and is certainly not consistently prudent, particularly when nettlesome issues such as race and gender come into play. Given the extent to which the conservative tradition in America was shaped by racialist and outright racist doctrines, by heterosexual-patriarchal notions of gender and family, and by xenophobic influences, the existence of African American, Latino, women, and homosexual conservatives is that much more fascinating.

Fighting for inclusion in the mainstream of the conservative movement, they have been amply confronted by the legacy of exclusion. At the same time, as I attempt to demonstrate, multicultural conservatism is structured by a series of positions and ideologies that strike me as internally consistent and, at times, even profound. In presenting themselves as public intellectuals and prophets to the nation, multicultural conservatives have sought to alter the course of American conservatism as well as the public discourse around issues of race, ethnicity, gender, and sexuality. While their philosophies are in keeping with some of the definitions of conservatism I have cited, women and minority conservatives have also drawn on the intellectual and political traditions of the communities that shaped them. In the process, they have taught the old dog of conservatism some new tricks.

Throughout, I use a variety of terminologies to describe multicultural conservatives. Most conventionally, I refer to them as "minority" conservatives. Although a number of scholars have raised questions as to the appropriateness of this term, it is nonetheless a convenient catchall for conservatives who are also African American, Latino, and homosexual. I also frequently use the phrase "women and minority" conservatives. This too is by way of convention and is not meant to imply that women and minority are mutually exclusive; there are a good many women conservatives who are black, Latino, or Asian. I have also employed the alternative designations "black," "African American," and "Afro-American," as well as "gay and lesbian" and "homosexual," and "Hispanic" and "Latino." This variance is primarily the result of variance in the language of multicultural conservatives. In general, black conservatives seem to prefer "black" and occasionally "Negro" to "African American," while some Hispanic conservatives adopt political positions that dispute the usage of "Latino" and especially "Chicano."

More substantially, a number of people have questioned my inclusion of women in the category of multicultural conservatism and my exclusion of other ethnic groups, such as Jewish-Americans, Native Americans, and Asian-Americans. In my defense, I argue that to leave out women such as Phyllis Schlafly and Midge Decter would distort the overall picture of the transformation of modern American conservatism, since Right-wing women have been central in critiquing feminism and in developing conservative ideologies and organizations. As for the exclusions, Jews have made important contributions to conservative discourses, and I do reference them in the text. Moreover, a number of neoconservatives—Irving Howe, Irving Kristol, and Nathan Glazer, for example—are Jewish and are fairly well represented throughout. Native American and Asian-American conservatives are cited less frequently.

Public expressions of political conservatism among Native Americans remain relatively rare; and while Asian-American conservatives may bring a distinctive contribution to the party, the burden of dealing with four other categories of individuals simultaneously was already enough of a challenge. But Asian-American conservatives are not completely slighted in these pages; they offer a small but interesting window into the frequently contentious relationships between conservatives and people of color and among conservatives of color themselves, especially over immigration. Additionally, Asian-American conservatives, much like Latino ones, enter into the narrative of and debate about the broader meaning of America in ways most liberals and leftists would no doubt find disturbing. For example, Susan Au Allen, perhaps the most visible Asian-American currently aligned with the Right, deploys a fairly narrow notion of what it means to be an American in her critique of affirmative action as a program that bars white men such as her husband from "equal opportunity, to make room for the blacks, Hispanics, the Native Americans, the Asians, the disabled and women."[6]

Au Allen and others who engage in a politics of assimilation are often regarded as "neoconservatives." While I have tried to employ the term "conservative" consistently, I do, when appropriate, switch to "neoconservative." This term (or "neocon") is commonly used to describe those men and women who came to the conservative movement after rejecting liberal and leftist positions and to distinguish them from older, "paleoconservatives." Noting this migration across the political spectrum, Irving Kristol, perhaps the most prominent neoconservative figure, once described a neoconservative as "a liberal who had been mugged by reality," to explain the transformation of former leftists-turned-conservative. The term is also by and large used to label those who joined the conservative movement and the New Right in the 1970s and early 1980s and who tend to have a political orientation that is more secular than religious, libertarian, and geared toward the defense of free market capitalism.[7]

These ponderous questions of terminology are relatively minor when compared to the overall conceptual difficulties of studying American conservatism. Some scholars have suggested that viewing American political culture through the lens of Left and liberal versus Right and conservative is a practice that sheds more heat than light. In this vein, David Horowitz urges us to move beyond the categories of Left and Right by rediscovering what segments of their constituencies share, namely a "common man" approach in the struggles against the centralization and concentration of power, big business, massive government, bureaucratization, and the disproportionate influence of the professional elite. The various forms of populist insurgency emanating from below, Horowitz argues, have had a much more profound impact on American politics since the late nineteenth century than any political ideologies produced from above.[8] While Horowitz's panoramic study offers some very useful insights, I disagree as to the efficacy of the Left/Right distinction.

The notion of a political spectrum moving from Left to Right still has some analytical and descriptive merit. True, all such categories have a level of instability and fluidity, but as a general framework they continue to shape (and perhaps to distort) the American political landscape. Further, it is hardly unimportant that the Left/Right distinction remains meaningful to those mainstream, multicultural, neoconservative, and paleoconservative persons whose ideas and actions generated the present study. Echoing Louis Hartz's implicit critique of Kirk and others who have labored to construct a tradition of organic conservatism in America, Horowitz does succeed in raising questions about the distinction between radicals and conservatives. Those individuals who have largely abandoned the traditional conservative defense of the status quo and who have adopted a more activist posture toward sweeping change do in fact demonstrate the extent to which the distance between radicals and conservatives (if not Left and Right) has been traversed.

As Paul Weyrich, one of the founders of the New Right, once proclaimed, "We are radicals who want to change the existing power structure. We are not conservatives in the sense that conservative means accepting the status quo."[9] Since the status quo that a good many Americans want to preserve embraces the New Deal and subsequent liberal policies, contemporary conservatives dream, as did the radicals in the 1960s, of creating a new world. This book, then, is about the "radical conservatives" of the New Right. While their views incorporate some of Kirk's principles, they are hardly confined to his pristine definitions. The radical conservatives who emerged in the 1950s and launched their bid for political ascendancy over the subsequent three decades are, as Horowitz suggests, unabashedly populist. In economic terms, they have tended to be libertarian, equating less government intervention in the market and in the lives of ordinary citizens with more freedom and greater prosperity. In social terms, they have tended to condemn the excessively secular and humanist bent of American culture and its corrosive effects on the traditional family, gender roles, and social morality. Here, too, government intervention is blamed for supporting the agenda of feminists, labor unions, liberal elites, and civil rights advocates.

Women, African American, Latino, and homosexual conservatives have entered into the radical conservatism of the New Right in a variety of ways. Some were propelled into the post–World War II conservative movement by anticommunism; others by the expansion of the welfare state; still others by a disillusionment with the Left and with the Democratic Party as well as by the rise of "identity politics." The question of whether they are *really* conservatives is, I think, secondary to the pivotal role they have played by aligning themselves with the New Right and the Republican Party and by working to transform our political culture. In their concerted efforts to delimit the role of the federal government in addressing matters of structural inequality and to cleanse the public sphere of "identity politics" via an enforced blindness to color and other forms of difference, women and minority conservatives have, especially since the 1970s, added a distinctive voice to the chorus against affirmative action, bilingual education, immigration, feminism, and an expansive vision of homosexual rights.

In this regard, this book is not only and not even primarily about conservatism; it is about the ongoing transformation of our public dialogue on the meaning and significance of race, ethnicity, gender, and sexuality. The conservative movement and the New Right are merely the location or site from which women and minority conservatives have waged a campaign against their leftist and liberal counterparts over what the relationship between identity and politics is and should be. Perceiving themselves as populists, radicals, insurgents, and prophets, African American, Latino, women, and homosexual conservatives also aspire, like Weyrich, to change the existing power structure and to transform the status quo. The books, articles, op-ed pieces, autobiographies, monographs, and speeches produced by conservatives constitute the raw materials for this book, and I have tended to take their self-definitions seriously. I would like to thank them all. I bear full responsibility for any unintentional distortions of their views.

Many thanks also to the numerous people who helped me to formulate, clarify, and express my ideas as I struggled with the complexities of multicultural conservatism. For good or ill, the topic elicited a range of passionate feelings and responses. Hence, this book is very much the product of hours and hours of conversation, debate, and argument with friends and colleagues—often over a tumbler of scotch or a pint of beer. Some individuals, including David Roediger and Eugene Genovese, have watched this project grow from its infancy. Others, including Robin Kelley, Neil Foley, George Shulman, Lisa Disch, Barbara Cooper, E. Frances White, Don White, Sharon Friedman, Stephen Stienberg, Vasu Varadhan, Scott McPartland, Randall Halle, Rick Perlstein, and Gerald Early, managed to carve out time from their frightfully busy schedules to offer invaluable advice, criticism, feedback, and encouragement along the way. The quality of the manuscript was also greatly enhanced by the talents of Norma Chanerl, who applied her craft to the final draft. Any failure on my part to heed their advice as well as any error in judgement remain entirely my own.

In a true embarrassment of riches, I have been fortunate enough to have been surrounded by two distinct and supportive communities of faculty, students, and staff: at the University of Minnesota and at New York University, especially within the Gallatin School of Individualized Study (may the Rebel Alliance live long and prosper!). Monthly meetings of the faculty reading group on testimony (including Tricia Rose, Derrick Bell, Fred Moten, Lisa Duggan, Paulette Caldwell, Martha Hodes, Phil Harper, and Robin Kelley) offered a much-needed source of wisdom and solace; along with good friends too numerous to mention by name, they managed to keep me both productive and sane. I am forever in their debt. So, too, with the staff at New York University Press, especially Editor-in-Chief Niko Pfund, whose unfailing belief in me and in this project never ceased to amaze me. Despite a vast array of cranky e-mail messages, self-doubt, and demands, Niko's wit, intellect, and kindness have been constant. Thanks for putting up with me.

I was equally fortunate to receive financial support from the Gallatin School's Faculty Enrichment Fund and from a National Endowment for the Humanities Summer Stipend. This project was also supported in part by a New York University Research Challenge Grant. The love of money may indeed be the root of all evil, but a grant or two sure comes in handy. Finally, I would like to thank my parents, Paul and Marilynn (Adams) Dillard, as well as my extended family, for teaching me, in word and deed, about honesty, integrity, and fairness. This book is dedicated to them in partial repayment for a lifetime of unconditional love.

Introduction

I can pinpoint this book's conception to the day I stumbled upon back issues of the *Lincoln Review* in the library stacks at the University of Michigan. The *Lincoln Review*, I was surprised to discover, is a quarterly journal of black conservative opinion published by, I was equally surprised to discover, the Lincoln Institute for Research and Education, a black conservative think tank in Washington, D.C. At the time—B.C.T. (Before Clarence Thomas)—I was virtually unaware of the existence of *a* black political conservative, let alone an entire cadre of them. I was certainly conscious of social and religious conservatism among African Americans, past and present, and of certain conservative impulses within black nationalist traditions. Yet I knew only vaguely of the work of Thomas Sowell, "the Black Milton Friedman," and regarded him as a quixotic nonconformist and something of a crank. Confronted with the evidence of the *Review*, with volumes stretching back to 1980, I found it difficult to continue my blissful ignorance.

I obsessively mulled over the question of contemporary black conservatism, reading Sowell's work, beginning with *Race and Economics*, published in 1975, and exploring the ideas of a diverse group of conservative authors, including Walter Williams, Anne Wortham, and Glenn Loury. With the nomination and eventual confirmation of Clarence Thomas to the Supreme

Court—a moment that served as a formal introduction of sorts of black conservatives to the American public—my nebulous curiosity congealed into concrete fascination. Slowly, I also came to realize that black conservatism was just the tip of the iceberg. In pursuing the historical and contemporary expressions of black conservatism, I began to find intriguing intersections and parallels among Latino, homosexual, and women conservatives who seemed to be in dialogue with black conservatives, with one another, and, ultimately, with the mainstream of the conservative movement.

In many ways, this conjunction of interests and ideologies appeared to be a recasting of the late 1960s, when leftist representatives of these social groups sought to make a common cause via coalition politics. As Dan T. Carter has observed, historians of the American Left have devoted a good deal of attention to how the civil rights movement influenced other progressive social movements of the 1960s and 1970s, including the second wave of feminism as well as gay and lesbian liberation. Yet, the "counterrevolutionary" effects of these movements are equally important.[1] One of these effects may very well be a coalescing conservative movement among women and minorities, assuming what once happened on the Left side of the political spectrum is now being replicated, to some extent, on the Right.

This book, then, is the product of my own attempts to grapple with a gradual realization that American political conservatism can no longer be viewed, and accurately represented, as the exclusive preserve of white, male, and heterosexual persons with comfortable class positions. Rather, it has become a multicultural affair as the past few decades have witnessed the growth of readily identifiable conservative discourses within African American, Latino, and homosexual communities and among women, both feminist and antifeminist. While there are historical precedents—especially those women and African Americans who have staked out politically conservative positions in the past—I suggest that the recent rise of a *multicultural* conservatism represents a new phenomenon. Indeed, working within scholarly, popular, and political circles, women and minority conservatives have begun to alter irrevocably the tone and complexion of contemporary conservatism.

The primary purpose of this book is to describe, document, and interpret this change within our political culture, as well as to assess the often hostile reception women and minority conservatives have received. In this effort, I have been influenced by a spate of recent studies urging historians of American politics and culture to focus more sustained attention on conservative movements and discourses, particularly among white urban workers in the North and among women from various classes and regions.[2] While these studies have raised provocative new questions and opened up new avenues of inquiry, they have largely ignored conservative tendencies among racial and ethnic minorities and among homosexuals (or "homocons," as they are sometimes referred to).

This lack of attention is not surprising, since, overall, multicultural conservatives have not exactly been embraced with unbridled enthusiasm in many quarters. As a result, their ideas have been underanalyzed. On the one hand, minority and women conservatives are generally marginalized within mainstream conservatism. The vast majority of compendia, monographs and critical studies of the conservative tradition in the United States virtually ignore the contributions of minorities and women,[3] even though the latter have often demonstrated a conservative faith in individualism and "family values," the free market, and the necessity of a limited government without intrusive social policies. They have also sided with the Religious Right on issues such as abortion, school prayer, sex education, and reproductive rights. In actively pursuing policies based on a public "blindness" to color, gender, and other forms of identity, women and minority conservatives have often been in the forefront of the conservative charge against the status quo of modern liberalism. Rivaling the famous multiracial Benetton advertising campaign, multicultural conservatives have presented themselves as poster children for the American Dream of individual upward mobility, proof positive that merit and determination can produce success.

Along with their mainstream allies, they have worked to repeal affirmative action and other race- and gender-conscious policies; to dismantle the welfare state for the sake of the poor; to discredit bilingual education; to stem the tide of special rights for homosexuals; and to counter such supposedly radical and therefore dangerous academic trends as queer theory, afrocentrism, Chicano studies, feminism, and anything else judged to undergird identity politics: a politics engendered by conceiving of individuals as members of oppressed and victimized groups. Despite a fairly impressive track record of swaying public opinion, even when women and minorities are cited or wooed by mainstream conservatives, this recognition tends to take a highly ghettoized form, bounded by what are regarded as exclusively minority and women's issues. Even Clarence Thomas has complained of finding no room at the inn of the New Right: "there was the appearance within conservative ranks that blacks were to be tolerated but not necessarily welcome. There appeared to be the presumption, albeit reputable, that blacks could not be conservative."[4]

On the other hand, minority and women conservatives are often regarded as pariahs within the racial, ethnic, gender, and sexual communities to which they, sometimes grudgingly, belong. They have been dismissed as traitors, as sell-outs, as self-loathing reactionaries who are little more than dupes of powerful white, male, heterosexual conservatives. Some critics have suggested that dark and sinister motivations lurk behind their ideas. In one of the more extreme denunciations, African American critic Amiri Baraka has chided black conservatives for being opportunistic "racists" who "camouflaged themselves as backwards Negroes, [and] who during the '60s upsurge of the Black Liberation Movement were pods growing in the cellars of our politics."[5] Baraka, like many other critics, expresses an inability to comprehend how any "self-respecting black man" (or presumably any Latina woman, any feminist, or any gay man) could be a political conservative. And yet, all of the self-identified conservatives who appear in these pages do in fact evidence highly complex and nuanced subject positions.

"Nuanced" is perhaps too weak a term. A rich diversity exists among women and minority conservatives, incorporating social and religious conservatism, libertarianism, free-market idealism, old-fashioned iconoclasm, and, among African American conservatives, a variant of black nationalism. In fact, some women and minority conservatives express views so individuated that they are loath to be labeled and lumped together at all. In selecting men and women who are in my estimation representative of what might be called the multicultural conservative *style*, I have focused primarily on self-identified conservatives. Some of these individuals are familiar figures: Phyllis Schlafly, founder of the Eagle Forum; Thomas Sowell, Glenn Loury, Walter Williams, Midge Decter, Clarence Thomas; Andrew Sullivan, former editor of the *New Republic*; and William Allen and Linda Chavez, both of whom served on the U.S. Commission on Civil Rights, for instance, need little formal introduction. Nor do increasingly prominent politicians within the Republican Party, especially the Mexican-American Congressman Henry Bonilla (R-Texas); J. C. Watts (R-Oklahoma); Helen Chenoweth (R-Idaho), and perennial presidential candidate Alan Keyes. Others, such as gay conservatives Bruce Bawer, Mel White, Marvin Liebman, and Richard Tafel, currently president of the Log Cabin Republicans; the Latino conservative Al Zapanta, chairman of the National Hispanic Policy Forum; the Asian-American conservatives Susan Au Allen, Matt Fong, and former Representative Jay Kim (R-California); black conservatives Elizabeth Wright, Star Parker, Anne Wortham, and Clarence Mason Weaver; and women conservatives such as Ruth Wisse,

Danielle Crittenden, and Katherine Kersten, director of the Center for the American Experiment in Minneapolis (who characterizes herself as a conservative feminist), are slightly less well known outside conservative circles but have contributed to the growth of multicultural conservatism.

Many of these individuals are involved in and indebted to the intricate institutional infrastructure of the modern conservative movement.[6] Linked by a network of think tanks, foundations, advocacy groups, Republican political action committees, and national and grass-roots organizations, as well as by newsletters, journals, magazines, web sites, and radio talk shows, women and minority conservatives have been awarded enormous access to the corridors of power and the byways of public opinion. Although conservatives are fond of claiming that they have been "silenced" by the liberal cultural and media elite, it is, as one journalist put it, "the loudest silence I ever heard."[7]

The roots of this confluence of interest lay in the mid- to late 1970s. Appalled by the prominence of radical feminists, gay and lesbian liberationists, and advocates of Black and Chicano Power, long-time conservatives and neoconservatives began to form their own organizations. In an early wave of this trend, the Republican National Hispanic Assembly was formed, in 1974, as part of the nascent outreach efforts of the Republican Party. By the late 1970s, new organizations among conservative women, such as Concerned Women for America, founded by Beverly LaHaye in 1979 to fight the influence of the National Organization for Women (NOW), and Anita Bryant's anti-gay Save Our Children, Inc., joined older groups like Phyllis Schlafly's Eagle Forum. Schlafly's ties to the conservative movement stretch back to the immediate post–World War II period. Her first job after finishing graduate school was with the American Enterprise Association (later the American Enterprise Institute) in 1945. Between 1952 and 1964, she ran unsuccessfully for Congress as a Republican and worked with a number of conservative groups. In 1964, her public profile got a considerable boost with the publication of her pro-Goldwater book, *A Choice, Not an Echo*, the bible of the Goldwater movement. After losing a bitter battle for the presidency of the National Federation of Republican Women in 1967, she began publishing *The Phyllis Schlafly Report* on a regular basis and continues to do so. The *Report* facilitated the building of a base of supporters who became the core of STOP-ERA (founded by Schlafly in 1972) and her Eagle Forum (founded in 1975).[8]

While closeted homosexuals, including Marvin Liebman and Mel White, labored to construct the postwar infrastructure of the modern conservative movement and the New Right, the late 1970s also witnessed the appearance of openly gay organizations such as the Concerned Republicans for Individual Rights, the Chicago Area Republican Gay Organization, and, in 1978, the Log Cabin Republicans (LCR). The genesis of the LCR grew out of the first Lincoln Clubs, organized in large part by Frank Ricchiazzi in response to a campaign against a California gay rights bill. Other clubs began to sprout up around the country and finally affiliated as the LCR.[9] That same year, 1978, J. A. Parker founded the Lincoln Institute, still the nation's leading black conservative think tank. Parker had previously worked with such mainstream conservative groups as the Young Americans for Freedom and in efforts to elect Goldwater in 1964.[10] He also worked as a Reagan volunteer in 1968 and 1976. In 1970, Parker established a consulting firm and continued to function as part of the conservative network, holding symposia on free enterprise zones, conducting a study of blacks and organized labor, and, for a time, representing the South African tribal homeland, the Transkei. (As with many black conservatives, his international anticommunism manifested itself most predominantly in relation to the African continent.) In 1980, he served as the Reagan transition team leader for the Equal Employment Opportunity Commission (EEOC) and, through the Lincoln Institute, helped to increase the visibility of other black conservatives, including Clarence Pendleton, Jr. (who went on to become chairman of the U.S. Commission on Civil Rights before his death in 1988) and Thomas Sowell.

In 1980, Sowell, along with Henry Lucas, the first black person to serve on the Republican National Committee, organized the Black Alternatives Conference, with significant funding from the network and the endorsement of high-ranking officials in the new Reagan White House. In bringing together black and white conservatives, Black Alternatives helped give shape and substance to their positions on race and society. It also provided a clear political alternative to leftists and liberals—a development much desired by the Reagan administration.[11] Indeed, the election of Ronald Reagan and the emergence of the Reagan Revolution was a boon for women and minority conservatives, especially in terms of political appointments. Clarence Thomas, who has acknowledged his intellectual debt to Sowell, served as assistant secretary for civil rights in the Department of Education from 1981 to 1982 and as chairman of the EEOC from 1982 to 1990. Latina conservative Linda Chavez, who began her career as a liberal aide on Capitol Hill and drifted rightward during her seven years in the employ of Albert Shanker, president of the American Federation of Teachers, eventually gained the attention of the Reagan administration with her writings in neoconservative journals. In 1983 she was selected to direct the Commission on Civil Rights and was subsequently brought to the White House as director of the Office of Public Liaison.

"Much of the analysis is finally bringing to light the dirty secret that Asians are truly a minority of a different color," exults *Asian Week* columnist Arthur Hu in jubilant tones, "they're !@#$% conservative." Well, yes and no. The development of a conservative contingent among Asian-Americans has been slow and sporadic but, as Hu suggests, shows signs of growth. Hu himself has been a big part of the process. He was the principal author of a 1989 complaint to the U.S. Department of Education that led to a federal investigation of the admission systems at the University of California at Berkeley and at UCLA. The complaint charged those institutions with establishing a quota system that discriminated against Asian-Americans and other qualified applicants. Like other conservative Asian-Americans, Hu backed the efforts to pass the anti–affirmative action California Civil Rights Initiative; favors probusiness, profamily, and antibilingual legislation; and, given that most Asians immigrate legally, offers, albeit typically cautious, support for measures against illegal immigrants.[12]

Hu is hardly alone. The former Democrat James Fang, whose wealthy family owns *Asian Week*, the San Francisco *Independent*, and a large venture capital corporation, changed his party affiliation in the late 1980s when Lee Atwater, then chairman of the Republican National Committee (RNC), publically appealed to him to cross over. Atwater had good reason to believe the switch was possible, since Fang's late father had cultivated ties to the GOP and his mother had served as a small-business commissioner in the Bush administration. Although Fang has yet to seek national office, he obtained a mayoral appointment as San Francisco's international trade director in 1991 and is presently director of the Bay Area Rapid Transit (BART) commission.[13] A family connection has also been influential in the political career of Matt Fong, whose mother, March Fong Eu, a well-known liberal Democrat, was California's secretary of state from 1974 to 1988. Matt Fong has banked on his mother's name recognition and her political connections. She declined to work on his losing run for state comptroller in 1990 and on his winning one for state treasurer in 1994. March Fong Eu was, however, an outspoken and vigorous advocate during his unsuccessful attempt to unseat Senator Barbara Boxer (D-California), a seat that had also eluded Fong Eu in 1988. Like Fang, Matt Fong remains an important voice for Asian-Americans inside the Republican Party and serves as an adviser to George W. Bush's presidential campaign in California.[14]

The most popular and well-known Asian-American conservative is, by far, Susan Au Allen. Raised in Hong Kong and educated in Catholic schools, she came to the United States in 1970 after her work with drug addicts came to the notice of the Nixon White House. At the urging of Elliott Richardson, Nixon's Secretary of Health, Education and Welfare, she decided to stay and pursue a J.D. at Antioch followed by an LL.M. in international law at Georgetown. In 1984 she was recruited to head the newly formed U.S. Pan Asian American Chamber of Commerce, a nonprofit business association designed to connect Asian-American entrepreneurs with more established business in the United States and abroad. Already well connected in Washington and in the international business community, Au Allen came to the attention of a wider public with a 1993 *USA Today* article in which she advocated the application of the "Asian technique of shame" to violent criminals in the United States: "In China, murderers are [tarred, feathered, and] put on flatbed trucks and driven around towns so citizens can express their outrage and contempt." Since then she has become a much sought-after pundit, appearing, for instance, on programs such as *To the Contrary* and offering an alternative voice to more established civil rights groups such as the Organization for Chinese Americans and the Japanese American Citizens League.[15]

Her testimony against Bill Lann Lee at his 1998 Senate Judiciary Committee confirmation hearing for the post of assistant attorney general for civil rights helped to derail Lee's permanent appointment. "Mr. Lee will advocate certain policies on race and gender issues that are contrary to the provision of equal rights and opportunity for all," she told the Committee. Lee's support for affirmative action and other programs "that have and will continue to have a deleterious effect on racial and gender harmony in general" was the primary focus of her ire. While such statements have only increased the animosity between Au Allen and Asian-American leftists and liberals, they have also won her the support of other conservatives such as Elaine Chou, a distinguished fellow at the Heritage Foundation, and the policy analyst John Liu.[16]

Although Asian-American conservatives are less publically involved in the Religious Right, its organizations—Traditional Values Coalition, Focus on the Family, Family Research Council, Concerned Women for America, the National Right to Life Committee, and others—offer additional venues for women and other conservatives of color. While individual fundamentalists, such as Jerry Falwell and Pat Robertson, and national religious organizations, such as the Southern Baptist Convention, were staunchly opposed to the civil rights movement in the 1950s and 1960s and to much of the civil rights agenda thereafter (including affirmative action and the application of sanctions against South Africa's apartheid regime), segments of the contemporary Religious Right pointedly reach out to African Americans and Latinos. The Promise Keepers, for example, which bisects both the Men's Movement and the New Right, gives a place of pride to "racial reconciliation." While men of color represent less than 10 percent of the massive stadium audiences at Promise Keepers events, they constitute half or more of the featured speakers and singers.[17]

Similarly, the Christian Coalition has in the past decade made direct overtures to African Americans and Latinos as well as to Catholics and Jews. The Reverend Earl Jackson, a Harvard-educated lawyer and former Boston talk-show host, currently serves as the Coalition's national liaison to African American churches.[18] Kay Coles James, another highly visible figure, has long-standing ties to the Religious Right. She was formerly a spokesperson for the National Right to Life Committee and a ranking official in the Family Research Council. During the Bush administration, she was appointed assistant secretary for public affairs at the U.S. Department of Health and Human Services and is presently dean of the Robertson School of Government at Regent's University, an institution of higher learning founded by Pat Robertson.[19] Along with Star Parker, a former (self-described) "welfare queen" turned Christian conservatives whose entrance into the Religious Right's network was mediated through her work with the Traditional Values Coalition, James is a sought-after speaker for conferences, symposia, and less formal gatherings.[20]

Besides Jackson, James, and Parker, individuals such as Representative J. C. Watts, Alan Keyes, journalist Armstrong Williams, and Roy Innis, executive director of the Congress of Racial Equality, have also received warm welcomes at Religious Right events. All invoke the centrality of religious commitment and an active faith in both American and African American culture. Uniting the particular and the universal, these black conservatives can be likened to their Catholic and Jewish counterparts. They draw explicitly on religious traditions that, while not necessarily perfectly aligned with fundamentalism and conservative evangelicalism, nonetheless provide the raw moral and cultural materials essential in formulating perspectives on issues ranging from abortion (a sin and a moral travesty on par with slavery and racial genocide) to capitalism (consistent with God's plan for his creation). Like Kay Coles James, they position themselves as "a strategic presence for Christ in the public sector."[21]

A number of things are important about this overview. First, the growth of this network of multicultural conservatives was wholly dependent on the existing infrastructure of the mainstream conservative movement and its impressive level of institutional progress in the 1970s.[22] Minority conservatives either held positions at established think tanks or had their independent efforts amply founded by conservative foundations. Sowell, for instance, was (and is) a senior fellow at the Hoover Institute. The black conservative Alan Keyes was a resident scholar at the American Enterprise Institute (AEI). Keyes was also former assistant secretary of state for international affairs before he entered the political arena during a 1988 run for the Senate. He served as head of the Citizens Against Government Waste and is founder and chairman of the Declaration Foundation.[23] Before founding the National Center for Neighborhood Enterprises in 1981, Robert Woodson was also an AEI fellow. Prior to his political conversion, Woodson was a liberal civil rights activists and served as an Urban League official from 1971 to 1977. The AEI also housed Jeane Kirkpatrick, before she was selected as Reagan's ambassador to the United Nations, while Midge Decter, currently director of the Committee for the Free World, sits on the board of the Heritage Foundation. Moreover, few conferences, symposia, and publications geared toward women and minorities fail to receive financial and moral support from the network.

Second, the majority of women and minority conservatives have ties to the Republican Party. While "conservative" and "Republican" are by no means interchangeable, the Republican Party, particularly during the Reagan and Bush years, functioned as a focal point for conservative efforts to win elective office and to pursue conservative legislation. Like Keyes, Linda Chavez also ran, unsuccessfully, in Maryland for the Senate. Keyes has gone on to run for president as an extreme prolife candidate in 1996 and again in the 1999–2000 primary season. In 1990, Representative Gary Franks became the first black Republican elected to Congress since 1932; he was followed by J. C. Watts in 1994. The party has also been an important venue for gay Republicans. The Log Cabin Republicans' Frank Ricchiazzi became, in 1982, the first openly gay Republican in California to sit in the state legislature. Efforts to organize the gay and lesbian contingent within the Reagan administration and the party under the name Concerned Americans for Individual Rights failed after the *New York Times* reported on their first meeting.[24] But, in 1986, Reagan hired gay

Republican Bob Kabel, a former aide to Tennessee governor Winfield Dunn, as his liaison to the Senate.

By the 1990s, women and minority conservatives were an even larger presence in electoral politics. Representative Steven Gunderson of Wisconsin—fiscally conservative, socially moderate, openly gay after being outed on the floor of the House by Bob Dornan—served from 1981 until his retirement in 1996,[25] while key positions are still maintained by Representatives Henry Bonilla (elected in 1992) and Senator Ben Nighthorse Campbell, the rare Native American Republican, also elected in 1992 and the first Native American of any political persuasion to serve in the Senate in over 60 years. In 1994 alone, seven Republican women were elected to Congress.[26] And this list does not even begin to account for the numbers of women and minority conservative elected to local offices.

Third, this network serves as a space for sharing nonfinancial resources to increase the public profile of African American, Latino, homosexual, and women conservatives. Not only do they frequently publish in mainstream conservative journals, including the *National Review, Public Interest, Commentary, Reason, First Things, Jewish World Review,* and *The Weekly Standard,* they also have established their own journals and newsletters. Black conservatives, for instance, have founded the *Lincoln Review* as well as *Issues and Views,* which has an economic-black nationalist bent, and *Headway* (formerly *National Minority Politics*). The *Phyllis Schlafly Report* stands alongside publications such as *Women's Quarterly* and *Ex Femina,* both published by the Independent Women's Forum, a newer conservative women's advocacy group. Most multicultural conservative organizations, like their mainstream counterparts, have their own newsletters to keep members current on activities and events. As cyberspace continues to present an accessible avenue for the exchange of information, more and more groups have established web sites, complete with links from one to another. One could spend the better part of a day jumping from site to site with remarkable ease.

Finally, in both the virtual and the physical world, the conservative network constitutes a shared communal space of support and encouragement. Any social or political movement that hopes to maintain itself and to increase its size must establish a movement culture with "free spaces"[27] to work out strategies, to mourn defeats, and to celebrate victories. There is some evidence that such a culture has begun to emerge among women and minority conservatives. Religious conservatives cultivate a "culture of opposition" via local churches, grass-roots organizations, and state and national conventions to create a movement culture. Despite tensions generated by race and ethnicity (for the movement culture remains predominantly white), as well as by denominational diversity (for the movement also remains largely Protestant), Catholics, Jews, and conservatives of color participate in the shared language of God and country.

Compelled by a desire to defend traditional values in the face of a secular humanist onslaught, they rely on their communal convictions to right the moral wrongs into which America has lapsed. They also envision themselves as a persecuted minority in the tradition of Martin L. King, Jr., and the civil rights movement and Cesar Chavez and the United Farm Workers of America.[28] By making these types of symbolic connections, the Christian Coalition has proven itself more adept than most at seeking to mobilize a shared language designed to mediate between the different lives of men, women, whites, blacks, Latinos, Jews, and Christians. Articulated through a "strategic vagueness," in which differences "come together within an emotional resonance under the umbrella of a relatively simple political framework," distinctions of race, ethnicity, and disparate religious identity are simultaneously invoked, symbolically, and masked, ideologically.[29]

This passionate simplification is also at work among secular conservatives, Republican moderates, and libertarians, where the shared language is informed by American "civil religion" with its appeal to individual rights (and responsibilities) and to public assimilation into the common culture of the nation without regard to race, creed, ethnicity, gender, or sexuality. Virtually excluded from the culture (if not necessarily the impetus behind shared language) of religious conservatives, homosexual conservatives tend to find relatively more comfort within this wing of the movement. One small but significant example of community building in this sphere is the Lincoln Leadership Award for Civic Virtue dinner, sponsored by the Log Cabin Republicans and honoring Ward Connerly for his efforts to defeat affirmative action in California. Held on February 12, 1997, in Washington, D.C., this well-attended celebration featured congratulatory speeches by leading conservative intellectual Michael Novak as well as by Robert Woodson, Newt Gingrich, and the LCR's Richard Tafel. In his long acceptance speech, Connerly made a point of thanking his numerous supporters and allies, including the Log Cabin Republicans, saying: "This award symbolizes the bond I have formed with Log Cabin Republicans. . . . We are joined at the hip."[30]

This is not to suggest there are not demonstrable tensions and conflicts within either the Religious Right or the New Right more broadly conceived. The conservative movement, overall, is predominantly white and

Christian and has, in both the past and the present, used racism, ethnocentrism, homophobia, and anti-Semitism to shape its narrative about the perils that confront American society and to achieve its goals. Yet, because conservatives, from the Christian Coalition to the Log Cabin Republicans, afford women and minority conservatives the opportunity to assent to a fairly ahistorical notion of national belonging, multicultural conservatives can, as a result and despite their more obvious differences from the mainstream of the movement, appeal to a collective vision of themselves as crusading rebels against the federal government and the cultural elite to explain their motivations.

Whether or not this ideological tendency, united by a broadly defined style of thought, a network of affiliated organizations, and a shared language, will coalesce into a full-blown political coalition remains to be seen. As with most emergent political movements, there is a core of true believers, or "card-carrying" members, as well as a contingent of fellow travelers who lend their considerable talents in often indirect ways. Hence, this book also engages the philosophies of individuals such as Richard Rodriguez, who has quite vocally refused the conservative moniker, as well as intellectuals such as Stephen Carter, Orlando Patterson, Katie Roiphe, Elizabeth Fox-Genovese, and Stanley Crouch. I gladly apologize up front for taking certain liberties with those whom I have classified as fellow travelers. While I want to respect their much-vaunted independence, I also want to recognize their contributions to constructing and legitimizing dissident, oppositional ideologies that have found a home, however problematic, within the mainstream conservative movement.

Finding a home—politically, ideologically, socially—is a recurring theme in this book, especially since so many multicultural conservatives have expressed feelings of marginalization. Whether they label themselves as "dissenters," as "conscientious objectors" to left-liberal orthodoxies, or as the vanguard of a new political consciousness, to be an African American and a conservative or a Latino who is also a conservative and a homosexual is to have an intriguing problem. For many, such combinations of identities and ideologies are inherently oxymoronic. Hence, in contrast to their white, male, and heterosexual counterparts, women and minority conservatives are continuously called upon to provide justifications of not only their political philosophies but their very existence as well. It is less than shocking, therefore, that, in the process of defining themselves and defending their politics, many women and minority conservatives have turned to history as a source of authenticity, authority, and legitimation.

Although I tend to be most interested in the post–World War II period and, more narrowly, the period since 1970, this book incorporates a broader historical dimension in two ways. First, I consider the various appeals to history and tradition found in the writings of women and minority conservatives. For instance, as Cynthia Kinnard documents in painstaking detail, antifeminism among women has a long history and constitutes a rich tradition to be appealed to by contemporary women.[31] Similarly, black conservatives have argued that African American culture has historically embodied a strong proclivity toward social conservatism and have laid claim to noted figures, including Booker T. Washington, Marcus Garvey, Zora Neale Hurston, and even Malcolm X as historical forebears. Even among Latino and gay and lesbian conservatives, there is an inclination to look back to and seek to reclaim a lost "Golden Age" of politics, an age dominated by a supposed consensus around the desirability of assimilation not as members of an artificially contrived cultural minority but as individuals, as citizens, as Americans.

This assimilationist sensibility, the argument goes, was derailed by the "destructive generation" of the 1960s.[32] And the vast majority of women and minority conservatives have been exceedingly critical of what is to their minds the excessive radicalism of liberationist movements among blacks, feminists, homosexuals, and Latinos. During this tumultuous period, conservatives believe, the demand for civil rights within a limited constitutional framework, along with acceptance of the necessity of cultural assimilation, gave way to calls for special preferences and a crippling dependency on the federal government's handouts. Hence, a major component of the multicultural conservative style urges a rethinking of this historical moment to encourage a new recognition of its shortcomings, as well as its negative impact on women and minorities.

There is a constant tension, it seems to me, between the parochial and the universalist thrust in this revisioning of history. That is to say, multicultural conservatives want to speak only as Americans, as individuals. Yet they are constantly forced to concede that the power of their critiques relies heavily on their socially constructed identities, despite the novelty of their political identities as conservatives. They speak not only as conservatives but, more important, as *conservative African Americans, Latinos, women,* and *homosexuals.* Political necessities dictate a fairly constant performance of these multiple identities. Cognizant of this dynamic, women and minority conservatives come close to exchanging one form of identity politics for another. Their value to the mainstream conservative movement resides not merely and not primarily in their conservatism but in their ability and willingness to speak to and for other women and minorities. As Barbara Leeden, executive director of the Independent Women's Forum, observed, "You can't have white guys saying you don't need affirmative action."[33]

Multicultural conservatives have positioned themselves as the true inheritors of *particular* intellectual pedigrees, while simultaneously striving to write themselves into the *general* sweep of the American conservative tradition. In this vein, the pervasive insistence that the "radical sixties" created a nightmarish monster that devoured an older ethic of assimilation stands them in good stead with the mainstream of the movement. "What emerged during the past few decades is no longer a civil rights 'movement' at all," argues Clint Bolick, a prominent white conservative attorney and head of the Institute for Justice, "but an establishment dedicated to perpetuating itself and expanding its power."[34] At least on this point, there is wide agreement among mainstream and multicultural conservatives. Still, the stakes are higher for women and minority conservatives. In their desire to convince women and minorities of the rightness (pardon the pun) of this proposition, multicultural conservative ideologies raise provocative questions about the connections between identity and politics, the claims of cultural authenticity, and whether there can ever be one single proper posture toward oppositional political struggles.

I also consider history as a partial explanation for the rise of a multicultural conservatism in the last few decades. In this regard, Amiri Baraka touched on the crucial relationship between the political upsurges of the late 1960s and the subsequent (re)articulation of a conservative critique. Baraka may be overly churlish in characterizing black conservatives as "pods growing in the cellars of our politics," but his statement does accurately portray the late 1960s and early 1970s as a period of fermentation for conservatives. While incorporating older traditions, contemporary conservatism is indeed a social product of recent American history. In a profound way, the existence of multicultural conservatism is indebted to the very movements its devotees reject. For instance, it is hard to imagine conservative women who hold prominent political positions and have high-powered careers without the prior success of feminism and the women's movement. Of course, even Margaret Thatcher could, without any apparent recognition of the irony, urge women to return to and to remain in the home.

Scholars such as Cornel West and Susan Faludi have tied present-day African American and women conservatives, respectively, to the "backlash" against leftist politics, embodied in the platforms of George Wallace, Barry Goldwater, and, ultimately, Ronald Reagan.[35] If it is hard to image conservative women without feminism, it is equally difficult to fathom their existence divorced from a brand of conservatism that capitalized on the fear of gender equity. The conservative counterrevolution employed gendered issues such as the Equal Rights Amendment, abortion rights, and the decline of the nuclear family as part of the ideological glue of the New Right. Rosalind Pollack Petchesky goes so far as to argue that if there is anything "new" about the current conservative movement in the United States, "it is its tendency to locate sexual, reproductive, and family issues at the center of its political program—not as manipulative rhetoric only, but as the substantiative core of a politics geared, on a level that outdistances any previous right-wing movements in this country, to mobilizing a nationwide mass following."[36]

Both exciting and capitalizing on anxieties about gender and gender relations, conservatives also profited from anxieties about race—busing, affirmative action, racial redistricting, and "forced" desegregation—as well as sexuality to further cement the movement. In the words of Ralph Reed, Jr., former executive director of the Christian Coalition, "issues of abortion and gay rights have been important in attracting activists and building coalitions."[37] It is precisely this intersection of issues and the intense debates they have generated that has defined a seemingly new brand of American conservatism. Likewise, this intersection is key in structuring my examination of the dynamic interplay and cross-fertilization of ideas among the four groups of individuals I identify under the rubric "multicultural conservatism." It is also important in my efforts to chart the ways their ideas intersect with, influence, and challenge the general tenor of mainstream conservatism. Although there have been some attempts to understand the conservative impulses among women and within African American, Latino, and homosexual communities separately, no similar attempt to bring together the historical and contemporary diversity of American conservatism in one book has been made. Only from a comparative perspective, however, can the phenomenon of multicultural conservatism become fully intelligible as an interlocking set of ideological, philosophical, and cultural propositions that cuts across the boundaries of race, ethnicity, gender, and sexuality.

While it is essential to explore connections between black, Latino, women, and homosexual conservatives, my interest in conservatism among African Americans tends to dominate key sections of my narrative. Along with conservative women, about whom a good deal has been written, black conservatives are a large contingent among the ranks of multi-cultural conservatives. Hence, I begin where I began years ago in the library stacks at U of M: with the challenge of understanding black conservatism. The first chapter, "Malcolm X's Words in Clarence Thomas's Mouth: Black Conservatives and the Making of an Intellectual Tradition," considers efforts among contemporary African American conservatives to construct their own distinctive historical and intellectual "canon."

When Clarence Thomas told a reporter he could not "see how the civil rights people today can claim Malcolm X as one of their own," because Malcolm X never said "black people should be begging the Labor Department for jobs," he touched off a storm of criticism from nonconservative scholars and politicians unwilling to have the legacy of Malcolm X spread quite so thin.[38] Thomas's statement is nonetheless indicative of the larger process of canon building by many black conservatives who attempt to root themselves squarely within the history of African American social and political thought. Implicitly recognizing that intellectual traditions are made, not found, and that they are the result of selective interpretation and, therefore, always open to re-invention, black conservatives and their fellow travelers have been steadily mustering arguments for their slice of a usable past.

This process, and the debates it has engendered, raises a number of provocative questions. What, for example, constitutes the political litmus test for inclusion in a black conservative canon? Just how conservative does one have to be? Who gets written in, and why? Who gets written out, and how? More broadly, was Thomas's adoption and adaptation of Malcolm X a positive marker of the flexibility and multivalence of African American political thought, or was it, as many have suggested, an act of self-interested misappropriation and corruption? How do we decide? Who, for that matter, is "we"? Further, does the existence of an African American conservative canon, even in its present decentralized and amorphous state, represent a crisis within African American politics, as some have argued, or does it, as I will suggest, merely represent the latest in a long line of debates structured around competing ideologies of identity, cultural authenticity, and strategies for economic, political, and social advancement?

The first chapter broaches these questions of claiming historical legacies and appealing to political and cultural inheritance; the second broadens the focus of my investigation to include the intersections among black, Latino, homosexual, and women conservatives as well as their coalition with the mainstream conservative movement. Chapter 2, "Toward a Politics of

Assimilation: Multicultural Conservatism and the Assault on the Civil Rights Establishment," explores the ways in which the critique of the post–1965 civil rights movement by black conservatives and their white mainstream allies has fueled a multifaceted attack on civil rights liberalism. By convention, the study of oppositional modes of consciousness and struggle has been most generally applied to those individuals and groups aligned with the Left. It is easier to think of groups such as ACT-UP and Queer Nation as inherently oppositional, but much harder to transfer this characterization to the conservative-homosexual Log Cabin Republicans. But what actually constitutes an oppositional political philosophy and strategy? What, exactly, is being opposed? To answer these questions I argue that one of the major themes that appears in the writings of African American, Latino, homosexual, and women conservatives is an unrelenting critique of and opposition to what is commonly referred to as the "civil rights establishment." This is also an arena through which Asian-American conservatives such as Arthur Hu and Susan Au Allen have made a distinctive contribution.

In his recent book *The End of Racism*, Dinesh D'Souza identifies the civil rights establishment as a "community of tens of thousands of people whose full-time job it is to promote civil rights. The civil rights establishment includes staffers at the Equal Employment Opportunity Commission, state government affirmative action officers, corporate and university diversity personnel, and the employees of the myriad private and public interest groups, all of whom work in concert to shape and enforce civil rights laws." D'Souza and his fellow conservatives envision a political world in which various organizations, from the NAACP and La Raza to the National Organization for Women and ACT-UP, work in collusion to subvert democracy and government, to silence (conservative) opposition, and to enrich themselves.[39]

In response, women and minority conservatives have mounted a concerted attack on the policies and power of the civil rights establishment—and the ideological orthodoxy said to support it—by claiming to speak on behalf of the silent and silenced majority of African Americans, Latinos, Asian-Americans, women, and homosexuals. This recasting of the strategy enlisted so successfully by Richard Nixon allows multicultural conservatives to insist that they are in fact much more representative of majority opinion than their leftist and liberal counterparts. One of the earliest contemporary expressions of this idea flowed from the pen of black economist Thomas Sowell, who has critiqued not only the institutional manifestations of the civil rights establishment but its vision as well.[40] According to Sowell and other conservatives, the very charge of racism, sexism, and discrimination has become a profitable industry that serves not the poor or disenfranchised but the leadership of the civil rights establishment itself to the detriment of the groups they claim to represent and of society as a whole.

While African American conservatives have been central in developing this critique, women, Latino, and homosexual conservatives have added their own distinctive voices to the chorus. Ruth Wisse has chided the women's movement for "contriving to define me as a member of a handicapped species" and has therefore "deprived me of my dignity and misrepresented my aims." Similarly, Linda Chavez has written that "the entitlements of the civil rights era encouraged Hispanics to maintain their language and culture, their separate identity, in return for the rewards of being members of an officially recognized minority group," and, because of this, "assimilation gave way to Affirmative Action." There is also a homosexual version of this critique that, like Chavez's, places the goal of assimilation over the benefits of differentiation, since, as Bruce Bawer has reasoned, "the aspirations of most homosexuals lie in precisely the opposite direction: More than anything else, we want people to see past the 'gay' label, and past whatever associations that label may carry in their minds, and to view us as individuals."[41]

Among Asian-American conservatives of different ethnic heritages and national origins, the point is, similarly, not to be like blacks and adopt an artificial group identity that bars the path to full assimilation. Enshrining the 1965 Civil Rights Act as well as the liberalization of immigration restrictions passed the same year, Au Allen has maintained: "The truth is America knows that a person is what a person makes out of himself or herself, not what color the person's skin." Further, invoking "Asian values" of hard work, thrift, and family, she wants us to believe a conservative brand of politics "actually represents the majority" of Asians in America.[42]

The assault on the establishment helps to define what multicultural conservatives are against. It also facilitates a fuller understanding of what they are for, namely a return to an older political paradigm guided by assimilation, individualism, and free-market capitalism. According to conservatives, the way out of our present morass entails depoliticizing race, ethnicity, gender, sexual orientation, and, to some extent, class in the public arena. Implicitly rejecting the notion that the personal is or should be the political and that public and private constitute a seamless whole, conservatives have urged a decoupling of these "separate spheres." Civil society—where ideally citizens meet as individuals and equals in the eyes of the law—needs to be, in essence, decontaminated from the private concerns of women and minority groups. (Of course, this dichotomy between private and public concerns is never as neat as it seems, as the case of abortion and reproductive rights demonstrates.) All the state need do is guarantee an equal opportunity to all citizens, not an equality of results.

This individualist ethic tends to deemphasize the realities of structural barriers to advancement, especially for African Americans, Latinos, and the poor, and to focus instead on heavily privatized strategies for individual and group reform, or "self-help" in a more common parlance. Hence, one hears a great deal about raising the "civilizational" level of the African American community to combat the culture of poverty and dependency and about making women stronger and more competitive in a male world and much less about harnessing the power of the federal government and even the public political will to solve social problems. It is the individual and not society who is in need of further restructuring. Legislative gains have already been secured. The doors to achieving the "American Dream" via merit and hard work are, conservatives repeatedly assert, open to us all. We need only rely on ourselves (and our private support networks) to walk through. The last remaining barriers, moreover, are mostly those erected by excessive government intervention in the workings of the free market. Affirmative action and welfare, along with minimum wage, cumbersome regulation of small businesses, tax disincentives, and closed shops must be done away with. Deregulating public education, especially through voucher schemes, stands alongside right-to-work legislation as further necessary corrective policies to allow character and the free market to work their magic.[43]

The critique of the civil rights establishment, which relies so heavily on public "blindness" to race, gender, sexual orientation, and even class, functions as yet another shared space among multicultural conservatives. It also functions as a position from which they have been able to exert a good deal of influence on mainstream conservatives, and on American political culture and public policy as well. The impact of the multicultural conservative style is undeniable. By positioning themselves within the ranks of the Right as both diehard devotees and lukewarm fellow travelers, in both subtle and overt ways they have been steadily expanding the boundaries of the sayable. To be able to preface potentially racist and sexist remarks with the phrase "As Thomas Sowell says . . ." or "As Linda Chavez has argued . . ." is to be able to cannibalize the moral authority of minority voices while skirting responsibility. The presence of women and minorities within the ranks of the movement has also helped to humanize and soften its rhetoric. By saying it first, multicultural conservatives have primed the pump for others.

The multicultural conservative critique of the civil rights establishment also raises the question of how women and minorities should be represented and by whom. By claiming to speak for the silent majority within their communities, women and minority conservatives have characterized themselves as more authentic than their leftist and liberal adversaries. To get at the crux of these concerns, the third chapter, "I Write Myself, Therefore I Am: Multicultural Conservatism and the Political Art of Autobiography," concentrates more narrowly on the questions of identity and authenticity. The focus here is not so much on public policy debates but on how multicultural conservatives have conceptualized and presented their public selves. Because so many minority and women conservatives have been so often denounced as traitors to their race, ethnic culture, gender, and sexual orientation, the style and substance of their autobiographical statements is a fruitful site of inquiry. Moreover, their appeals to cultural authenticity and to personal experience provide an important foundation for their political positions, reinscribing, somewhat ironically, connections between the personal and the political, the private and the public.

The manner in which minority conservatives choose to construct their life stories in their autobiographies is also key to a fuller understanding of the challenges they represent to both the Left and the Right. Bruce Bawer addresses this question in his semiautobiographical text *A Place at the Table: A Gay Life in America*. "Because I happen to be gay," Bawer writes, "the far right expects me to keep my personal life a deep, dark secret, while the far left expects me to buy into its entire political platform or risk being designated a 'self-hating' homosexual."[44] Like many minority conservatives, Bawer rejects the imposed dichotomy between identity and ideology and chooses to map out a space of his own. In the autobiographical writings of homosexual conservatives such as Bawer, of African American conservatives such as George Schuyler and Star Parker, of Latino conservatives such as Richard Rodriguez, what emerges are political identities that do not fit comfortably into any preexisting categories. Not all of them are conservative to the same degree or in the same ways; there exists among them no single party line. Yet each of them has had to confront the same sort of double-bind of identity and politics articulated by Bawer, and each has used that confrontation as a source of political critique.

Although the first three essays are centered more fully on race and ethnicity, gender and sexuality have been equally important in the ideas of multicultural and mainstream conservatism. The fourth chapter, "Strange Bedfellows: Gender, Sexuality, and 'Family Values,'" focuses on the fissures that have been created within the New Right by issues such as homosexual marriage and lifestyles and the disintegration of the family under the "burden" of divorce and female-headed households. Along with their mainstream counterparts, African American, Latino, and women conservatives have pointed to the social and cultural necessity of rebuilding and strengthening the family; this cause has been central to the political project of the Religious Right. Homosexual conservatives, however, have found their own call for inclusion in the institution of marriage to be the subject of some derision within the conservative movement. In this and other ways, the relationship of homosexual conservatives to the mainstream of the movement is much more problematic than that of women and racial and ethnic minorities. Their response to the Religious (and secular) Right's divisive use of the AIDS epidemic and the politics of sexuality is thus of particular import.

As Chris Bull and John Gallagher maintain, the gay movement and the Religious Right have been perfect enemies in the political and culture wars of the 1990s.[45] Given this reality, where, then, can or should homosexual conservatives stand? In the debates over what the family is or should be, gender relations and the question of sexual orientation have become explosive issues, pitting conservative women against feminists and homosexual conservatives against the Religious Right on the one hand and "queer theorists" (many of whom view marriage as an inherently heterosexist institution) on the other. Beyond the ongoing debates over gay and lesbian marriage, this chapter also assesses attempts by the Religious Right to reach out to minority communities, especially African Americans and Latinos, by using homosexuality as a wedge issue. As the use of the documentary *Gay Rights, Special Rights* (a piece of political propaganda that warns African Americans about how homosexuals have appropriated the trappings of their movement) reveals, sexuality has become a site around which the nonlibertarian segment of the conservative movement is attempting to erect a diverse coalition. "Many important white conservative organizations," writes the Heritage Foundation's Adam Meyerson, "are stepping up efforts to attract black membership. Focus on the Family is organizing an urban ministry program dedicated to restoring the black family. The Christian Coalition is aggressively signing up black and Hispanic members. The Traditional Values Coalition . . . unites black and white pastors in opposition to government efforts to legitimate homosexuality." As Meyerson sees it, this confluence of interests and ideologies is an "earthquake" that will "rock American politics."[46]

What the future holds for these attempts to build a truly multicultural conservative movement, despite internal difficulties and disagreements among its members, is a pressing political question, one on which I take the opportunity to speculate in my conclusion. While writing the four essays that constitute the body of this text, I have endeavored to be as fair and impartial as possible, even though I remain as dubious as ever about many of the political and philosophical positions women and minority conservatives have adopted. Ideas do indeed have consequences, and the ideas that shape and shore up multicultural conservatism have had an impact on society via our debates about public policy, about the proper function of the federal government, and about the broader realms of identity, authenticity, and political struggle.

What I have aimed for here is a balanced account of conservative discourses among women, African Americans, Latinos, homosexuals, and, occasionally, Asian-Americans, one that locates these discourses, as well as the identities and politics that emerge from them, historically, culturally, and ideologically. For many, myself included, multicultural conservatism comprises a complex body of ideas, practices, and challenges, but it is a development that needs to be understood and assessed. In the end, I hope to leave the reader with a far more complicated vision of the diversity of American conservatism, a vision that takes the history and the political implications of conservative thought among women and within minority communities seriously, albeit critically.

A voice on the bare heights is heard/ the weeping
and pleading of/Israel's son,/ because they have perverted the way,/ they have forgotten the Lord/ their
God./ Return, O faithless sons,/ I will heal your
faithlessness.   —*Jeremiah 3:21–22*

I don't see how the civil rights people today can
claim Malcolm X as one of their own. Where does
he say black people should be begging the Labor
Department for jobs?   —*Clarence Thomas, 1991*

CHAPTER I

Malcolm X's Words in Clarence Thomas's Mouth

Black Conservatives and the Making of an Intellectual Tradition

I want to begin with a sustained exploration
of black conservative thought, primarily because black conservatives have
played such a central role in the development of a multicultural conservative style. While distinctive in many respects, the black conservative critique of liberalism and the federal government is not extraordinarily new
or innovative, particularly in its appeal to tradition and to Americanism.
Emergent social and political movements often seek to legitimate themselves and their ideologies by appealing to historical precedents and fore-
runners. Throughout U.S. history, a diverse array of groups (women,
workers, immigrants, African Americans, homosexuals) have pushed for
their rights by inserting themselves into national narratives and by depict-
ing themselves as good sons and daughters of the founders. Given the persuasive power of this rhetorical style, it is not surprising, for instance, that,
when early women's rights crusaders gathered at Seneca Falls in 1848, they
devised a political manifesto and call to arms that mirrored the Declaration of Independence in both form and philosophical content. "We hold

these truths to be self-evident," the Seneca resolution states, "that all men *and women* are created equal; that they are endowed by their Creator with certain inalienable rights."[1]

This endeavor to press for inclusion by citing the sacred texts of the nation on the one hand and the unfinished business of American democracy on the other has been an enormously successful strategy for reform; it has helped to transform the country while strengthening America's "civil religion."[2] This strategy derives its moniker—the American jeremiad—from seventeenth-century New England Puritan sermons that depicted America as a wilderness or harsh testing ground bestowed upon God's chosen people, who had a special destiny to erect a City upon a Hill to serve as a beacon of hope to the world.[3] If America is to succeed, then it must live up to its initial promise; America must muster the will to continuously reform itself when it falls into sin and transgression. Thus, the jeremiad is best thought of as a form of prophecy, warning of the consequences of God's vengeance if repentance is not forthcoming. Generations of reformers have defined the sins of the nation in secular terms, including slavery, various forms of discrimination and exclusion, and policies and practices that circumscribe individual liberty and equal opportunity. For those populations defined as outside or marginal to the national community, the jeremiad was and remains a fruitful way to demonstrate loyalty and to secure rights.

African Americans have been exceptionally adept at crawling inside the jeremiad form and appropriating its twin appeals to the judgement of God and to the Declaration of Independence and the Constitution. In the late eighteenth and the first half of the nineteenth century, slavery was interpreted as the seminal sin: an offense in the eyes of God, an abuse of natural liberty, and, perhaps most significant, contrary to the meaning of American democracy. In the hands of Frederick Douglass the jeremiad was elevated to a political art form. Speaking before an antislavery audience on the Fourth of July, 1852, Douglass railed against the present generation for falling away from the course laid out by the founding fathers, who "loved their country better than their own private interest."[4]

> Your fathers have lived, died, and done their work, and have done much of it well. You must live and die, you must do your own work. You have no right to enjoy a child's share in the labor of your fathers, unless you do your work. You have no right to wear out and waste the hard-earned fame of your fathers to cover your indolence.[4]

Douglass begins his address using pronouns—you, your—emphasizing the distance between himself, an ex-slave, and his audience, but he subtly closes the gap by invoking the right to call himself a "fellow citizen" and to use the collective "we."

In the course of his speech, Douglass cites the Declaration of Independence, the Bible, and the Constitution (which does not, he argues, support or condone slavery) to expose the hypocrisy of a free, yet slave-holding nation. "At a time like this," Douglass expounds, "scorching irony, not convincing argument is needed."

> O! had I the ability, and could reach the nation's ear, I would today pour out a fiery stream of biting ridicule, blasting reproach, withering sarcasm, and stern rebuke. . . . We need the storm, the whirlwind, and the earthquake. The feeling of the nation must be quickened; the conscience of the nation must be roused; the propriety of the nation must be startled; the hypocrisy of the nation must be exposed; and its crimes against God and man must be proclaimed and denounced.[5]

As the social theorist Michael Walzer points out, the jeremiad "begins with revulsion but ends with affirmation." The aim of prophecy, accordingly, is to arouse remembrance, recognition, indignation, and repentance.[6] "Return, O faithless sons," Jeremiah wails at his audience. The prophet distances himself from his stiff-necked people but in the end reaffirms his bonds with his community: "I will heal your faithlessness." Douglass's text follows this paradigm perfectly. For, while he charges the sons and daughters with slandering the memory of the founders, he nonetheless closes on a note of hope.

"I do not despair of this country," Douglass concludes. "I, therefore leave off where I began, with hope. While drawing encouragement from the Declaration of Independence, the great principles it contains and the genius of American institutions, my spirit is also cheered by the obvious tendencies of the age." Douglass expresses no doubt that redemption (abolition) is possible. Nor does he question that America will reform itself and act in accordance with its millennial obligation to bring the light of freedom to the world, including Africa. At the very end of the speech Douglass couples American exceptionalism with African messianism: "Africa must rise and put on her yet unwoven garment. Ethiopia shall stretch out her hand unto God." It's a nice twist, a rhetorical flourish that contains a blatantly racial, internationalist perspective that in no way detracts from the uniquely American quality of the speech.[7]

Black conservatives have struggled to reinvent this jeremiad form, appealing not only to God and country but also to heroic figures from America's and Afro-America's past. Like Douglass, they too strive to speak as prophets to the nation and urge a return to America's hallowed principles before we are destroyed. Again like Douglass, they have devised a style that speaks simultaneously to their dual heritage as African Americans. Uniting Douglass with Abraham Lincoln, "the Great Emancipator" and the consummate Republican, black conservatives position themselves as rightful heirs of two deeply intertwined traditions. They have a pronounced tendency to claim Lincoln as their own—the premiere black conservative think tank, the Lincoln Institute, bears his name; the Republican Party is often referred to as the Party of Lincoln—yet they have been equally willing to access African American traditions. Herein lies the rub.

Efforts by black conservatives to create an intellectual tradition from *within* the African American canon have been far more controversial. Clarence Thomas was on far safer ground when he asserted his affinity to Lincoln than he was when he did the same with Malcolm X.[8] His statement challenging the right of "civil rights people today" to claim Malcolm X as "one of their own" brought forth ringing denunciations from black leftists and liberals. Equating Thomas's stance with a stylized marketing ploy, the Columbia law professor and *Nation* columnist Patricia J. Williams wrote that "Clarence Thomas is to Malcolm X what 'Unforgettable. The perfume. By Revlon' is to Nat King Cole," thereby suggesting that Thomas is little more than an insubstantive simulacrum of the Real Thing.[9]

In this, Williams was hardly alone, as she and others continuously emphasized the political stakes of Thomas's (mis)appropriation of African American political culture. Linking Thomas with other black conservatives, Amiri Baraka has chastised "The Sowells, Walter Williams, Crouches, Playtoy Beenyesmen, Glenn Lourys, Roy Innises, Melvin Williams, Juan Williams, and Thomas Ass Clarences" as "racists," and as "pods growing in the cellars of our politics."[10] Although not all opinions were as extreme (at least in print), the general climate of opinion among leftist African American intellectuals appears to be that Thomas and other "neoaccomodationist-conservative black spokespersons," to borrow a phrase from Manning Marable, represent a crisis of contemporary black political culture.[11]

Marable, along with other black leftists such as Adolph Reed, has been especially vigilant in denouncing the efforts of black conservatives to seek legitimation in the past. They claim, overall, that black conservatives have no organic relationship to the African American past and no real political, cultural, or emotional ties to African Americans in the present. Instead, Marable and Reed claim, black conservatives have simply inserted themselves into a predominately white discourse on race, a move for which they have been duly compensated by various forms of patronage; they are nothing more than the black face of the white Right.[12] The larger question of what it means to misappropriate the past as well as how one adjudicates a proper from an improper solicitation has been subtly relegated to the background of this debate. What is much less remarked upon, and what Baraka's assessment of Thomas and others only alludes to, is that this "crisis" is also part of an ongoing confrontation over the meaning of African American liberation, and indeed the meaning of race, especially since the 1960s.

Thomas's attempt to wrap himself in the mantle of Malcolm X is but one small indication of black conservative canon building. Responding to the charge that they have no philosophy, no authenticity, and no relevance to African American political culture, black conservatives have sought to substantiate their ideas (and their very existence) by enlisting prominent figures, including not only Malcolm X but also Booker T. Washington, Frederick Douglass, Marcus Garvey, Zora Neale Hurston, and Martin Luther King, Jr. As Elizabeth Wright, editor of the black conservative newsletter *Issues and Views*, has put it, "making claim to historic figures in order to promote a position or cause is an age-old practice."[13] It is also a practice that makes a good deal of strategic sense as they struggle to legitimate their views. For the would-be prophet is always bound by tradition and counts on the immediacy of a shared history in the minds of her listener.

Where African American leftists see misappropriation and crisis, black conservatives see opportunity. Striving to turn the tables on the "black liberal establishment," Alan Keyes writes:

> Ironically, in the efforts to damn Thomas as an ingrate biting the hand that feeds him, the [African American] leadership revealed the posture they think most appropriate for black Americans: on our knees thanking 'massah gubmit' for benefits and favors. . . . His [Thomas's] main offense was simply that he never promoted the agenda of the union bureaucrats and left-liberal Democrats who seem to control the elite voices that are supposed to speak for black Americans.[14]

Such pronouncements, which incorporate the quasi-populist rhetoric of a "silent majority" as well as the rhetoric of "Uncle Tomism," are exceedingly common in the efforts of black conservatives to discredit their adversaries. Indeed, no single figure has been as maligned as Uncle Tom, whose very name has come to symbolize race traitors, sellouts, and those who pursue their own self-interest over the collective interest of the "race."[15] That liberals and leftists as well as conservatives all appeal to this rhetorical tradition is odd but understandable, since no other figure has been as politically serviceable in the realm of ad hominem attack. Further, "Uncle Toming" one's opponent has played a role in the various intraracial debates that have structured black political thought and activism since Uncle Tom was first created in the pages of Harriet Beecher Stowe's novel.

Ultimately, this struggle among contending African American intellectual and political forces extends far beyond the debates about the Thomas-Malcolm X connection and draws in some of Afro-America's most noted nineteenth- and twentieth-century thinkers and activists. Although no African American version of *The Portable Conservative Reader* exists,[16] we can certainly begin to chart and evaluate the efforts of some black conservative thinkers to define what amounts to a distinctively accented, and for them *politically useful*, canon. African American conservatism is still a relatively small tendency, as opposed to a cohesive movement, and there is a good deal of ideological difference among self-identified conservatives. In fact, the variations within black conservatism are as complex as those within the mainstream conservative movement, incorporating libertarianism, anticommunism, and economic nationalism, as well as social and religious strains, among others. Such variations do, however, coalesce into a broadly shared style of thought.

Black conservatives are knitted together first and foremost by racial identity, even when that identity is paradoxically rejected in the name of an extreme individualism or in the name of achieving the goal of a color-blind society. Libertarians and conservative integrationists, for example, tend to view racial consciousness and racial practices as barriers to assimilation for African American individuals. This version of black conservatism privileges a universal (and "American") vision over a more parochial and particular one.[17] In perhaps the most strident formulation of this idea, black libertarian Anne Wortham, a frequent contributor to the *Lincoln Review*, has argued that racial consciousness is damaging to individuals, to the very concept of individualism, and to society. In her study of the "new ethnicity," she maintains that the "tragedy of the most recent phase of intergroup relations in American history is that ethnic and racial minorities—particularly Blacks who have known the worst sort of oppression and exploitation by the state—chose to institutionalize the primacy of group rights over individual rights."[18] In fact, Wortham launched her academic career denouncing the dangers of "ethnoracial consciousness." For her, this form of group consciousness, inspired by the social fiction of race, is both racist and profoundly hostile to individual self-consciousness. "What links consciousness and ethnocentricity," she writes, "is the basic attitude that one's ethnic and/or racial group is the center of everything, and all others scaled with reference to it."[19] In sum, ethnoracial consciousness is a flight from the reality of one's own being, a form of escape motivated by a deep-seated fear of individual freedom.

Into this "integrationist" category one could also insert a fairly wide range of authors and critics, including Stanley Crouch, Orlando Patterson, Randall Kennedy, and Shelby Steele. With the exception of Steele, they have been generally hesitant to identify with conservative political causes or with the New Right. Their various critiques of racial consciousness, however, have strengthened the conservative discourse around the necessity of color blindness. Here, too, one finds an occasional appeal to African American canonical figures, especially Ralph Ellison and Frederick Douglass, even though these fellow travelers have been less engaged in conservative canon building as a political project. While Wortham offers us a philosophical exploration of the pitfalls of group consciousness, Crouch displays more of a cultural one. In his nod to tradition, he has placed Ellison at the very center of his perspective about race and identity. In his 1994 eulogy of Ellison, he says:

> Ralph Ellison, *alone* of the world famous Afro-American novelists, never denied his birthright, his complex responsibilities as a participant in the analyzing of American meaning, which is the job of the intellectual, and the remaking of American life in the hopefully immortal rhythms and tunes of art, which is the job of our aesthetically creative. Ellison had no interest in the overpaid chitlin circuit of professional alienation and guilt-mongering. He knew that all distinct ethnic roots have been transmuted by the tragedy of American collision and the intricate—sometimes romantic—cultural blues of collusion.[20]

Using the hybridity of American culture, symbolized by the blues, jazz, and Ellison's musings, as a metaphor for the rich mixtures that constitute a fully American identity, racism and racial chauvinism become for Crouch the dissonant chords in the life of the nation.

In contradistinction stand those black conservatives who are unwilling to reject group-based racial identities to this degree. Indeed, the summary judgment that all black conservatives strictly adhere to the goal of a color-blind society dramatically overstates the case. Authors such as Glenn Loury walk a fine line between the wholesale embrace and the wholesale rejection of a group-based racial identity. As Loury said at a conference on rethinking race, "We are all racialists now . . . we do well to remember that no one in America can afford to be truly color-blind. The very fact that I stand here before you, defined as a black neoconservative, being praised and honored for the courage to 'do the right (wing) thing,' even as I am branded a traitor by many blacks, reveals the power of race in our political lives."[21] More than any other conservative figure, Loury has objected to the duplicitous use of color-blindness; that is, the use of the doctrine as a way to ignore racial inequalities and to subvert reasonable policies to address them. Rejecting the notion that race is everything, he has been equally critical of the notion that race is nothing.[22]

Loury's position is as distinct from those of the libertarians and of the color-blind integrationists as it is from that of the conservative black nationalists. Proclaiming that "black conservatives are the real nationalists," Elizabeth Wright, along with Walter Williams and other frequent contributors to *Issues and Views*, has been waging a battle to wrestle the mantle of black nationalism from Louis Farrakhan and assorted afrocentrists—even though there are obvious similarities between them. Farrakhan and the Nation of Islam are religious fundamentalists and economic nationalists. The Nation's economic philosophy, like that advocated by *Issues and Views*, is a version of black entrepreneurial capitalism; its social philosophy stresses the patriarchal family, supports the death penalty, and deems homosexuality to be sick and unnatural. But there the comparison stops.

The problem with Farrakhan and the Nation for Wright and other black nationalist conservatives are the qualities that render him, in their eyes, a black fascist: his continued support of the separate black state ideal, his denunciation of interracial sex as an offense to the value of racial purity, his anti-Semitism and his antiwhite rhetoric. Wright, in particular, is often hostile to immediate integration preferring, instead long-range social and economic strategies within black communities. Yet, she is unwilling to bestow any inherent or transcendental characteristics to race. Nor does she see any necessity for an adversarial relationship between black and white Americans. Echoing Richard Nixon's redefinition of black nationalism as black capitalism, this perspective values race and a cohesive racial identity merely as a pragmatic necessity. Race is, in effect, reduced to a historically resonant and useful category for organizing collective self-help initiatives. Hence, racial essentialism and most forms of afrocentrism, like the Nation of Islam's, are rejected in a manner that holds out the possibility of transcending race at some point in the future. In this conscious (if uneasy) blending of black nationalism and Americanism, race is substantially depoliticized in the public sphere. It should have little or no bearing on public policy and federal legislation. Where race matters most, the nationalist-conservatives insist, is in the private sphere of black community life, simply as a means to an end.

When viewed through the lens of the embrace of an American identity, the distinction between nationalist-conservatives and integrationist-conservatives is not at all stark. Both variants position themselves squarely against the ideologies that emerged during and after the Black Power movement, particularly those that embraced a confrontational style and that asserted race as the foundation of interest-group politics. Both tendencies also coalesce around dismissing racism as the *primary* cause of contemporary racial inequality. "It's not racism," proclaims the Reverend Walter J. Bowie, a conservative Baptist minister, "it's just us." He continues:

> Time and time again we have heard that America is a racist country, and that the greatest problem we face as Black people is racism. This has been repeated so many times that many have come to accept it as 'gospel.' I want to raise a dissenting voice and challenge this assumption that some have accepted uncritically.[23]

This rejection of the primacy of racism does not mean most black conservatives would hold that racial discrimination is no longer a factor in American society. What it does mean, by and large, is "racism is not a sufficient cause for ghetto poverty and other social problems experienced by the black poor."[24] Instead of racism, black conservatives of various stripes have pointed to other practices and institutions, including the federal government's antipoverty and affirmative action programs, and to "liberal racism," as well as to the "culture of poverty," as more reasonable explanations for conditions that affect the African American poor.

In this way, black conservatives have sought to issue their jeremiads to the nation. Consider, for example, the founding statement of the Lincoln Institute, duly printed on every cover of the *Lincoln Review*. The Institute was founded "to study public policy issues that impact on the lives of black middle America, and to make its findings available to elected officials and the public." It continues:

> The Institute aims to re-evaluate those theories and programs of the last decades which were highly touted when introduced, but have failed to fulfill the claims represented by their sponsors—and in many cases, have been harmful to the long-range interests of blacks. The Institute is dedicated to seeking ways to improve the standards of living, the quality of life and freedoms of all Americans.

The target is not racism but once highly touted federal programs that delimit the freedoms of African Americans and indeed all Americans. In studiously avoiding the language of racism, members of the Institute and editors of the *Review* have inserted themselves into a broad narrative about America and the possibility for individual upward mobility and assimilation by anyone.

Focusing explicitly on the lives of "black middle Americans" and implicitly appealing to older patterns of ethnic assimilation and progress, black conservatives seek to replicate the successes of other ethnic groups that have become more fully integrated into the public life of the nation. Such progress, many black conservatives suggest, was possible only at the expense of group identity and ethnic cohesion. As Thomas Sowell has maintained, "Ethnic identity has sometimes been thought to be a potent—if not paramount—factor in group progress. But groups with much identity . . . have not generally done better than groups with less concern over such things." He concludes, "It is by no means clear that either cultural persistence or group advancement has been promoted by making cultural distinctiveness a controversial issue."[25] Moreover, asserting cultural distinctiveness forestalls the ability of a group to lay claim to Americanism, with its spirit of optimism and individualism. "It's high time we stopped acting like a victimized minority," chides Emmanuel McLittle, editor of *Destiny*, one of the newer and smaller black conservative magazines, "and started making inroads into the mainstream of American life."[26]

In this updated version of racial uplift, an older ideology that also sought to "civilize" black Americans, the focus is less on structural barriers to advancement and more on the glories of self-help, personal responsibility, moral fiber, and, of course, good old-fashioned hard work. As a doctrine rooted in the oppressive realities of the post-Reconstruction and Jim Crow eras, racial uplift, however, has always been a problematic concept.

On the one hand, it has certainly been deployed to buttress racial solidarity, a positive vision of black identity and *collective* self-help within communities. On the other hand, middle-class advocates of uplift have all too often failed to appreciate fully, and thus have reproduced, the racial (and potentially racist) assumptions of white cultural superiority, the masculinist assumptions of patriarchal authority, and the elitist assumptions that progress for the "talented tenth" would automatically signal progress for the race as a whole.[27] Racial uplift, past and present, also has a pronounced tendency toward pathologizing the poor.

Contemporary black conservatives have been quick to acknowledge their debt to a highly individualistic reading of the doctrine of uplift as they continue to carve out an intellectual tradition of their own. In formulating arguments about race, class, politics, and policy, a variety of black conservatives have looked to the past for guidance, sustenance, and legitimacy. Despite their diversity, the processes by which they have attempted to carve out a tradition of their own raises a number of provocative questions, especially about the political and philosophical "litmus test" for inclusion. In what follows, I present an overview of the current state of an emerging black conservative canon, with particular emphasis on how and why some figures are included while others are excluded. By surveying the ways in which black conservatives and their nonblack allies have mined the African American tradition from Booker T. Washington to Martin L. King, Jr., my goal is to present a more detailed analysis of the black conservative jeremiad and, in the end, to begin to assess its weaknesses and strengths.

Booker T. Washington, W. E. B. Du Bois, and the Search for "First Principles"

During the last ten years, you have often described yourself as a black conservative. I must confess that, other than their own self-advancement, I am at a loss to understand what it is that the so-called black conservatives are so anxious to conserve.   —*A. Leon Higginbotham, Jr., 1992*

In many respects, Higginbotham's expression of confoundment as to what black conservatives are "so anxious to conserve" is itself rather obfuscating.[28] Although he makes no direct reference to it in his text, Higginbotham restates an observation that appeared in Kelly Miller's 1908 essay, "Radicals and Conservatives." In that essay Miller recounts the reaction of "a distinguished Russian" who "could not restrain his laughter" on hearing that some African Americans adopted conservative positions. "The idea of conservative Negroes was more than the Cossack's risibilities could endure," Miller related. "'What on earth,' he exclaimed with astonishment, 'have they to conserve?'"[29] Almost eighty years later, Higginbotham reinterprets an insult to African Americans as a whole as an insult to contemporary black conservatives who feel they have more to conserve than their own self-advancement.

Black conservative thinkers have not let this deprecating challenge go unanswered. Glenn Loury, for example, is quite eager to conserve certain long-standing traditions within African American political, intellectual, and moral reasoning. Variants of black conservatism stretch back to the years of slavery through Reconstruction and incorporate figures such as Isaiah Montgomery, who voted in Mississippi's constitutional convention to limit black rights and who was a chief supporter of Mound Bayou, one of the most successful southern black towns between 1880 and 1920. Montgomery supported the "wisdom" of reducing the number of Negro voters through various restrictions because, he implied, this would encourage them to obtain knowledge and wealth.[30] Yet, at the foot of these traditions stands Booker T. Washington, who also emphasized wealth, property, and education over civil and political rights.

In his defense of Clarence Thomas, Loury points to the "historic resonance" of the recent debates regarding Thomas's suitability as a judicial replacement for Thurgood Marshall. "This argument," Loury writes, "has pitted liberal civil rights advocates (for decades now the established orthodoxy among respectable exponents of black opinion) against advocates of a conservative philosophy for advancement based on direct empowerment of the poor, relying significantly on self-help and dubious about the ability of government programs to resolve the deepest problems affecting black society."[31]

Loury argues that the terms of this debate between liberals and conservatives remain essentially the same at the end of the twentieth century as they were at the century's start. Like Kelley Miller, Loury distinguishes between the radical political emphasis of W. E. B. Du Bois and the early NAACP and the conservative, accommodationist approach of Booker T. Washington and the Tuskegee Institute. While Loury certainly concedes that history has hardly proven Washington right and Du Bois wrong in any definitive way, he still maintains that Washington's doctrines, especially the idea that "Brains, property, and character for the Negro will settle the question of civil rights," offers the best foundation for contemporary African Americans.

Moreover, Loury has been actively cultivating a public philosophy and a public persona that draw explicitly on Washington's rhetorical style. Critiquing the more confrontational versions of black political activism, including Malcolm X's, Loury asserts the ethic of persuasion is in danger of being lost. "What Washington understood," Loury insists, "and what remains as true today as it is difficult to say out loud, is that cultivating the sensibilities of whites is directly in the interests of blacks. Because we live in a democracy," he concludes, "we bear the burden of persuading our fellows of the worth of our claims upon them."[32] In essence, Loury is reasserting the necessity of the jeremiad form as a rhetorical and political strategy, with its stress on the connections between the prophet and his nation. It is the very style of address, then, that becomes a marker of a "reasonable" conservatism that can be translated into an oppositional stance against the Left's supposedly irrational stress on racism and victimization.

Loury is hardly the only black conservative to note the usability of Booker T. Washington and to situate Washington as a sort of standard bearer able to define the general parameters of which people and what ideas should be included in a black conservative tradition. Unfortunately, most have been content to reproduce the already overly dichotomized view of the differences between Washington and Du Bois. Not only does such a view tend to drain out historical specificity; it also tends to misrepresent Du Bois's position on social, economic, and moral strategies for black advancement.[33] The same is largely true among nonblack conservatives who have commented on what they view as the paucity of moral leadership in contemporary African American communities.

Dinesh D'Souza, for example, makes a good deal of this "historic debate" between these two figures. The terms of that debate are drawn in the starkest manner possible, and D'Souza comes perilously close to transforming "Du Boisian" into an epithet.[34] Telescoping the entire history of civil rights struggles into a choice of Du Bois over Washington, he insists that in revisiting the original debate "we can discover options exercised and options forgone." He concludes that African Americans "would be in a different situation today if the civil rights leadership had opted for Washington instead." In his opinion, only black conservatives—and black nationalists—evidence the proper respect for Washington and his legacy.[35] Hence, only Washington is allowed to represent the supposed road not taken, the road that privileges culture and civilization over politics and civil rights.

Du Bois's willingness to rail against what he saw as the moral deficiency of segments of the African American population is sometimes noted in passing, despite the fact that moral uplift played a significant role in structuring Du Bois's views, especially in early works such as "The Conservation of the Races" (1898). Moreover, rarely is his call for self-segregation and economic cooperation, expressed in speeches such as "A Negro Nation within a Nation" (1935), given any credence among contemporary conservatives. Faced with the crisis created by the Great Depression, in that speech Du Bois maintains "the main weakness of the Negroes' position is that since emancipation he has never had an adequate economic foundation."[36] Agreeing in principle with Washington's efforts to provide a "comprehensive economic plan," Du Bois also insisted that Washington's plan was severely undermined by the concentration of industries, land monopoly, and of the mechanization of agriculture and of the industrial workplace.[37] Joining the economic with the political, Du Bois called for the creation of an "economic nation within a nation," from which African Americans could "work through inner cooperation to found its own institutions, to educate its genius, and, at the same time, without mob violence or extremes of race hatred, to keep in helpful touch and cooperate with the mass of the nation."[38] For Du Bois, the point was not only to improve individuals and uplift black communities but also to transform society and its institutions.

Given such programmatic statements, contemporary conservatives are too swift to write Du Bois completely out of their intellectual canon. At the very least, Du Bois inserts a cautionary note about the nature of capitalism into the excessive glamorization of Washington and the free market. Viewed against the backdrop of American conservatism overall, it might be more accurate to say not that Du Bois was radical and Washington conservative but that they both have something to contribute to the articulation of conservative philosophies, albeit of different types. In the early part of his long and varied career, Du Bois was arguably closer to an older, more organic version of conservatism, skeptical of market capitalism and rampant materialism, while Washington was more in tune with the turn-of-the-century transformation of American conservatism via its gradual embrace of laissez-faire capitalism.[39] In later years, Du Bois, whose "conservatism" was always closer to an anticapitalist position, does come to wed his ideas to international socialism. Still, some aspects of his Depression-era perspectives closely parallel many of the positions adopted in a less complex form by contemporary conservatives.

Instead of presenting a more nuaunced vision, conservatives most commonly cast Du Bois in the role of (radical) villain in contrast to Washington's (conservative) heroism, with all points of commonality between the two sacrificed on the altar of a neat dichotomy. Such an approach creates more potential for confusion than it clears up. Given the variety of positions adopted in the past, and the plurality of interpretations possible in the present, neither Du Bois nor Washington fits easily into contemporary formulations of Left and Right, radical and conservative, villain and hero. Establishing a stark dichotomy between Du Bois and Washington nonetheless serves an ideological function in the conservative iconography of Washington. "Booker T. Washington is the specter of truth that haunts the black community," writes Elizabeth Wright in a special issue of *Issues and Views* dedicated to "Our Greatest Warrior."[40] *Issues and Views*, an economically oriented black conservative newsletter, wants to wage a concerted campaign to "save" and defend what contributors consider to be the most valuable aspects of Washington's legacy, most notably his stress on "economic nationalism."

It is Wright's opinion that most blacks have been "taught by fellow blacks a distorted version of Washington's message of self-help and [are] ignorant of his life's work."[41] Yet she cites no concrete examples of this distortion and chooses to ignore the bulk of existing scholarship on Washington, Tuskegee, and the legacies of both, while nonetheless maintaining that most African Americans are conditioned to belittle Washington. The primary thrust of Wright's writings is much more polemic than scholarly, incorporating the supposed silencing of Washington's legacy—ignoring all evidence to the contrary—into a tirade against a "self-interested middle-class":

In the lives of Booker T. Washington and the thousands who were influenced by his philosophy, we learn not only where we came from, but what we might have been as a race, had not a self-interested middle class and leadership opted for an easier way out—thus taking us off course and derailing our progress. While feigning concern for the poor, these crusaders assign responsibility for the poor to every conceivable branch of government and corporate entity in America. As they diligently avoid playing the critical role of economic catalyst to develop black communities . . . they preach about the responsibilities of others, and their determination "not to let the white folks off the hook."[42]

Such arguments deploy the language of class and intraracial class tensions as a weapon, but the critique is based not so much on class as a social category as it is on class as an ideology. The middle class per se is not at fault, only that portion deemed to be self-interestedly dedicated to a politics of liberalism in which the state has the potential to become a positive agent of social change and social welfare.

The problem in the end is not so much that this politically defined segment of the middle class is self-interested (hardly a novel charge) but that it is self-interested *in the wrong ways*. Moreover, Wright raises the old charge of racial dilution and "Uncle Tomism," resorting to the sorts of ad hominem insults traditionally leveled against Washington and his followers. The "new Toms" are those self-interested middle-class liberals content to live on the federal government's "plantation." As Wright has argued, "Instead of following his [Washington's] example, instead of building ourselves as a people, we have this generation of self-promoting *octoroons* who are making a good living playing the white man."[43]

In contradistinction to their nonconservative counterparts, black conservatives present themselves as largely middle-class dissidents who are the rightful and more authentic crusaders for the poor. This black conservative vanguardism, which is so reminiscent of the call for a "Talented Tenth," has been channeled into a battle between competing factions of the black middle class itself. The most contested terrain between these two competing factions is poverty, with both sides dismissing the other with insinuations of corruption, complacency, and opportunism. Poverty, black conservatives charge, has become a profitable industry perpetuated by liberals as a way to enrich themselves. In this as in other ideas, contemporary conservatives have drawn sustenance from Booker T. Washington.

Decades ago, Washington denounced his detractors by asserting that some African Americans had become black professionals by virtue of becoming professional blacks who "make a business of keeping the troubles, the wrongs and the hardships of the Negro race before the public." Today, Wright and others have updated this canard, transforming it into an ideological battering ram designed to discredit their foes. In the mainstream press and in their own journals and newsletters, this has become a major component of the black conservative critique of liberal social policy, civil rights activists, and anyone deemed to have opposed Washington's philosophy, in both the past and the present. Further, by demonizing a "self-interested middle class," black conservatives can dubiously insist that one of the chief barriers to black advancement is that poverty has become an industry and that it is the industry itself that must be dismantled before any real progress can take place.[44]

In his book on the Afro-American jeremiad, the historian David Howard-Pitney notes that there are at least two interlocking strains of this tradition: one geared toward white audiences and reaffirming the nation's millennial promise and destiny, the other castigating blacks for their failure in the realm of self-improvement and the "duties of Christian citizenship."[45] Washington studiously avoided the call for biting ridicule, blasting reproach, and stern rebuke that marked Frederick Douglass's jeremiad to the nation. Instead, Washington reserved the harshest chastisement for a black population that was "in the most elemental of civilization, weak." Thus, before African Americans could fully assimilate into America as citizens, the race must be uplifted. "The wisest among my race understand that the agitation of questions of social equality is the extremist folly," Washington proclaimed in his famous Atlanta Exposition Address, "and that progress in the enjoyment of all the privileges that will come to us must be the result of severe and constant struggle rather than artificial forcing."[46] Black conservatives, for better or worse, have followed this Washingtonian paradigm.

There are of course other ideological components of black conservatism. On the basis of a fairly selective use of Washington's philosophy, one is encouraged to view an interlocking set of ideas about black advancement—self-help and, more important, an anti-government stance, a commitment to entrepreneurial capitalism, and the Gospel of Wealth—as contributing factors in establishing a "litmus test" that defines the contours of a black conservative tradition. Washington has also been enlisted in defining an appropriate posture regarding race and racial consciousness, one in which race pride and racial cohesion may be a necessary means to an end but not an appropriate end in itself. Moreover, and again following Washington's example, the suggestion is constantly made that one must also have inspired the animus of black leftists and liberals, who have "shouted down every pragmatic black person who has stressed economic independence over mindless integration."[47] The prophet is, after all, one who speaks unwelcome truths with tough love in his heart; she is not always respected and embraced in her own time.

Beyond Washington: Building a Black Conservative Canon

Having used Washington (and excluded Du Bois) to establish the general parameters of black conservatism, the contributors to *Issues and Views* and others are able to put forth cases for appropriate additions to an emerging canon. For example, Marcus Garvey, "a steadfast admirer of Booker T. Washington," is valued for his dedication to black capitalism, capital investment, and free enterprise, even though his own business enterprises were less than successful. The ideological differences between Washington and Garvey, particularly their views on race, do not seem to matter much in this context. "Like Washington," Wright summarily argues, "Garvey viewed economic independence from whites as an essential goal. He saw in the desire for integration a diversion that could undermine the spirit of solidarity among blacks, which he believed essential if they were to cooperate and pool their resources as other groups did."[48]

If Washington needs to be saved from obscurity, then Garvey needs to be saved from what Wright calls "pseudo-nationalists" who reproduce Garvey's image "on everything from banners, to posters, to T-shirts," while privileging his "radicalism" in terms of race over his "conservatism" in terms of economics. For Wright, there is no perceptible contradiction between black conservatism and black nationalism of the sort practiced by Garvey. The trouble with Wright's position is not that such a perspective emphasizes the conservative tendencies of black nationalism. From nineteenth-century figures such as Edward W. Blyden, Martin Delany, and Alexander Crummell to twentieth-century figures such as Garvey, Malcolm X, and Louis Farrakhan, black nationalism has certainly incorporated a generally conservative focus on the necessity of male-headed households, strong families, religious devotion, a rigid moral code of behavior, and black capitalism.[49] Instead, the problem with Wright's perspective is that it occludes the more radical implications of Garveyism and other forms of black nationalism, most notably its forceful critique of white racism.

Garvey did not in fact believe racial justice to be possible in the United States because people of African descent would always be a numerical minority. For Garvey, the Negro could not "resort to the government for protection for government will be in the hands of the majority of the people who are prejudiced against him, hence for the Negro to depend on the ballot and his industrial progress alone, will be hopeless as it does not help him when he is lynched, burned, jim-crowed and segregated."[50] In terms of the so-called debate between Washington and Du Bois, Garvey favored neither man's approach; both tied the Negro to the promise of America, which Garvey could not abide. Further, he viewed racism as a quasi-natural phenomenon, emanating not only from circumstance but from the natural affinity one feels for one's own racial group. It was this sort of essentialist race feeling that Garvey attempted to tap into with the motto of the Universal Negro Improvement Association: "One God, One Aim, One Destiny."

While the focus on white racism and the often concomitant rejection of an American identity has led some black conservatives such as Anne Wortham to dismiss nationalists such as Garvey altogether, Wright and others have struggled to write them into a black conservative canon. Alan Keyes, for instance, funnels almost all of African American intellectual history, including Garveyism, into the conservative "values that form the essence of the black-American character." In so doing, he skirts the issue of Garvey's pronounced racial chauvinism and his virulent critique of the unremitting nature of white racism. In a similar vein, Wright has argued that Garvey's opinions on race were less a matter of a radical philosophy than a "pragmatic linking of race pride to the goal of economic liberation—and his guidelines for using the free market to achieve that goal."[51] Here again, the difficulty with such an interpretation of Garvey and Garveyism stems from selectivity. Garvey's fidelity to the concept of race was surely more than a matter of mere pragmatism. Garvey was, to paraphrase Washington, among that class of colored people who insist on keeping the wrongs of the race before the public. He was, in the popular opinion of the time, a "Black Moses" of his people, the one who could lead them to the promised land. Garvey also tended to endow race with an almost mystical quality in the tradition of nineteenth-century black nationalism. His reclaiming of a lost, but ennobling, past in ancient Africa and especially Egypt prefigures the more recent development of afrocentrism, which many contemporary conservatives feel bound to reject as a racial fantasy.[52]

Indeed, unlike Booker T. Washington, who engaged in a modified version of the American jeremiad, Garvey advocated a racial ideology that precluded such endeavors. For Garvey, America (or any other Western nation) could never be the true home of the Negro. "What have Negroes to conserve?" he once asked, considering the realities of racism in the United States. The search for a home in the world is over, Garvey insists: "We have found a place; it is Africa, and as black men for three centuries have helped white men build America, surely generous and grateful white men will help black men build Africa."[53] In proposing this new nation in Africa, Garvey drew less on American traditions than on the recovery of African ones. Believing the Negro to have been robbed of his past, he often wrote and spoke of what the ancient civilizations of Egypt had given to the world, especially to Greece and Rome. Therefore, Garvey could issue a direct appeal to the black race to see itself as it really is; to help Africa stretch its hands forth unto God and to take its proper place in the world of racially distinct and powerful nations.[54]

Although Garvey's racial chauvinism seems too blatant to simply ignore, this aspect of his philosophy is barely remarked on by contemporary black conservatives. Some portions of his views are expressly more valuable than others. But the articles on Garvey that have appeared in *Issues and Views* do raise another hallmark of black conservatism, namely a relentless rejection of communism and anything that presages a "collectivist" ideology. In general, black conservatives view communism as a system that, in Garvey's words, "robs the individual of his personal initiative and ambition or the result thereof."[55] Communism, however, is broadly defined to include practically anything opposed to capitalism and the free market, up to and including the idea that the federal government should play an overt role in the socioeconomic advancement of individuals and groups. To buttress this anticommunist, promarket ideology, black conservatives have also drawn on lesser-known individuals. S. B. Fuller, for example, who parlayed a door-to-door sales operation into a multimillion-dollar conglomerate that included a Chicago department store and a New York real estate trust, is held up by present-day conservatives as an exemplar of pragmatic African American conservatism.

Fuller emerges as a highly usable figure. Raised in poverty in Louisiana, he managed to overcome racial barriers, thus conforming to the rags to riches *individual* self-help script, and he often publicly denounced "the grandstanding rhetoric of black 'leaders' who never addressed the reality of economics."[56] The suggestion is, as with all good black conservatives from Booker T. Washington on, that Fuller was ostracized by black liberals for insisting that "a lack of understanding of the capitalist system, not racial barriers, was keeping blacks from making progress."[57] Contemporary black conservatives have drawn on an array of individuals such as Fuller, who form a tradition of entrepreneurship stretching back to the eighteenth century.[58]

While the majority of examples of early black conservatives are drawn from the economic sphere, attempts have been made to mine the cultural arena, including writers such as Zora Neale Hurston and Claude McKay.[59] The inclusion of Zora Neale Hurston in a black conservative canon has been much more muted and subtle, but it is no less compelling. Hurston makes only a cameo appearance in conservative texts such as Dinesh D'Souza's *The End of Racism*, and she appears only fleetingly in publications such as *Issues and Views*. In fact, one of the few articles by a conservative author in which Hurston is given sustained attention appeared in the *Lincoln Review*, and in it Hurston shares the spotlight with Clarence Thomas.[60]

Most Hurston scholars seem to be fairly comfortable in dismissing evidence of her conservative political views as "naive and dangerous," and as relatively unimportant. For instance, while the Hurston scholar Mary Helen Washington notes that Hurston's anticommunist articles in the *Saturday Evening Post* and the *American Legion Magazine*, as well as her support of Robert Taft in 1952, "[document] a developing political conservatism," she feels called upon to explain, and perhaps to explain away, the more disturbing dimensions of Hurston's ideas. "This growing conservatism, which was interpreted as antiblack, is difficult to explain," Washington writes.

> Hurston always saw herself as a self-made success, and she had the kind of individualism and egoism that generally accompanies that belief. . . . Thus, she was able to dismiss slavery as an anachronism, which no longer concerned her, since all the slaveholders were long since dead and she was too busy getting on with the future to care. It was a naive and dangerous viewpoint, and one that led directly to her right-wing politics.[61]

To the degree that individualism, a tendency to downplay the effects of slavery and racism, and a desire to chart one's own nonconformist course have been depicted as central to some variants of black conservatism, Washington is correct to view Hurston in this light. But what Washington accepts as an aspect of Hurston's life that is now difficult to explain is precisely what some conservatives have identified as part of Hurston's important contributions to African American and American political culture.

Writing in the *Lincoln Review*, Bill Kaufman characterized Hurston as "a proud daughter of the South, a patriotic black nationalist, and a believer in limited constitutional government," who "scorned the incipient welfare state as 'The Little White Father.'" Kaufman also makes a great deal of Hurston's 1928 essay, "How It Feels to Be a Colored Me," in which she notes that she is not "tragically colored" and that she does not belong to "the sobbing school of Negrohood who hold that nature somehow has given them a lowdown dirty deal"[62]—statements that Mary Helen Washington has characterized as "exasperating" and, when read today, enough to "make one's flesh crawl." Kaufman also notes, not surprisingly, that Hurston (like Booker T. Washington, Garvey, and S. B. Fuller) was chastised by the NAACP and others for her "heterodox" views.

Contemporary conservatives could also find ample comfort in Hurston's anticommunist views, which grew out of her long-held suspicions of the Communist Party for its "insulting patronage" of "pitiable" blacks.[63] Like their mainstream counterparts, black conservatives were rabidly anticommunist during the Cold War. Some, such as the Lincoln Institute's J. A. Parker, cut their political teeth in organizations such as Young Americans for Freedom, and since its inception the Institute has had close ties to the World Anti-Communist League.[64] Whereas white conservatives focused primarily on the Eastern bloc and on Latin America, black conservatives maintained similar positions on the need to keep Africa free of the communist menace. Both adopted Jeane Kirkpatrick's now famous distinction between dictatorial regimes, which are repressive but allow for domestic pressure toward social change, and totalitarian ones, which close off all forms of internal dissent. Employing this paradigm, conservatives were able to justify supporting dictatorships as long as they were sufficiently anticommunist and pro-American.

Since anticommunism, both foreign and domestic, crops up time and time again in the development of black conservative traditions, Claude McKay, a contemporary of Hurston's and a member of the cadre of black writers associated with the Harlem Renaissance, could also be written into the black conservative canon under this guise. As with Hurston's, McKay's anticommunism is a prime source of attraction. According to one assessment, not only did McKay "prematurely [see] through the sham of the Communist Party, which sedulously wooed him," but when he denounced the party and the Soviet Union for their duplicity in matters of race, he suffered through a "campaign of vilification that had been mounted against him."[65]

Like Garvey, McKay was a West Indian immigrant who was attracted to the ideologies and practices of Booker T. Washington. Believing that "the answer for his people was in an improved economic status," McKay enrolled in Washington's Tuskegee Institute, although his sojourn there lasted a brief six months.[66] While recognizing McKay's artistic accomplishments, it is as a critic of communism and "totalitarian liberals" that he is vaunted by the conservatives. We are told by the conservative cultural critic Ralph de Toledano that, were McKay alive today, he would reject federal programs such as affirmative action as an "insult" to blacks and a "tacit confession" that blacks were somehow inferior and could not rise to the level of their talents without "a handout from a white master race." Although de Toledano bestows upon McKay an impossible knowledge of contemporary developments, black conservatives who desire to claim McKay as a predecessor are on somewhat safer grounds with his anticommunism. And much is made of the fact that McKay, having been ostracized for his political views by communists and by black spokespersons in the late 1940s, joined the Catholic Church in part because "it is the greatest political organization in the world and a bulwark against the menace of Communism."[67]

Conservatives have traditionally depicted communism as anti-individual, antidemocratic, prostatist and ultimately un-American. Therefore, anything associated with communism is necessarily dangerous and subversive.[68] Unlike McKay and Hurston, post–Cold War black conservatives are less concerned with actually existing communism than with a style of thought that, to their minds, conjoins communism and liberalism via a predisposition toward paternalism. White liberal paternalism, or "liberal racism," as it is often designated, is in fact a cornerstone of the black conservative critique of left-liberal orthodoxies.[69] For contemporary conservatives Hurston's "Little White Father" is still an ever present and troubling aspect of American political culture and has become one of the dimensions that links contemporary black conservatives to the historical figures they seek to claim. Their genealogical project, however, is far from complete. For instance, if Garvey, Hurston, and McKay have been suggested as part of the intellectual lineage of black conservatism partly on the basis of their anticommunist views, then one wonders why George Schuyler has been so obviously left out.

Schuyler, who was also part of the Harlem Renaissance and who went on to become one of the most noted black journalists of his day, is perhaps the most clearly conservative figure available. He was a staunch anticommunist and in the 1950s and 1960s identified with the political conservatism of the far Right, joining organizations such as the New York Conservative Political Association and, eventually, the John Birch Society.[70] Yet Joseph Conti and Brad Stetson, the authors of one of the only recent attempts to present a book-length study of contemporary black conservatism, mention Schuyler only once.[71] Not only did Schuyler entitle his autobiography *Black and Conservative*, but, given the centrality of anticommunism in the making of a black conservative tradition, his omission is doubly curious.

True, Schuyler, a committed iconoclast, is a difficult figure to pin down, but no more so, one would suppose, than McKay or Hurston. His long career as a public figure encompassed numerous twists and turns, as he moved from the socialist-oriented and anticolonial Left in the 1930s to the anticommunist Right in the 1960s. In this regard, Schuyler's trajectory is similar to that of the "New York intellectuals" who traveled from the anti-Stalinist Left in the 1930s and came to form the core of neoconservatism in the 1970s and 1980s.[72] In fact, Schuyler worked with many of these intellectuals in the American Committee for Cultural Freedom before he resigned in 1954, in part because of the ACCF's criticism of McCarthyism. Moreover, like Booker T. Washington before him and contemporary conservatives after him, Schuyler was highly critical of the "civil rights industry" of his day. For Schuyler, the category "civil rights activist" became, in the 1950s and 1960s, nearly synonymous with a dangerous and subversive collectivism. As he writes in his autobiography, "from the beginning of the so-called Negro Revolution and the insane antics identified with it, I had taken the same position editorially and in my column that I had throughout the years."

> I had opposed all the Marches on Washington and other mob demonstrations, recognizing them as part of the Red techniques of agitation, infiltration, and subversion. This was indicated by the fact that invariably they were proposed, incited, managed and led by professional collectivist agitators, whose only interest in the workers was to exploit them; backed by the proliferation of "liberals" of position and influence who always run interference for them [blacks] by "explaining" and defending their course.[73]

Although present-day conservatives seem reluctant to acknowledge it, ideologically there is not much difference in kind between Booker T. Washington's criticism of professional blacks who keep the hardships of the Negro race before the public, Schuyler's denunciation of collectivist liberals, and their own contemporary critique of the "civil rights industry" in modern American and in African American politics. Nor was Schuyler's position as quixotic as it might seem at first blush. Schuyler was not alone in raising such questions about King and about the modern civil rights movement. From the vantage point of the present it is easy to forget how controversial the civil rights movement (and King) was, not only among white Americans but within African American communities as well. One of King's chief African American detractors was the Reverend J. H. Jackson, pastor of Olivet Baptist Church, once the largest black congregation in Chicago and the nation. After 1955 Jackson was head of the powerful National Baptist Convention (NBC), then the largest and most influential organization controlled by blacks.

Although Jackson was close to the King family and Martin Luther King, Jr., initially served as one of his lieutenants, the relationship between the two ministers soured and eventually erupted into open hostility. It was King's desire that the NBC serve as the primary institutional base of the civil rights movement, but Jackson, a committed gradualist, had other ideas and blocked all attempts by King's supporters to gain control of the organization. Not only did Jackson deny support to early campaigns such as the Montgomery bus boycott, but, during the sit-ins and freedom rides, he rebuked those who "talk too much about racial integration and not enough about racial elevation."[74] Following a nasty battle between King supporters and Jackson loyalists during a national gathering of the NBC and a resulting melee that precipitated the accidental death of one of the delegates, Jackson publicly charged King with lawlessness in the "move for freedom" and subsequently stripped King of his prestigious title of vice president of the NBC's Sunday School Board, a tactic that amounted to excommunication from the organization.

The breach between the Reverends Jackson and King was never re-paired. Agreeing to some extent with Schuyler, Jackson also denounced the 1963 March on Washington as a dangerous and unwarranted form of protest. And again, like Schuyler, Jackson was opposed not to the idea of civil rights per se but to what he judged the unduly radical methods used in securing them. Viewing Schuyler in this light helps to make his critiques slightly more understandable, if not necessarily more palatable.

Martin Luther King, Jr., and the "Heroic" Days of the Civil Rights Movement

One possible explanation for Schuyler's absence from the conservative intellectual canon hinges on the question of how the post–World War II civil rights movement should be represented. Contemporary conservatives have taken great pains to demarcate the "heroic" phase of the movement—the 1954 *Brown* decision to the legislative victories of 1964 and 1965—from the subsequent "corruption" in the late 1960s with the rise of Black Power, "identity politics," and the pursuit of "special preference." In attacking the earlier phase of the movement, a phase now heralded by conservatives as embodying the best traditions of American democracy, Schuyler is, in retrospect, less useful to today's conservatives. The difficulty with Schuyler, it might be said, is that he was no Martin L. King, Jr. Indeed, while Schuyler presently suffers from underexposure in the texts of conservative authors, quite the opposite is true for King.

King remains a powerful symbol. With the exception of Frederick Douglass, no other African American orator and activist has been as astute in appropriating the jeremiad form. King's vision was truly prophetic, and his moral appeal to the nation was undeniable. In his frank rebuke of his generation's apostasy, King placed African Americans at the moral center of America's destiny. As King wrote in his "Letter from Birmingham City Jail," one day "the South will know that when these disinherited children of God sat down at lunch counters they were in reality standing up for the best in the American dream and the most sacred values in our Judeo-Christian heritage, and thusly, carrying our whole nation back to those great wells of democracy which were dug deep by the Founding Fathers in the formation of the Constitution and the Declaration of Independence."[75] King also displayed an equal facility in speaking directly to black Americans, urging them not to waver in their resolve, to meet violence with nonviolence, and to forsake the prison of bitterness, shame, and hatred.[76]

A heavily redacted and simplified version of King's vision of a society where individuals would be judged on the content of their character and not on the color of their skin is used as a mantra among those conservatives who believe in the possibility of a color-blind society. Shelby Steele used it as the title of his 1992 bestseller, *The Content of Our Character*, and it has been deployed with equal vigor in such texts as Representative Gary Franks's *Searching for the Promised Land: An African-American's Odyssey*; the radio talk-show host Ken Hamblin's *Pick a Better Country: An Unassuming Colored Guy Speaks His Mind about America*; and Alan Keyes's *Master of the Dream: The Strength and Betrayal of Black America*. All of these works, and others like them, share two broad propositions: first, that the dream of integration and color blindness has been betrayed by liberals and leftists who corrupted the course and goals of the civil rights movement in the post-1965 era; and, second, that contemporary conservatives are our best hope of retrieving this earlier promise.

One need look no further than the recent drive to end affirmative action within the University of California system and the subsequent victory of Proposition 209, officially (and ironically) titled the California Civil Rights Initiative (CCRI). The success of these initiatives was dependent on the redefinition of the original goals of the civil rights movement.

At its core, this redefinition insists on the rejection of structural politics and on the rejection of the idea that the federal government can and must act positively and affirmatively to ensure racial justice. Turning away from the national political arena, conservatives push instead a privatized social agenda that places the bulk of blame or praise on the shoulders of individuals—not institutions, not society, not, in the end, "we" Americans at all.

In this sense, the black conservative jeremiad shares little with most versions of the Afro-American ones, apart from the distinctive pattern established by Booker T. Washington. It lacks, that is to say, a corporate, communal dimension—what we Americans all must do—expressed as shared sacrifice and strenuous commitment. Thus, solving the American dilemma is relatively painless, at least for the vast majority; all we must "do" is to repeal race-conscious legislation, cut welfare, and simply stop talking about race. Indeed, whenever possible, we should collectively celebrate the achievements of African Americans and congratulate ourselves on the nation's openness to black progress. As with Booker T. Washington's assent to accommodation over structural transformation, the success of these rhetorical strategies and of initiatives such as the CCRI was also dependent on the vocal support and activism of black conservatives, most notably Ward Connerly, a businessman, University of California Regent, and, most recently, head of the newly founded American Civil Rights Institute.[77]

Echoing decades of black conservative reasoning, Connerly pressed the case that racism is no longer a chief factor in delimiting black advancement and that remedial federal programs are harmful to American democracy and to those very individuals such programs were designed to assist. "While others are assimilating," Connerly has said, "blacks are getting further and further away from one nation indivisible."[78] The desire for assimilation is key here and might be said to represent an attempt to infiltrate the privileges or "wages" of whiteness by emphasizing one's American-ness, one's individuality, and one's worth.[79] Only by assimilation through color blindness and individual merit is one allowed to hold out the possibility of pursuing one's individual liberty. In this updated version of "passing," crossing the color line, socially and politically if not physically, and liberating oneself from the race (and The Race) becomes the path to freedom.

To legitimate these positions, Connerly and others have dissected King's words and deeds to suit their own agenda. Conservatives can even point to the stamp of approval bestowed by one of King's nieces, Alveda Celeste King, who believes it is time "for African American conservatives to emerge into the light of a new day ... and speak out for the values that the Republican Party so wholeheartedly embraces."[80] At the same time, in their speeches and essays, rarely does one find any mention of the "other" King—the King who expressed fears that the "Dream" had become a nightmare; the King who expressed no affinity for assimilation or the free market. In a 1967 keynote address to the National Conference for a New Politics, King deconstructs the "myth that capitalism grew and prospered out of the Protestant ethic of hard work and sacrifices."

> The fact is that capitalism was built on the exploitation and suffering of black slaves and continues to thrive on the exploitation of the poor, both black and white, both here and abroad. . . . The way to end poverty is to end exploitation of the poor. Ensure them a fair share of the government's services and the nation's resources. We must recognize that the problems of neither racial or economic justice can be solved without a radical redistribution of political and economic power.[81]

Hence, King's vision was far less individualistic than Connerly's or that of the majority of conservatives who constantly pay homage to King and who conceptualize him as a lonely detached warrior, rather than as a man deeply rooted in a particular culture. Further, as this quotation suggests, the King of the 1965–1968 phase of his life was angrier than before. He had come to see America as a fundamentally sick society in desperate need of extensive structural reform. Believing the dream to have become a nightmare, King was forced to admit: "Yes, I am personally the victim of deferred dreams, of blasted hopes."[82] While one can seek to reconcile these two distinct Kings, preciously little effort is made among conservatives to do so. In the end, they simply take the version of King most suited to their own purposes and designs. Hence, the later King has unfortunately been undervalued and ignored by conservatives whose selectivity distorts King's legacy. And, to complicate the matter even further, yet another vision of King has been put forth in the texts of conservatives.

Not all conservatives can be said to value the so-called color-blind, assimilationist King. In the writings of nationalist-minded conservatives a "darker" King can be found, one who is only faintly praised and aggressively condemned. For nationalists such as Elizabeth Wright, "King and the other civil rights leaders, so called, are to blame for destroying our schools, our businesses, our communities," by embracing the doctrine of integration.[83] Color blindness may be well and good in the national, public, and political arenas where all individuals are equal in the eyes of the law, but a pragmatic appeal to race and racial cohesion to rebuild black institutions, to restore black neighborhoods, and to repair the social and moral fabric of black communities is equally if not more important.

Again, where race matters is not in discussions of what the state should do to rectify past discrimination and present inequalities but only in discussions of what African Americans should do to help themselves. In order to depoliticize race in the public sphere, matters of racial discrimination and racial uplift must be rendered as an exclusively private affair, thus shielding the state as well as the American public from an engagement with nettlesome issues of racial justice. An insistence that all men and women, whether "black," "white," or "other," be regarded only as individuals in the public sphere may have an idealistic and even admirable quality, but it also tends to obscure the material significance of ideological and social constructions of race, gender, and class.

Rearticulating this attempt to confine race to the private sector, Dinesh D'Souza opines on the "tragedy" of King's life; his failure to pursue what D'Souza calls "the second dimension of [King's] project: a concerted effort to raise the competitiveness and civilizational level of the black population."[84] In this reading of King's prophetic intent, King failed to speak to the moral deficiencies of African American peoples. Thus, the "problem" with King is that he was no Booker T. Washington. While they may disagree over what a Heritage Foundation–sponsored conference called "The Conservative Virtues of Martin L. King," the central message of the black conservative jeremiad remains the same: that the time for African Americans to demand redress and justice from the government is now past, that those who have failed to walk through the doors of opportunity have only themselves and their dysfunctional communities to blame. It is this message and this message alone that has been distilled from the African American traditions in social, political, and moral thought to create the essence of a black conservative canon.

Conclusion

Ultimately, this debate over King—and other historical figures—is a double-edged sword. For black conservatives this strategy of claiming canonical figures makes perfect sense. To be accorded the same sort of credence among African Americans that they are granted in the media, in public policy circles, and within the New Right, they must seek a greater degree of authenticity, legitimacy, and moral authority. What better way to do so than to position oneself squarely on the shoulders of "heroic" and revered men and women from the past? In this manner, black conservatives can declare, in essence, we are one of you, we share your interests and can best outline a course for our collective advancement. Such a strategy could, in fact, be persuasive. All too often nonconservative critics have faulted black conservatives for lacking an institutional base within African American communities and for their failure to gain local, state, and national office—so far.[85] That black conservatives have yet to achieve such prominence among African American voters and supporters in the past does not ipso facto mean that they will fail to do so in the future.

Nor is this strategy without some positive dimensions. First, this process of canon building can assist nonconservatives to better understand how various black conservatives position themselves along the political spectrum. As the disagreement over King and his legacy amply bears out, all black conservatives do not think and speak with one mind. Second, for better or worse, black conservative voices have begun to broaden conservative and nonconservative discourses in American political culture. Their presence has at least opened the possibility of a truly inclusive and multicultural movement on the Right and an ideologically diverse movement on the Left. At the very least, their presence reminds us of the richness of the African American tradition(s) and the myriad ways that tradition can be interpreted and deployed. Bringing another perspective to the table is not so much an indication of crisis as an opportunity for reevaluation, assent, and, of course, dissent.

The other edge of the sword is a bit sharper, however, for those who do dissent from both the conservative reinterpretation of the past as well as their present political pronouncements. As the nation continues to move away from a concrete commitment to substantiative, as opposed to merely procedural, equality and away from the goal of a truly multicultural, as opposed to a naively color-blind, society, dissenters are confronted with the necessity of meeting the various challenges posed by conservatives. Leftist scholars and activists have been far from silent on these matters. Critical race theorists such as Derrick Bell and Kimberle Crenshaw and social historians such as George Lipsitz, Robin Kelley, and David Roediger, along with a host of economists, sociologists, and policy analysts, have struggled to expose the dangers of color blindness and the policies it supports.[86]

From a variety of perspectives, all have argued that color blindness and initiatives such as the CCRI represent a movement away from a meaningful engagement with issues of race and racial discrimination. Mindful of the good intentions that drive the desire to move "beyond race," they assert that color blindness merely allows us to ignore the racial construction of whiteness, often by diverting our attention to the "social pathologies" of African Americans, and thus reinforces its privileges. As the legal scholar Cheryl Harris notes in her seminal article "Whiteness as Property," at the very historical moment "that race is infused with a perspective that reshapes it, through race-conscious remediation, into a potential weapon *against* subordination, official rules articulated in law [and in far too many of our public debates] deny that race matters."[87] While color blindness might seem to promise individual freedom and even redemption from the confines of race, Harris and others insist that it simultaneously denies the ongoing centrality of race and racism in structuring social and economic life.[88]

Along with their conservative counterparts, many of these leftist scholars have returned to the figures that make up the African American canon and to history itself for guidance and inspiration. And they, too, desire to speak as prophets, like Frederick Douglass, to a nation grown cold to and intolerant of African American claims that the state and all of society has a responsibility to empower the disadvantaged. "I am convinced that we need to get that sense of entitlement back," writes Robin Kelley in his strongly worded rebuke of black conservatives (or "negrocons" as he refers to them). "Call me old-fashioned, but opposing strong government supports in favor of some romantic notion of self-reliance is tantamount to relinquishing our citizenship."[89] Recalling all the major battles and victories waged for and with the assistance of the federal government—abolition, Reconstruction, industrial unionism, nonracist social welfare programs, and civil rights—Kelley insists that African Americans not lose sight of their right to demand social, economic, and political equity from the state.

Similarly, and with a more direct appeal to a canonical figure, Manning Marable urges a "Du Boisian" strategy toward issues such as affirmative action, which would "argue that despite the death of legal segregation a generation ago, we have yet reached the point where a color-blind society is possible, especially in terms of the actual organization and structure of white power and privilege."[90] Cumulatively, their work reveals that, while Elizabeth Wright may be correct that laying claim to historical figures is an age-old practice, such appeals to and uses of the past are always open to contentious debate. Indeed, these sorts of debates, occurring generation after generation, are precisely what has given African American political thought the rich diversity it has always enjoyed. Having played such a large role in structuring our collective past, it would be disingenuous to suppose they will not, whatever the cost and despite all risks, continue to do so well into our future.

Such debates—at least those involving canonical figures—have been less important among women and other minority conservatives. Oddly enough, despite a potentially rich field of opportunities, appeals to women of the past appear only fleetingly in the writings of politically conservative women and even less frequently in the writings of conservative Latinos and homosexuals. One notable exception, however, can be found in the desire of homosexual conservatives to connect themselves to Abraham Lincoln. Like black conservatives, they frequently refer to the Republican Party as the Party of Lincoln, and at least one conservative homosexual organization appropriates the mythology of Lincoln in its name—the Log Cabin Republicans.

Yet, the debates about and among African Americans, black conservative positions on race and individualism, public policy, and the public sphere, along with self-help and moral uplift, are all echoed in various forms within the writings and speeches of other multicultural conservatives. Speaking in their own distinctive voices, with their own particular appeals to America's past, women, Latino, and homosexual conservatives also aspire to cleanse the public sphere of the language of difference in favor of an American identity premised on a public blindness to gender, sexuality, and ethnicity. As the following chapter demonstrates, the conservative jeremiads being produced by homosexuals, women, Latinos, Asian-Americans, and blacks share a willingness to contest the meaning of history and progress as they strive to return us to the promise of American democracy—if only we would turn away from and repent of our wicked ways.

The civil rights movement, rather than working to improve the lives of black Americans, to restore a healthy family life, to rid the inner city of crime and drugs, has preferred to make common cause with white liberals whose goal was an expanded welfare state rather than a society in which individuals could go as far as their abilities would take them.
—*Editor's Comment, "Twenty Five Years after the March on Washington: The Growing Irrelevance of the Civil Rights Movement,* Lincoln Review *(1988)*

CHAPTER 2

Toward a Politics of Assimilation

Multicultural Conservatism and the Assault on the Civil Rights Establishment

As I suggested in the previous chapter, the critique of the post-1965 civil rights movement has been key in the articulation of a black conservative jeremiad. But this narrative is not the exclusive property of African Americans. Among conservatives in general, the 1954–1965 phase of the movement is generally characterized as a heroic attempt to reform American democracy and to secure the civil and political rights of all Americans regardless of race. Unfortunately, according to conservatives, as civil rights leaders and organizations became part of the establishment, they turned away from the shared American consensus on race and race relations. At the moment of their greatest success, civil rights advocates embraced race-conscious policies and initiatives as well as divisive language emphasizing the intractability of racism and structural discrimination. This gross overpoliticization of race, conservatives charge, has led left and liberal civil rights advocates to reject the movement toward color blindness as well as the doctrine of individual equality of opportunity in favor of group-based equality of results.

Thomas Sowell, among others, has argued that many Americans who supported "the initial thrust of civil rights, as represented by the *Brown v. Board of Education* decision and the Civil Rights Act of 1964, later felt betrayed as the original concept of equal individual *opportunity* evolved toward the concept of equal group *results*."[1] Following Sowell's lead, black conservatives insist that this change not only "betrayed" the movement's initial supporters but also betrayed African Americans as a whole by wedding them in the end to a harmful agenda based on group rights, victim status, and a crippling dependency on the federal government.

While black conservatives have been key in the development of such narratives, its earliest articulation can be found in the broad contours of thought that came to define the "neoconservatism" of intellectuals such as Nathan Glazer, Irving Howe, Irving Kristol, and Norman Podhoretz. Predominantly white, male, and Jewish, these theorists, policy analysts, and cultural critics revolted against what they viewed as an excess of egalitarianism in American political culture, the radicalization of the (New) Left, and the transformation in the tenor of the civil rights movement. Yet, it was Daniel Patrick Moynihan more than any other single figure who laid the intellectual foundations for the neoconservative critique of the post-1965 civil rights movement. Arguing that equality of opportunity almost always ensures inequality of results, he chastised black activists and politicians for not realizing and assenting to this basic liberal truth.

"The point of semantics," Moynihan insisted, "is that equality of opportunity now has a different meaning for Negroes than it has for whites."

> It is not (or at least no longer) a demand for liberty alone, but also for equality—in terms of group results. In Bayard Rustin's terms, "It is now concerned not merely with removing the barriers to full *opportunity* but with achieving the fact of *equality*." By equality Rustin means a distribution of achievements among Negroes roughly comparable to that among whites.[2]

Should this natural evolution of the movement occur, Moynihan warned, "there will be no social peace for generations."

The men and women who would come to be labeled neoconservative certainly supported the early phase of the civil rights movement, with its demands for federal legislation to ensure civil and political liberties without regard to race, color, religion, or national origin. Many drew parallels between blacks and Jews, between racism and anti-Semitism, to fashion morally persuasive arguments against all forms of discrimination and prejudice. Yet, in the mid-1960s they began to part company with the Left over issues of structural discrimination, economic justice, poverty, and social welfare. Arguing that poverty and extralegal forms of discrimination could not be legislated (or spent) away, they stood in increasingly staunch opposition to programs such as affirmative action and many of the era's Great Society federal initiatives. Affirmative action became, in Nathan Glazer's now famous formulation, "affirmative discrimination," a monumental restructuring of public policy to take into account the race of individuals. Moreover, neoconservatives charged, policies such as affirmative action reinscribed a new quota system comparable, in their eyes, to the informal system that had kept Jewish individuals out of schools, occupations, and institutions.[3]

Similarly, the Great Society initiatives were critiqued for taking the emphasis off individual achievement, responsibility, and hard work, turning instead to a mass of ill-conceived and ineffectual programs. The overly ambitious agenda of these programs resulted in inflation, worker alienation, racial tensions, and lingering ills. The problems of race and poverty, neoconservatives insisted, could not be addressed solely or even primarily by the machinations of the federal government. We must look instead to the cultural realms for explanations and solutions. Thus, in book after book and article after article, neoconservative intellectuals hammered away at the dysfunctional status of the black family, the culture of welfare dependency, the lack of skills and ambitions, and other negative patterns of behavior to account for the persistent inability of some black Americans(and other ethnic minorities) to achieve.[4] Foreshadowing future developments, Moynihan argued, in a 1967 essay, that true liberals should ally with conservatives against radicals. Because true liberals understand that their essential interest lies in the stability of the social order, and because that stability is under assault from radical leftists, "they [liberals] must seek out and make much more effective alliances with political conservatives who share their interest and recognize that unyielding rigidity is just as great a threat to continuity of the social order as an anarchic desire for change."[5]

With black allies such as Sowell, these new-style conservatives carried this argument into the heart of the mainstream conservative movement, encouraging more traditional ("paleo-")conservatives to herald the early phase of the civil rights movement as well. This, despite traditional conservatism's initial opposition to the *Brown* decision and the fact that arguments over the 1964 Civil Rights Act dramatically split the ranks of the Republican Party, helping to pave the way for the racially encoded conservative populism of Barry Goldwater in 1964, George Wallace in 1968, Richard Nixon in 1972, and Ronald Reagan in the 1980s. Even hard-core conservatives such as Patrick Buchanan have come, at this late date, to praise the movement. "In retrospect," writes Buchanan in *Right from the Beginning*, "the civil rights movement was liberalism's finest hour. . . . If they have stumbled and blundered terribly since, they knew what they were doing then. And what they were doing was right."[6]

That was then; this is now. For our purposes, what is most important about these historical developments is the degree to which the critique of the post-1965 civil rights movement marks a point of intersection between black and white (or "mainstream") conservatives and, as I will argue, among Latino, homosexual, and women conservatives as well. A broad perspective on these intersections and corollaries reveals that at least since the mid-1970s, a powerful enemy known as the "civil rights establishment" (CRE) has emerged as one of the chief targets of various factions within the conservative movement—despite, or perhaps because of, the politics of race, gender, ethnicity, and sexual orientation.

Clint Bolick, a white conservative attorney and a leading opponent of affirmative action, sees the rise of the civil rights establishment as directly bound to the transformation in the post-1965 movement. Unlike its predecessor *movement*, Bolick argues, the current establishment has lost the moral legitimacy of a universalist paradigm by favoring a particularist politics, thus "transforming the meaning of civil rights from those fundamental rights we all share as Americans into special rights for some and burdens for others." Moreover, this civil rights establishment holds a virtual "monopoly over the mantle of civil rights," which allows its representatives to "dictate the terms of the debates" and to silence the voices of those who seek to challenge the orthodoxy the establishment imposes.[7]

Said to be located at the nexus of a diverse array of groups such as the NAACP, the National Organization for Women, La Raza, and ACT-UP and of radical academics and university administrators, as well as the remnants of the New Deal coalition, this establishment has been accused by conservatives of perpetuating a dangerous and subversive vision of liberalism, one well outside the shared American understanding of civil rights and one that perverts the American political system. Dinesh D'Souza, for instance, sees a sort of Machiavellian conspiracy at work. "Groups like the NAACP work in coalition with other activist groups such as the National Organization for Women, the National Education Association and the AFL-CIO to win political and financial benefits through horse trading.

For example, the NAACP might support a feminist bill on comparable worth in exchange for NOW's backing for a racial preference measure. There is nothing unusual about such bartering, of course, except that it converts civil rights from a moral ideal that transcends partisan politics into another special interest cause that may or may not warrant public support.[8]

Leaving aside the question of whether civil rights has *ever* been a cause that transcends partisan politics, the conservative assault on the civil rights establishment bears a striking resemblance to the critique of the so-called liberal establishment in generations past. In fact, while the language employed by Bolick, D'Souza, and Sowell has a distinctly contemporary ring, the broader thrust of the critique is far from new. During the formative years of the modern conservative movement and the emergence of the New Right, attacks on what was derisively termed the liberal (or "Eastern")[9] establishment helped to congeal the nascent movement's various factions into a more or less coherent, and oppositional, force. As Sidney Blumenthal has noted, the construction of modern conservatism was predicated on collective fears of the supposed power wielded by liberals over the federal government and American society from roughly the New Deal on.[10]

"The chief point about the Liberal Establishment is that it is in control," complained M. Stanton Evans, a prominent conservative at mid-century. Writing in 1965, as one phase of the civil rights movement was coming to an end and a new phase was developing, Stanton also chastised the establishment for its presumptuousness in "guiding the lives and destinies of the American people." "It wields enormous power, immeasurable power" he continued, "its control embraces the instruments of public scrutiny. It directs and instructs popular opinion."[11] Similarly, William F. Buckley, Jr., founder of the *National Review*, could confidently state that liberals "exercise great power (I cannot imagine a day's events free of their influence). I go so far as to say theirs is today the dominant voice in determining the destiny of this country."[12]

Against this hydra-headed monster of power and influence, mainstream conservatives juxtaposed themselves as anti-elitist, antistatist, rebellious insurgents. Their rebellion was based not only on their long-standing opposition to the New Deal and the welfare state. The conservative critique of liberalism was also augmented by the vast societal changes precipitated by the civil rights movement and concomitant anxieties over race relations.

Again, with the assistance of neoconservatives, this conservative "populism" increasingly came to disparage connections among the Black Power movement, feminism, the Chicano liberation movement, and gay and lesbian radicalism. In so doing, conservatives presented a picture of a society in peril of being torn asunder by a host of subversive and "un-American" radicals bent on foisting ill-conceived and equally un-American policies on an unsuspecting public.

This associative tactic is clearest in the editorial turn taken by *Commentary* in the late 1960s and early 1970s. The opening salvos in what would become an all-out war against the New Left began around 1966, featuring indictments of younger activists by the likes of Tom Kahn, Nathan Glazer, and Diana Trilling as well as Bayard Rustin, whose harsh critique of the Black Power movement appeared in the fall 1966 issue.[13] Throughout the late 1960s, *Commentary* continued to vacillate between Left and Right, condemning the radicalization of liberalism with one hand and seeking to preserve vestiges of liberal anticommunism with the other. Even the editors of *The National Review*, the flagship journal of postwar conservatism, noticed this erratic tendency and issued a welcome under the banner, "Come On In, The Water's Fine."[14]

As other commentators have noted, after 1971, Podhoretz appeared to be dictating *Commentary*'s editorial policy by consulting a veritable laundry list of New Left sins. Environmentalists were denounced; activist professors and clergy were ridiculed; feminism and gay liberation were lampooned, as were the Black Panthers, McGovernites, antiwar protestors, and anyone or anything that supported or glamorized the counterculture, including the Democratic Party. Unlike the mainstream conservatives whom they were increasingly coming to resemble, the contributors to *Commentary* claimed to have an intimate, insider's understanding of their adversaries, some of whom were in fact old friends. "We knew what they really thought and felt," Podhoretz later explained, "which did not always coincide with what they considered it expedient to say in public; and we knew how to penetrate their self-protective rhetoric."[15]

Surveying the terrain of contemporary liberalism, neoconservatives also found the corrupting influence of the New Class—a host of intellectuals, bureaucrats, social workers, academics, lawyers, and consultants—immersed in the drive for power and prestige for its own sake and at the expense of the public. Michael Harrington, in his 1968 book, *Toward a Democratic Left*, idealistically argued in favor of an educated New Class, drawn from the ranks of postwar baby boomers, as the foundation for a new

American liberalism. For both social and demographic reasons, Harrington believed that such a group could be encouraged to reject extreme self- and class interest and to work instead on behalf of the poor and working classes. In their critique, neoconservatives were less impressed by Harrington's optimistic reading of the potential of the New Class to erect a good society.

Instead, the coming of the New Class was a source of danger. As neoconservatives saw it, the ranks of this class were "massively expanding as the sixties generation came of age," and this expansion was fueled by a growing number of federally sponsored programs and initiatives of dubious merit.[16] While claiming to embody compassion for the poor and downtrodden, the New Class was in reality out only for its own gain. Here again, neoconservatives were instrumental in bringing a new language (if not necessarily a new vision of the dangers of liberalism) into the mainstream of the conservative movement and, more significant, in establishing a pattern followed by African American, Latino, and homosexual conservatives.

Made to bear the brunt of radical activism of the 1960s and the cultural and economic malaise of the 1970s, the "civil rights establishment" thus came to displace the liberal establishment as a target of conservative ire. This shift in focus from traditional liberalism to civil rights liberalism (and racial conservatism) is far from inconsequential; much of this struggle among liberals, leftists, and conservatives turns on the very definition of civil rights and the meaning of race. No longer willing to contest civil rights activism per se, many conservatives, like Bolick and Buchanan, now voiced their support for the goals of the pre-1965 movement but only those that were well within a limited constitutional framework and that emphasized individual rights. Such an ideological shift allowed conservatives to claim the mantle of Martin L. King, Jr., and to praise his dream of an interracial democracy in the name of fairness, merit, and individualism, while simultaneously attacking leftists and liberals for betraying it.

What this establishment is viewed as being and doing, and why a diverse group of conservatives are so dedicated to discrediting and dismantling it, is the primary focus of this chapter. I want to suggest that multicultural conservatives have introduced a provocative wrinkle into the discourses of conservative dissent from liberalism and the liberal establishment, one that problematizes assumptions about identity politics and cultural authenticity as well as notions of "insiders" and "outsiders." While they are as concerned as mainstream conservatives with the potential damage to the American polity posed by the civil rights establishment, the central focus has been on the establishment's corrupting influence on the very women and minorities it claims to serve.

Indeed, much of the power of what I have called the multicultural conservative *style* resides in the ability of black, Latino, homosexual, and women conservatives to premise their criticism of the establishment on their own identities as members of groups about whom they have an insider's knowledge. This from-the-inside-out approach, to paraphrase the title of black conservative Glenn Loury's recent collection of essays, constitutes a critique of one form of identity politics while subtly replacing it with another.[17] Like Podhoretz and the Old/New Left, a number of women and minority conservatives—especially those neoconservatives once aligned with liberal and leftist causes—promise to penetrate the self-protective rhetoric of the CRE, giving us a good look at the man behind the curtain.

In their opposition to the philosophies and practices of the CRE, women and minority conservatives have also revived the old "silent majority" argument used to such effect by Nixon. "In these difficult years," intoned Nixon in his first inaugural address, "America has suffered from a fear of words: from inflated rhetoric that promises more than it can deliver; from angry rhetoric that fans discontents into hatreds; from bombastic rhetoric that postures instead of persuading." In the midst of this avalanche of words, Nixon promised a government that would "listen in new ways—to the voices of quiet anguish, the voices that speak without words, the voices of the heart—to the injured voices, the anxious voices, the voices that have despaired of being heard."[18] Capitalizing on the fears and anxieties of working- and lower-class whites caught up in a nostalgia for a supposedly simpler time, Nixon mobilized their seething resentment against black militants, rowdy feminists, subversive antiwar protesters, pointy-headed intellectuals, and other sophisticated wordsmiths who seemed engaged in a twisted conspiracy to destroy America.[19]

Multicultural conservatives have merely tapped into this older strategy and applied their own spin to it. In the process, they have raised questions about representation and the right to speak on behalf of a group. Like Nixon, they have promised to listen to those anguished voices that speak without words. Thus, they have urged a rethinking of the radicalism of the 1960s and the politicization of race, gender, ethnicity, and sexuality in our public life and in our universities, while offering a solution to the problems caused by the establishment, namely the embrace of a politics of assimilation, individualism, and free-market capitalism. Like their white (and Jewish) counterparts, they have brought new perspectives to old conservative arguments. Pursuing their own agendas, women and minority conservatives have provided an invaluable service to the New Right by reformulating preexisting strategies and opening up new political terrains.

Who's Afraid of the CRE?

Simply stated, the civil rights establishment takes up too much space; it generates a din so loud that more reasonable voices cannot be heard. As with many of the arguments that have come to mark the multicultural conservative style, black conservatives have played a leading role in developing the criticism of the CRE as a totalitarian and nonrepresentative force in American and African American political culture. "The civil rights leadership," chides black conservative Robert Woodson, "has been very successfully imposed a gag rule on the black community: unless you espouse the liberal Democratic ideology, you're out of step, and we'll accuse you of being anything but a child of God. People have been intimidated by that."[20] Woodson, head of the National Center for Neighborhood Enterprise, a pro-free-market, grass-roots organization he founded in 1981, also blames the "official script" of the civil rights establishment for foreclosing an honest discussion of the problems of the black urban poor.

This official script has led, according to Woodson, to the growth and perpetuation of a federally sponsored industry of poverty that victimizes the black and Latino urban poor. "What we have built in the name of the poor," Woodson argues, is a *Poverty Pentagon.*

> And in this huge conglomerate of programs for the poor, the principal beneficiaries are not the poor but those who make their living from the poor. We have, in many cases, programs that do not improve the conditions of the poor but actually exacerbate the very problems they were designed to solve.[21]

Woodson's position grows out of a disillusionment with the course of the post-1965 civil rights movement. As a social worker active in protest organizations in the 1960s and an Urban League official from 1971 to 1977, his criticisms of the movement—particularly its "embrace of integration and busing" and its focus on "issues that were important to middle- or upper-income blacks, [which] did little for lower income blacks"—are common ones.

Woodson is also a leading member of the cadre of black intellectuals who aligned themselves with the New Right, occupying a position at the American Enterprise Institute and participating in organizations that have structured the intellectual wing of the modern conservative movement since the late 1970s.[22] This group, including academics and activists such as Woodson, Sowell, Loury, Walter Williams, Elizabeth Wright, and Anne Wortham, have all come to question the proprietary nature of the establishment on race matters. As the sociologist Murray Friedman has noted, they do not share any one social or political philosophy. "What permits them to be classified together, however, is that in their work on poverty they have avoided generalized indictments of American society and eschewed purely racial explanations of the plight of poor blacks."[23] In one way or another, they have also all claimed that the CRE is no longer representative of the majority of African Americans.

In a host of articles and speeches, black conservatives have repeatedly pointed to the growing irrelevance of the civil rights movement and the establishment that has supported it. Now is the time, they insist, to leave the "plantation" cultivated and maintained by the federal government and its establishment lackeys. This potent rhetorical strategy resonates with African American political culture and is a powerful metaphor for antistatist political struggles. Its structure is deceptively simple: Dependency (slavery) equals almost everything associated with the federal government's welfare and antipoverty and race and gender-based initiatives. In *It's Okay to Leave the Plantation: The New Underground Railroad*, C. Mason Weaver, a black conservative talk-show host and political commentator, defines the "plantation mentality" as a "system that discourages independence and character and encourages reliance on masters or appointed tribal chiefs in our community."[24]

Weaver's book chronicles his transformation from a "Berkeley liberal" in the 1960s and early 1970s to a conservative Christian Republican in the 1980s. Pushing the plantation metaphor to its virtual breaking point, the inner-city becomes a "plantation run by black overseers (black leaders) who went to the master (government) for us"; picking cotton is analogous to "allowing our votes to be picked by one party"; slavery is equated with welfare, drug use, and crime, while birth control and reproductive freedom are devalued as nothing more than a form of racial genocide. The black community today, Weaver argues, "controls 99% of the problems we face," and on the basis of this supposition he urges a new form of self-abolition.[25] The new emancipation can be effected only when the majority of the black community recognizes its power and responsibility and joins individuals, like Weaver, who have already escaped via the underground railroad and embraced the philosophies of the Religious Right and the Republican Party.

Many black conservatives, especially those with a socially conservative and Christian perspective, emphasize the importance of rebuilding the black family and the Black Church, improving education (particularly through voucher schemes), and strengthening civic and community life, but black conservative women have been exceedingly diligent in this arena. Ezola Foster, for example, privileges her roles as wife, mother, and educator to buttress her critique of liberal social policy. A former Democrat and a public school teacher in South Central Los Angeles for more than thirty years, Foster is also the founder of Americans for Family Values (formerly Black Americans for Family Values). As a public advocate for conservative policies, she rails against the proliferation of welfare, abortion, liberal immigration laws, the Democratic Party, and most members of the black establishment, whom she characterizes as "snake oil salesmen." "Today's welfare system," Foster asserts, "is like the slave trade," aided and abetted by immoral sex education, promiscuity, teen pregnancy, and single-female-headed households. Foster, who claims to be more of a radical conservative than Pat Buchanan(!), advises less talk about rights and entitlements and more about responsibility, especially for women, along with the necessity of school prayer, educational reform through vouchers, and right-to-work and prolife legislation.[26]

In articulating these views, Foster has been joined by other black conservative women such as Teresa Doggett and Star Parker. Unlike Foster, who became disillusioned with the Democrats, Doggett has been a lifelong member of the Grand Old Party. "Conservative," says Doggett, who has run for elected office in Texas on the Republican ticket, is the only label she attaches to herself. "I never brought up in the race that I was a woman or an African American. Everybody is sick of those labels." Doggett, whose husband, John, created a minor scandal in his testimony against his former Yale Law classmate Anita Hill in the Hill-Thomas controversy, has always been a Republican. Raised in a middle-class black family in Kansas, she claims to have never even met a liberal before moving to Washington, D.C., after college. Although she has "no trouble supporting special programs to help those who have limited opportunities and advantages," Doggett is virulent in her insistence that "basing these programs on race and gender makes no sense at all."[27]

Similarly, Star Parker, a former welfare recipient turned conservative Christian, also advocates a "tough love" policy on welfare, abortion, school choice, and affirmative action. Likening Democrats to pimps and black liberals to whores, Parker blames them, along with second-generation welfare "addicts," for the destruction of the black community.[28] What distinguishes Parker's voice from her cohorts is her ability to speak from direct experience. In her autobiography, she depicts herself as having been a stereotypical welfare queen, using her benefits to obtain four abortions, an apartment with a Jacuzzi, and a substantial profit selling Medi-Cal stickers on the black market. Until, that is, she found God, married, worked her way off welfare, became an energetic convert to conservatism, and began to work with the Traditional Values Coalition, one of the premier groups within the Religious Right.

Such attacks on the civil rights establishment, using metaphors of slavery and dependency as well as personal experience, have offered a powerful format for other minority and women conservatives. Some have drawn a direct correlation between post-1965 African American politics and the "troubles" of their own social groups and communities. This correlation is clearest in the writings of the Latina conservative Linda Chavez, who has attacked the civil rights establishment—and especially groups such as La Raza—with a venom rivaling that of any of her conservative colleagues. Chavez, executive director of the U.S. Commission on Civil Rights during the Reagan administration and presently head of the Center for Equal Opportunity, sees a direct, and negative, relationship between the post-1965 African American movement and the ideologies of the "Hispanic" left; she suggests that the former negatively influenced the latter. "So long as Hispanics remained a separate and disadvantaged group," Chavez asserts, "they were entitled [like blacks] to affirmative action programs, compensatory education, government set-asides, and myriad other programs."[29]

"Assimilation," Chavez concludes, "gave way to Affirmative Action" and politics of group identity and victimization. Assimilation on the political level and a return to self-help within communities are the dual strategies that link black and Latino conservatives. Whereas black conservatives urge a return to the vision of the pre-1965 stage of the civil rights movement, Chavez also wants to retrieve an earlier understanding of Hispanic-American politics. Above all, she wants to return to a point before the 1971 *Cisneros* decision artificially transformed Hispanics into a legally defined and protected minority group. In that decision, *Cisneros v. Corpus Christi Independent School District,* a U.S. district court ruled that Mexican-Americans constituted an identifiable minority group entitled to special federal assistance. For conservatives, this official recognition as a disadvantaged minority relegated Hispanics to the status of wards of the state, paved the way for the creation of a more powerful ethnic lobby, and challenged the assimilationist ethic of older, more moderate organizations.[30]

Chavez views the post-*Cisneros* Latino contribution to the power of the civil rights establishment as emanating not from grass-roots activism or any majority opinion among the groups labeled "Hispanic." For her, such a majority opinion would have been a logical impossibility since "[b]efore the affirmative action age, there were no Hispanics, only Mexicans, Puerto Ricans, Cubans and so on."[31] In her desire to expose the nonrepresentative nature of the Latino Left, she charges that advocacy organizations such as the Mexican American Political Association, the Alianza Federal de Mercedes, the Crusade for Justice, and La Raza were solely the product of college-educated radicals in league with powerful and wealthy foundations, especially the Ford Foundation. "These new foundation-supported groups," Chavez declares "could afford to pursue their own agenda, without the broad, popular support from the Hispanic community—and they did."[32]

By supporting federal antipoverty initiatives, by defending and expanding the welfare state, by writing Hispanics into the Voting Rights Act and affirmative action guidelines, and by pursuing federal funding for bilingual education programs, these organizations became, in Chavez's words, "a cadre of ethnic power brokers" rather than the legitimate representatives of the Hispanic Americans. In his book *Ethnic America,* Thomas Sowell also blames the rise of these leftist organizations for slowing the pattern of assimilation among Hispanics. And, like Chavez, he views their members as radical separatists who linked themselves with the Black Power movement and therefore did not represent the sentiments of the majority. Writing specifically about groups such as the Brown Berets, he claims that "most Mexican Americans have literally never heard of these various organizations, however seriously the media treats their assertions in the name of 'Chicanos.'"[33]

As with other conservatives, the meaning of culture and the nature of cultural values are equally important in their critique of the Establishment. "Inherently, the Hispanic voter is a conservative voter," argues Carlos Rodriguez, a GOP political consultant. "Republican issues don't have to be translated to the Hispanic community because inherently those issues—faith, family, and hard work—are the ones they already identify with."[34] Guided by this principle, organizations such as HALTO (Hispanics Against Liberal Take Over), founded by Daniel Portado and based in California, and the more substantial Republican National Hispanic Assembly, the Hispanic outreach arm of the Republican National Committee, seek to stem the destructive tide of affirmative action and welfare, illegal immigration, and bilingual education.

Conservatives such as Chavez view the federal government's sponsorship of bilingual education as a prime example of how the CRE's "misguided policies" work primarily for the benefit of the power brokers themselves. Once again, the New Class rears its ugly head. According to Chavez, who was a former president of U.S. English, an English language advocacy group, the millions of dollars funneled into bilingual education function to provide jobs program for an educated Hispanic elite that occupies many of the positions as teachers and administrators. "The number of Hispanic children in bilingual programs grows each year," Chavez writes, "as does funding for the programs at the local, state and federal levels."

No other ethnic group, including the 250,000 immigrants who come here from Asia each year, is clamoring for the right to have its language and culture maintained in this country at public expense. Although Hispanics have succeeded in doing so—for the time being—theirs will be a Pyrrhic victory if it is gained at the expense of their ultimate social and economic integration.[35]

Like Chavez, who speaks no Spanish, other minority conservatives, including the late Senator S. I. Hayakawa (R-California), cofounder and honorary chairman of U.S. English, have claimed to be deeply offended when the government assumes that naturalized citizens do not understand English. They have also derided Latino advocates of bilingualism as "professional Hispanics as distinguished from Hispanic professionals," distancing Latino leftists from the supposed vast majority who do support measures such as the English Language Amendment.[36] Indeed, bilingual education has emerged as one of the more explosive issues separating Latino liberals and leftists from conservatives. Raul Yzaguirre, president of the National Council of La Raza, has denounced organizations such as U.S. English in the sternest terms possible. "U.S. English," he has said, "is to Hispanics as the Ku Klux Klan is to blacks."[37]

While it is easy to write off such characterizations as extremist rhetoric, in 1988 the *Arizona Republic* published excerpts from a confidential memo written by U.S. English's cofounder, Dr. John Tanton, an ophthalmologist from Petoskey, Michigan. Offering a defense of "our common language," Tanton's memo also raised the specter of a Hispanic takeover and the concomitant fear of "race suicide." "As Whites see their power and control over their lives declining," he wrote, "will they simply go quietly into the night? Or will there be an explosion? . . . We're building in a deadly disunity. All great empires disintegrate, we want stability."[38] Not only did the publication of Tanton's views seem to justify the worst claims made against the organization; it also spurred Chavez's resignation as president. She claims ignorance of Tanton's ideas and now disavows any sympathy with legislative initiatives to create "language police." Rather, as a conservative with libertarian leanings, she advocates limiting bilingual education and abolishing bilingual ballots. Hispanics who do not learn English, she continues to maintain, will not be able to avail themselves of equal opportunities. "Those who do not, will be relegated to second-class citizens."[39]

It is in this way, among others, that Asian-American conservatives have contributed to the articulation of multicultural conservatism. Asian-Americans sympathetic to the Right have used Chavez's work on Latinos as a model. "Asians who wonder about the cult of victimization adopted by [liberal] Asian activists would do well to see how this attitude disadvantages the Hispanic community," writes columnist Arthur Hu. "They get political points by showing what a lowly race they are instead of being proud of progress that is being made." Invoking a fusion of traditional Asian values and Americanization, Asian-American conservatives have been as dedicated to antibilingual education as Hayakawa ever was and tend to oppose illegal immigration in the most strenuous ways possible. Further, they have demonstrated, as a group, little willingness to bristle at the classification of Asian-Americans as a "model minority" and as "honorary whites," most notably in the context of the affirmative action debate. That this technique is also deployed to buttress the proposition that conservatives are not against all people of color is likewise of little apparent concern. As with Chavez and others, the preferred strategy is to pursue the glories of assimilation at all cost.[40]

Cultural cohesion at the expense of a culture of assimilation is also a theme developed by Richard Rodriguez. "But the bilingualists simplistically scorn the value and necessity of assimilation," Rodriguez contends. "They do not seem to realize that there are two ways a person is individualized. So they do not realize that while one suffers a diminished sense of *private* individuality by becoming assimilated into public society, such assimilation makes possible the achievement of *public* individuality. . . . Only when I was able to think of myself as an American, no longer alien in *gringo* society, could I seek the rights and opportunities necessary for full public individuality."[41]

While I am fully aware of Rodriguez's contention that he is not a card-carrying conservative, he has added a certain amount of texture to the views advocated by Chavez, Sowell, and other multicultural conservatives. To this extent, I have suggested that he be viewed as a "fellow traveler." Not only does his writing on public policy and identity bisect and reinforce conservative Hispanic opinion, but since his "coming out" he has also provided aid and comfort for conservative homosexuals. Appealing again to his defense of public individuality, he has critiqued the culture of gay identity that undergirds the existence of areas such as the Castro district for implying "that sexuality was more crucial, that homosexuality was the central fact of identity."[42]

Rodriguez's position on Latino identity directly parallels his views on gay identity. Both, when premised on and defined by group consciousness, must be opposed in the name of individual freedom. Both forms of group consciousness, moreover, conspire to define America as alien. Such a stress on individualism and assimilation is common among homosexual conservatives overall. In a fairly rare contribution by a lesbian, Norah Vincent reiterates the need for homosexuals to move beyond the confines of a gay or lesbian identity. "If lesbians truly want *equal* rights and *equal* treatment," she writes, "they should step into the real world, make a case for their humanity first, and above all, learn to take a joke."[43] But how, one might reasonably ask, should they make their case? Gay and lesbian conservatives stand in a slightly different relationship to the overall critique of the civil rights establishment. Since homosexuals have not had the same relationship to the state as other minority groups, their criticisms are somewhat preventive. Like other conservatives, however, they tend to cast a cold and critical eye toward a politics of difference. Disparaging homosexual groups and individuals associated with the CRE who advocate a gay, lesbian, or transgender culture as separate and distinct from American culture, conservative authors such as Bruce Bawer have argued that homosexuals would be better served if they were to abandon their efforts to make such categories socially or politically relevant.

In *A Place at the Table: The Gay Individual in American Society,* Bawer considers the idea that some gays—"like blacks before them"—might seek to establish affirmative action programs, but he quickly rejects the suggestion on the grounds that the "great majority of homosexuals, I suspect, would strongly oppose them." Bawer's reasoning is all too familiar. "Quota systems," he writes, "subordinate individual identity to group identity; they reinforce the tendency to view someone who happens to belong to a minority group not as an individual but as a member of that group." What most homosexuals want, Bawer assures us, is not the recognition of gay culture or special preferences but precisely the opposite: "More than anything else, we want people to see past the 'gay' label, and past whatever associations that label may carry in their minds, and to view us as individuals."[44] Unfortunately, according to conservatives, what "most homosexuals want" remains unrecognized and therefore unrepresented by liberal gays and lesbians.

Log Cabin Republicans (LCR) is the most prominent organization seeking to rectify this situation by giving gay and lesbian voters a voice within the Republican Party, the conservative movement, and American political culture overall. Founded in 1978, it is currently the largest conservative homosexual group in the nation, with more than fifty chapters across the country, a national office in Washington, D.C., and a political action committee. Advertising itself as a "home for mainstream gays and lesbians," the LCR has prepared a statement of purpose that declares:

> We care deeply about equality and we hold Republican views on crime, fiscal responsibility and foreign policy. We believe in individual rights rather than group rights. We believe in limited government rather than big government. We believe that all Americans should be able to participate fully in the political process. We represent the next generation for the gay and lesbian community. No longer will we be told where we must live, how we must dress, and how we must vote. Now there is a political alternative.[45]

The guiding philosophy of LCR is not so much liberal as libertarian. In terms of homosexual politics, the group supports the passage of antidiscrimination legislation, the repeal of sodomy laws, and the right to marry with all of the legal and social benefits that marriage bestows. In the main, what distinguishes the LCR philosophy from those of other gay rights groups—apart, that is, from its location within the Republican Party—is its libertarianism. Following the strict division between the public sphere and the private one that traditional libertarians have maintained, gays and lesbians associated with the LCR endorse proposals allowing for individual equality as public individuals and protecting against discrimination and government intervention into their private affairs. In fact, one of the founding members of the Log Cabin Republicans is Dorr Legg, an early gay rights activist and a leading libertarian thinker, who made history in 1958 by winning a Supreme Court case that resulted in his being allowed to send his gay-oriented magazine, *One*, through the mail.

While Legg was an advocate of basic civil rights for gays and lesbians—a necessary precondition for equality and full integration into public life—he was adamantly opposed to any attempt to force homosexuals to "desperately contort themselves into simulacra of heterosexuality."[46] And on this key point turns the distinction between libertarians and assimilationists. Some gay conservatives, following Legg's lead, believe in a flamboyant "individualism of the queen"; others, such as Rich Tafal, president of the national LCR, and the gay Christian conservative Mel White, advocate traditional social values of God, country, and family. There is nonetheless substantial agreement that such matters are private concerns and therefore beyond the purview of government and its minions in the civil rights establishment.[47]

There is also widespread agreement among conservative homosexuals that gays and lesbians—not to mention bisexual, transsexual, and transgender individuals—do not constitute a minority group with a distinct culture. Nor do they countenance the so-called ideologies of victimization fostered by the Left. Writing against any politics that presupposes gay and lesbian oppression—"every minority's word for practically everything, a one-size-fits-all political designation used by anyone who feels unequal, aggrieved, and even uncomfortable"—Jonathan Rauch disputes the very reality of this claim, as well as its usefulness to the gay rights movement. Jumping on the bandwagon of oppression, he argues, implies that to be gay is to suffer. "It affirms what so many straight people, even sympathetic ones, believe in their hearts: that homosexuals are pitiable." That alone, concludes Rauch, echoing the concerns of other gay conservatives, as well as black and Latino conservatives, "is reason to junk the oppression model, preferably sooner instead of later."[48]

This challenge to blacks, Hispanics, and homosexuals who claim leadership positions within the CRE is also well represented among conservative women, despite major philosophical differences between the women over their "proper place" in American society. In *Women of the New Right*, Rebecca E. Klatch identifies two major schools of thought among conservative women. The first group, social conservatives, is close to the orientation of the Religious Right. In general, their worldview is deeply rooted in religious, primarily Christian, beliefs, an understanding of the heterosexual two-parent family as the sacred unit of society, and a perspective that celebrates the role of women as wives and mothers. Laissez-faire conservative women, on the other hand, tend to view the world in terms of the political and economic liberty of the individual and are, therefore, closer to neoconservatives and the libertarian branch of the conservative movement. They are also more likely than socially conservative women to embrace some of the basic tenets of feminism—or at least those that facilitate the full assimilation of women into mainstream society. As Klatch notes, both currents share a deep distrust of the intrusive power of the federal government as "a symbol of America on the road to decline." For social conservatives, "Big government signifies the promotion of immorality, the endorsement of Secular Humanism, and the usurpation of traditional authority," while laissez-faire conservative women view "Big government as an impediment to the individual's economic liberty and as an intrusion on the individual's political liberty."[49]

This difference in worldviews (which also bisects the conservative movement overall) has produced tensions among conservative women as well as a multiplicity of organizations. The positions adopted by the Eagle Forum and Concerned Women for America (CWA) are most representative of social and religious conservatives; laissez-faire or neoconservative women have tended to join and maintain leadership positions within a variety of nongender-specific New Right groups, although some have found a comfortable niche in the Independent Women's Forum, which has been described as "too conservative for traditional women's organizations and too secular for conservative groups like the Eagle Forum and the [CWA]."[50] Both factions are nonetheless united in opposition to the CRE and establishment feminism.

Coming from different perspectives, conservative women agree that the power of the CRE, especially its feminist wing, needs to be checked and diminished. "In a profound way," writes Sylvia Ann Hewlett, a member of various conservative think tanks, "feminists have failed to connect with the needs and aspirations of ordinary American women." Recalling her conversion to the conservative cause, she asserts: "I realized that the ERA, though it might appeal to elite and chic career women who belong to NOW, might actually get in the way of helping ordinary women."[51] Not surprisingly, NOW looms large in the imagination of conservative women. In an often repeated story (probably apocryphal), Beverly La-

Haye, founder of CWA, pinpoints her conversion to conservatism to a 1979 interview of Betty Friedan by Barbara Walters. Angry that Friedan held herself up as the spokeswoman for all American women, LaHaye dedicated herself to matching and countering the power of NOW. Having struggled for years to create a grass-roots movement with an influential lobby, CWA presently has more than six hundred thousand members organized into more than twelve hundred prayer/action chapters and an operating budget of more than $10 million.[52] Backed by this impressive and well-coordinated network, the women of CWA have promised to promote and defend the interests of the silent majority of ordinary (and God-fearing) women.

While the ideologies of (socially) conservative women run counter in many ways to those of black, Latino, and gay conservatives—stressing the special role of women in the private sphere as opposed to assimilation into public life as individuals—and while they are equally concerned with the power of feminists and their supporters within the civil rights establishment, it is primarily among laissez-faire women that one finds an attempt to appeal to other women "who are human beings first, women second."[53] Moreover, it is among this constituency that stronger parallels to black, Latino, and homosexual conservatives exist. Anita Blair, president of the Independent Women's Forum (IWF), drew this connection when she asserted that "feminism has become a word like racism,[describing] a person who irrationally puts her sex above others."[54] In conjunction with CWA, Blair and the members of the IWF, which sees itself as a "corrective" to traditional feminism, aspire to "help women who feel that they are sort of conservatives in hiding" and are actively seeking alternatives to NOW.[55]

Their connection to racial conservatives was evident in the IWF's founding. The organization grew out of a coalition called "Women for Clarence Thomas," which defended Thomas against Anita Hill's sexual harassment charges, hoping to demonstrate that not all women found Hill's charges credible.[56] Nor do IWF members limit themselves only to gender issues. In the organization's brief existence, it has produced policy statements on affirmative action, especially for women but also minorities, on crime, education, welfare, and other topics. In so doing, the IWF, along with other conservative women's groups, has played a leading role in developing both mainstream and multicultural conservative ideologies. And here too one finds a critique of the establishment undergirded by the critique of New Class bureaucrats who exploit ordinary men and women for their own ends.

Deconstructing the Radical Sixties

The Sixties, I have come to believe, are something of a political Ror-
schach test. Tell me what you think of that period, and I shall tell you
what your politics are.   *—Joseph Epstein, 1988*

This election marks the definitive end of the Stonewall-generation of
politics. . . . Now that the old generation has been repudiated, the next
generation of Gay leaders has the opportunity to refine the movement.
           —Rich Tafel, after the 1994 midterm congressional elections

By claiming to speak for the (silenced) majority, conservatives have attempted to depict leftist individuals and groups as merely part of a radical
and marginal fringe while conservatives proceed to carve out spaces for
themselves at the center. For mainstream and multicultural conservatives,
the deficiencies inherent in identity politics lie not with how certain
(nonwhite) group identities have been historically constructed and continuously reinforced by social discourses but with the attempts of minority groups to "capitalize" on these partially enforced identities for their
own advancement. Any social or political movement that placed group
identity at its foundation—especially the liberation movements of the
1960s—created, conservatives assert, an untenable situation from which
we have yet to recover. The combined strength of these movements has
led to the disuniting of America, the balkanization of society, the endangerment of democracy, and a privileging of narratives of victimology.

In this vein, women and minority conservatives have confronted the
radicalism of the 1960s and early 1970s. Indeed, the view that the 1960s
produced a "destructive generation" and a host of detrimental social policies, beginning with the Great Society, looms large in the conservative assault on the CRE. One of the more interesting dimensions of the multicultural conservative style is the reading of recent American history implied in their collective assessment of the Left. Black, Latino, women, and
gay conservatives have converged around the contention that radical and
liberationists movements need to be revisited, reassessed, and recast. While
focusing on different facets of these movements—Black Power, Chicano
movements, feminism, gay and lesbian liberation—women and minority
conservatives are united in their depiction of them as aberrant.

Tafel's assessment of the 1994 midterm elections and his insistence that
in it gay and lesbian voters repudiated the "Stonewall-generation of poli-

tics" is premature, at best, but nonetheless representative of the conservative attempt to disparage and displace their adversaries. By trivializing the sixties generation, multicultural conservatives share a predisposition to urge that we move forward by looking further backward and recovering an older political sensibility. This older sensibility is defined most generally by the goals of assimilation and integration; by an emphasis on sameness despite race, ethnicity, and sexual orientation; by a stress on patriotism, loyalty, and "American" values; and by the attainment of civil rights within a limited constitutional framework.

"Today," complains gay conservative Bruce Bawer, "Stonewall is not only commemorated but mythologized." Many gay and lesbian activists, Bawer continues, "talk as if there was no gay rights activism at all before Stonewall, or else they mock pre-Stonewall activists as Uncle Toms."[57] Instead of disparaging the pre-Stonewall past, homosexual conservatives have argued that older organizations such as the Mattachine Society offer a far sounder guide for contemporary gay and lesbian politics. Founded in April 1951 by Harry Hay, Mattachine was the first modern gay rights organization in the nation. Originally classifying homosexuals as "one of the largest minorities in America today," and seeking to develop an "ethical culture . . . paralleling the emerging cultures of our fellow minorities—the Negro, Mexican and Jewish people," Mattachine initially encompassed a radical, group-based solution to discrimination. By 1953, however, tensions between political radicals such as Hay, who viewed homosexuals as a separate and distinct minority, and political moderates and conservatives, who adopted an individualistic, assimilationist position, had reached a critical level. In the aftermath of this political and ideological struggle, Hay and other radicals, many of whom, like Hay, had ties to the Communist Party, were defeated and purged.[58]

After 1953, the Mattachine Society pursued a politics of accommodation to the "straight norms" of heterosexual society, arguing that gays and lesbians should "adjust to a pattern of behavior that is acceptable to society in general and compatible with the recognized institutions of home, church and the state." This mainstreaming of the new movement and the concomitant desire for integration "not as homosexuals, but as people, as men and women whose homosexuality is irrelevant to our ideals, our principles, our hopes and aspirations," became the prevailing ethos of the movement before the Stonewall riot in 1969 invented a new age of activism.[59] While the militant activist spirit was kept alive by libertarians such as Dorr Legg and his *One* magazine, their views were marginal, at best, within the homophile movement. Moreover, with the radicalization of the movement after 1969, younger activists bypassed the libertarianism of Legg and recovered, instead, the group-based approach of Harry Hay.

Carl Wittman's "Refugees from Amerika: A Gay Manifesto," which appeared in 1970, offers a vision of gay identity and gay politics tied almost exclusively to a representation of homosexuals as an oppressed minority. Appropriating Black Power ideologies, the gay ghetto, although formed for mutual self-protection, constitutes an occupied territory policed by straight cops, hemmed in by straight laws, and exploited by straight money. "To be a free territory," Wittman professes, "we must govern ourselves, set up our own institutions, defend ourselves, and use our own energies to improve our lives." To foster his claim of homosexual victimization, he subjects "exclusive heterosexuality" to criticism, seeing in society's demand that all members be straight and procreative a ruthless desire for social control and exploitation. In the end, Wittman calls for coalition building with Black liberationists, feminists, Chicanos, "hip and street people," as well as with homophile groups ("reformist and pokey as they might sometimes be, they are our brothers") to fight various forms of interlocking and mutually reinforcing structures of exclusion and discrimination.[60] And this, conservatives argue, is precisely the problem with post-Stonewall radicalism.

Gay and lesbian conservatives find themselves hemmed in between the radicalism of the gay Left and the homophobia of the Christian Right. The intervening years between 1969 and today also witnessed a homophobic backlash against gays and lesbians, codified in 1977 by the singer and orange juice spokeswoman Anita Bryant. Her voter initiative drive against a Dade County, Florida, ordinance protecting gays and lesbians from discrimination served as a lightning rod for the emergent antigay movement. Building on her friend (and fellow evangelical Christian) Phyllis Schlafly's anti-ERA campaign, Bryant launched Save Our Children, Inc., a grass-roots organization that set the tone for New Right antigay advocacy for decades.[61] As a result of both the post-Stonewall generation, on the one hand, and a new wave of discriminatory movements among social and religious conservatives, on the other, contemporary homosexual conservatives occupy a difficult spot rhetorically and strategically.

Eager to achieve leadership positions in the struggle for fundamental civil and human rights—the right to marry and adopt children, legal protection from gross discrimination in housing and employment, the right to serve openly in the military, and the elimination of sodomy laws—as good conservatives, they also want to distance themselves from the CRE and its perversion of civil rights. They must pursue a flexible strategy that, as Andrew Sullivan put it, has less to do with the "often superfluous minority politics of the 1991 Civil Rights Act" and more to do with the "vital fervor of the Civil Rights Act of 1964."[62] In pressing this case, homosexual conservatives strive to portray themselves and the silent population they represent as ordinary white middle-class Americans—a strategy that runs the risk of further marginalizing gays and lesbians who are working class, poor, and members of racial and ethnic minorities, as well as drag queens and transgender individuals. To this extent, gay and lesbian conservative arguments are as informed by class and by middle-class norms of behavior as black or Latino ones.[63]

In the conservative revisioning of history, the post-Stonewall generation of activists emerges as aberrant in the general sweep of modern history, while the period from roughly 1953 to 1969 constitutes, in retrospect, a sort of Golden Age of gay and lesbian politics. This narrative strategy celebrating a time before the descent into ineffectual radicalism embodies multiple layers of signification. It provides a basis from which to critique the post-Stonewall generation of activists and offers an alternative guide to a seemingly postradical (and perhaps postgay) future. This strategy also has the added benefit of paralleling the mainstream conservative nostalgia for the 1950s as a period of peace and prosperity for average Americans. Indeed, nostalgia has proven to be a powerful rhetorical tool, especially in the hands of Richard Nixon and Ronald Reagan. In his 1969 inaugural address Nixon promised to listen to the anguished voices of the silent majority; in his own 1981 inaugural speech Reagan promised to protect the populace from "special interest groups." In the course of twelve years, Nixon's noisy, militant rabble had matured into Reagan's powerful lobbies. In speech after speech Reagan reached back and rearticulated national symbols and American narratives, proclaiming that once again, it could be "Morning in America," that we could rebuild our "City upon a Hill"[64]—if only we could keep the special interests at bay.

A conservative-inflected longing for a Golden Age is also embodied in the corpus of Hispanic conservatism. "Back in the '60s," recalls Henry Bonilla, the first Mexican-American Republican to be elected from Texas, "when the Beatles were the most popular fad in America, about the most unpopular thing you could find in Texas was a Republican." Growing up in the barrios on the south side of San Antonio, Bonilla, whose father and grandfather were Democrats, did not know a single Republican.

Indeed, back then it seemed like the Republicans were uninterested and suspicious of minorities and the poor while the Democrats tried to show us that they cared about our needs, offering us a message of hope and equality. They talked about providing jobs, education, housing, medical care and security for every American. They were the champions of civil rights and equal opportunities. In short, the Democratic Party promised it would solve the nation's problems with its programs.[65]

Although liberal rhetoric sounded attractive, Bonilla argues that the good intentions of liberal policies created a hell of higher taxes and discriminatory tax policies, increased regulations, and intrusive programs for Mexican-Americans. Instead, he concludes, what most Hispanics want are those things traditionally valued in Latino culture: "respect for the institutions of marriage and family, a strong faith, emphasis on education and the importance of hard work and responsibility." Having turned Left in the 1960s, Hispanics, chides Bonilla, must now look to the Right to protect their interests as Americans.

Latino conservatives such as Bonilla and Chavez urge, in effect, a return to the assimilationist patterns set by organizations such as LULAC (League of Latin American Citizens). Founded in 1929 by mostly urban and middle-class Mexican-Americans, LULAC sought to foster the goals of basic civil rights and Americanization in Texas and other southwestern states. Restricting membership to U.S. citizens—thus distinguishing its members from immigrants and migrant workers—the organization emphasized English-language skills, cultural assimilation, and loyalty to the American nation. LULAC, along with other groups founded in the interwar period, represented a new sensibility distinct from the philosophies of older Mexican-American voluntary associations, such as mutalistas and honorific societies, that had cultivated a sense of separateness. LULAC and newer groups broke with this trend. "Although most were generally proud of their ethnic heritage," according to the historian David Gutierrez, "they believed that Mexican Americans had focused too much on maintaining their ethnicity and culture in the United States, and, in the process, had hindered their progress as participating members of American society."[66] Like the early NAACP, LULAC turned toward legislative initiatives against discriminatory practices in education, employment, and voting and immigration policy while simultaneously pushing programs geared toward ethnic uplift and accommodation.

A less rosy reading of this preradical past has been offered by the cultural historian Neil Foley, who sees in the "rise of the so-called Mexican American generation of the 1930s, '40s and '50s" an insistence on "their status as whites in order to overcome the worst features of Jim Crow segregation, restrictive housing covenants, employment discrimination and the social stigma of being 'Mexican,' a label that, in the eyes of Anglos, designated race rather than one's citizenship status."[67] Having been unduly racialized—that is, rendered nonwhite by the U.S. Bureau of Census in 1930—they feared being relegated without recourse to the same deplorable status as blacks. Being nonwhite not only made Mexican-Americans targets of increased discrimination; it also weakened their claims to legal protection as American citizens. During the Repatriation Movement of the 1930s, for example, the government decided that all persons born in Mexico or of Mexican-born parents "who are not definitely white, negro, Indian, Chinese or Japanese, should be returned as Mexicans."[68] A good deal rode on the vague definition of "not definitely white." While Foley characterizes the policies and social philosophies of organizations like LULAC as a "Faustian pact with whiteness" for their attempts to gain the privileges of whiteness, often at the expense of blacks, assimilation (and deracialization) made and continues to make a good deal of strategic sense to some Mexican-Americans. For Chavez and other Hispanic conservatives, it is this sensibility that needs to be redeemed and restored.

In heralding a Golden Age, homosexual and Latino conservatives have used the African American civil rights movement as a prime example of a politics gone awry, but no more so than black conservatives themselves. For instance, a number of black conservatives participated in the two "Second Thoughts" conferences, both organized by two ex-radicals turned conservatives, Peter Collier and David Horowitz, and founded by various conservative foundations. The first, held in 1987, encompassed former radicals who looked back and critiqued New Left movements in the 1960s; a special panel focused on members of the (now) Old Guard of neoconservatism.[69] While published proceedings from this event include essays by Glenn Loury and Julius Lester, the second conference, "Second Thoughts about Race," presents a far deeper and more sustained attack on African American radicalism.[70]

Second thoughts about race are almost invariably second thoughts about Black Power and black cultural nationalism in the late 1960s and 1970s. Among black conservatives, these forms of racialist thinking are roundly denounced for their emphasis on cultural differentiation and racial separateness, and for delegitimating the goals of integration, individualism, and merit. The fellow traveler Stanley Crouch, in his contribution to the Second Thoughts conference and in other venues, has been exceedingly vocal in developing this argument. He insists that the racial essentialism that undergirded Black Power elevated "blackness" above all else while defining itself against "white" (American) culture. In the process, everything associated with "white middle-class standards" was rejected out of hand. The result of this shift in consciousness, which he continues to see as pervasive, was an excessive glamorization of marginalization and ghetto life; a justification of lowered expectations in a society deemed to be thoroughly racist; and an aversion to "acting white" in terms of educational excellence, speech, dress, and comportment. He writes:

> The battle with so-called 'white middle-class standards' that we still hear discussed when the subjects of everything from school performance to rap records are addressed is itself a distortion of the goals of the Civil Rights Movement. This battle would lead us to believe that there are differences so great in this society that we could actually accept a separatist vision in which the elemental necessity of human identification across racial, sexual, and class lines would be replaced by the idea that people from various backgrounds can only identify with those from their own group. Such a conception avoids King's idea that people should be judged by the content of their character and not by the color of their skin—or, if we extend that to sex, by gender.[71]

King's famous line about judgments based on character and not color was also taken up by Shelby Steele, who issued a ringing condemnation of the foundations of "blackness" that emanated from the 1960s. As Steele sees it, in the late 1960s "blackness itself was transformed into a grandiose quality" of racial superiority, thus turning the notion of white supremacy on its head while still maintaining the racial binary of black versus white. "White was the color of alienation and black was the color of harmony and moral truth."[72]

The more compelling conference presentations, however, revolved around the debate as to whether the civil rights movement did cease or should have ceased to exist. For Walter Williams, the movement stopped in 1965, having achieved its goals. Also focusing on deviant behavior and desultory cultural messages, Williams blames the civil rights establishment for its insistence that the problems of crime and drug use and the lack of educational achievement and employment opportunities are in fact *civil rights* issues at all. The work of the state is done; constitutional protections have been amply extended across the color line. "If we continue to think of black educational problems as a civil rights issue, we will continue with policies like busing and integration, trying to get more money for public schools, college affirmative action programs for young blacks who cannot meet traditional academic entry requirements and banning employment tests."[73] Viewing racism as endemic and parading it as the font of all ills, Williams asserts, only allows us to ignore the "*self-induced*, day-to-day destruction of our youngsters."

Surveying, like Williams, the contemporary landscape of urban America, the conference participants returned again and again to the late 1960s to locate the sea change in racial politics that created or at least exacerbated current problems. Supplanting the vision of King with that of H. Rap Brown, Huey Newton, and Stokely Carmichael, black conservatives attest, paved the way for the rise of race merchants within the CRE. This change also had the ill-fated consequence of privileging political state-backed and financed solutions over antistatist social and cultural ones.

Finally, there is widespread agreement among black conservatives that Black Power and black cultural nationalism inhibited the ability and desire of African Americans to identify with American culture, history, and traditions. Far from seeing America as a land of opportunity and valuing its democratic traditions, the radicalism of the late 1960s and 1970s depicted America as corrupt and exploitative. In widening the psychological gulf between themselves and America and placing themselves in an adversarial relationship with the nation, black cultural nationalists, conservatives argue, created a legacy that presented black Americans not as rightful heirs of America's promise but as victims of America's brutality.

This frame of mind led, they believe, to a form of racial power brokering (a black New Class) in which the point is to get as big a piece of the government pie as possible, thus precluding working toward the common good of society. Julius Lester, who was a SNCC organizer in the 1960s and who claims to have little affinity with political conservatism, managed to sum up the general tenor of the Second Thoughts on Race conference on this score:

What happened to the civil rights movement is that it abdicated responsibility for the society as a whole and opted for the sloth of blacks being eternal victims who want to lay claims on the emotions and sympathies of others, who no longer are aware of or even care to work toward something that might be agreed upon as the common good but, instead, focus exclusively upon their own concerns as if there were no others that also demand the nation's legitimate attention.[74]

While some conservative women, such as Carol Iannone, have shared in this discourse on Second Thoughts—about the sixties experience and about the implications of radical feminism—others, such as Schlafly, Sylvia Ann Hewlett, Midge Decter, and Beverly LaHaye have long been featured warriors of the Right. As a pronounced ideological movement, the most recent wave of what might be called "gender conservatism" began to take shape in the early 1970s. It, too, juxtaposed itself to radical tendencies of the period. Decter, a frequent contributor to *Commentary* published *The New Chastity and Other Arguments against Women's Liberation,* one of the first scathing critiques of "second wave" feminism, in 1972. It was just one small sign of things to come, particularly in the wake of the 1973 *Roe v. Wade* decision that legalized abortion and inadvertently launched a widespread movement to overturn the decision. The critical turning point, however, came in 1977, with the International Women's Year conference in Houston. After the conference endorsed an essentially feminist platform, which supported abortion and reproductive rights, a host of New Right women's groups were organized in response. By 1979, when President Jimmy Carter hosted the White House Conference on Families as a sort of legislative follow-up to the IWY's program, conservative women came out in force for an alternative conference held in protest.

In 1980, conservative women, backed by the growing influence of the Religious Right, were able to force an anti-ERA plank into the platform of the Republican Party—the first time the Party had supported such a measure.[75] With the timing of these events in mind, it is difficult to support the proposition that the antifeminism of the New Right was actually a "backlash." Since both movements emerged simultaneously, each feeding and reinforcing the other, at best New Right antifeminism is a sort of "sidelash." At any rate, the success of antifeminism and the sentiment it has generated throughout popular culture and public policy is undeniable, especially among younger women reared in a "postfeminist" environment.

Geared toward those who came of age in the 1980s and 1990s—after the major victories of the modern women's movement and during the reaction against its more radical implications—some conservative women have attempted to craft an attractive alternative to the Left. It is here that one finds the most pervasive deployment of a Golden Age narrative. To the extent that conservative women indulge in the manufacture of a nostalgic view of a preradical feminist past, they appeal to what Katherine Kersten defines as "classical feminism." Kersten, the director of the Center for the American Experiment, in Minneapolis, is a member of the first generation of "liberated" women and is therefore unwilling to fully demonize the gains won by feminism. "Conservatives," she observes "can too easily fall into a reflexive defense of the status quo." Hence, it needs a version of feminism to provide "a counterweight, asserting that when justice and equality are at issue, we must seek reform boldly and prudently."[76]

For Kersten, classical feminism was both bold and prudent. Accepting the proposition that biology is not destiny, classical feminism is grounded in the idea of a universal human nature—regardless of gender differences—that confers inalienable rights and equality of opportunity on all individuals. In her call for a new conservative feminism, Kersten is careful to lay claim to intellectual foremothers such as the nineteenth-century classical feminist Margaret Fuller, who wrote: "What Woman needs . . . is as a nature to grow, as an intellect to discern, as a soul to live freely. . . . We would have every path laid open to Woman as well as Man."[77] Having already secured equality before the law and basic civil rights, guided by the doctrines of classical feminism, women must now seek to reform a *culture* that encourages divorce, illegitimacy, and a lack of self-sufficiency and personal responsibility.

> But the conservative feminist is careful not to make the mistake of seeking exclusively political solutions to problems that are essentially social and culture in nature. She believes that changing individual behavior is the key to reducing the ills that consign an increasing number of women to second-class citizenship. She knows, of course, that passing a law can be easy, while influencing behavior is notoriously difficult.[78]

The conservative feminist, Kersten concludes, resists the temptation to assign blame to a hostile "system" and is the "architect of her own happiness." While it ignores the economic and social-structural barriers that many women confront, such an approach might strike a cord with the so-called postfeminist generation. Among younger women who are more recent converts to the cause, one thinks immediately of the positions adopted by fellow traveler Katie Roiphe. Recalling her freshman year at Harvard in 1986, she writes: "I didn't spend much time thinking about feminism. It was something assumed, something deep in my foundations." Yet, the brand of feminism she encountered on campus was dramatically different from the values instilled by her mother and grandmother. "The feminism around me in classrooms, conversations, and student journals was not the feminism I grew up with," Roiphe continues:

> Take Back the Night marches and sexual harassment peer-counseling groups were alien, and even sometimes at odds with what I thought feminism was. All of a sudden feminism meant being angry about men looking at you in the street and writing about "the colonialist appropriation of female discourse."[79]

Roiphe's critique may be representative of a new style of antifeminism among conservative women, but the discourse is dominated by an old guard of women who never expressed much sympathy for feminism in the first place. Phyllis Schlafly, for instance, who helped to put New Right women on the map, continues to characterize women's liberationists as a disaster. Such women have always seen not only radical feminism but a good deal of the modern women's movement as a dangerous threat to women and society.

Despite generational and ideological differences, conservative women have gone to great lengths to discredit their leftist counterparts as antifamily, pro-abortion, and antimale and as a bunch of totalitarian and elitist prudes who neither know or care about the day-to-day concerns of ordinary women. In a nutshell, feminists are deemed to be essentially antiwoman. "Traditional feminism has burned out," declares Barbara Leeden; "we've got to get away from the idea of women as victims and whiners." Consigning women to the lowly status of victims in need of constant protection, adds Laura Ingraham, "stands on its head the cause that true feminists originally championed: equal opportunity for women."[80] Until, that is, feminism got derailed and returned women to the yoke of paternalism. Convincing women to rethink and reject radical feminism as a form of dependency and paternalism is, like the black conservative critique of liberal racism and "plantation" politics, an essential part of a larger political project. It is time, according to Linda Chavez, to move out of the barrio; now is the moment, argue gay conservatives, for homosexuals to reject the gay ghetto. Whether conservative women—along with conservative blacks, Latinos, and homosexuals—can use this approach to successfully recruit younger women such as Roiphe and to create a truly cross-generational movement that incorporates women from different classes, regions, and racial, ethnic, and religious backgrounds remains to be seen. In this vein, the desire to reinterpret the radical sixties in a negative light serves in and of itself as a ground for ideological coalition building.

The Multicultural Conservative Assault on Multiculturalism

For twenty years, the most important battle in the civil rights field has been for the control of the language.
—*The Heritage Foundation,* Mandate for Leadership II:
Continuing the Conservative Revolution *(1984)*

All social movements must at some point face the challenge of recruiting younger activists. From older organizations such as the Young Americans for Freedom, in the 1960s, to chapters of the College Republicans and other campus-based groups, to the rise of conservative student papers such as the notorious *Dartmouth Review,* the mainstream conservative movement has met this challenge head on. Throughout the 1980s college campuses across the nation became a prime site of ideological battles waged in the name of the "culture wars." As conservatives continue to warn students and their parents about cadres of tenured radicals and the perils of political correctness, the lack of free speech, and the politics of illiberal education, the university continues to be a key element in mobilizing conservative reaction.

The multicultural conservative critique of political developments since the late 1960s reinforces and has been reinforced by attacks on intellectual developments within the academic sphere. Variants of afrocentrism, feminist theory, Chicano and Latino studies, and queer theory—often derided as "victim" or "oppression" studies—have become an additional source of animus for black, women, Latino, and gay conservatives, respectively. Taken together, what this amounts to is a multicultural conservative critique of multiculturalism.[81] Women and minority conservatives have been able and exceedingly willing to venture into areas of critique into which mainstream conservatives did not often venture with the same degree of confidence.

In the late 1960s and 1970s, the emergent New Right and its neoconservative cousins were as concerned with the dynamics of race, gender, ethnicity, and sexuality as any good panel at a MLA conference. Yet, before the dawn of a more or less coherent multicultural conservatism, mainstream conservatives were generally forced to content themselves with the road of least resistance, namely ignoring blacks and other minorities in terms of votes while simultaneously helping to create and capitalize on the white—especially male and working-class—backlash against them.[82] With the rise of multicultural conservatism, however, mainstream conservatives have been given the opportunity to translate their oppositional views into the internal realm of racial, ethnic, gender, and sexual politics. In the process, women and minority conservatives have proved to be invaluable soldiers in the battle for control of the language.

Many of the arguments are by now familiar, and I do not wish to belabor the matter where summaries will suffice. The general tenor of the conservative critique of multiculturalism has been succinctly presented in texts such as Roger Kimball's *Tenured Radicals,* Dinesh D'Souza's *Illiberal Education,* and Allan Bloom's *The Closing of the American Mind.* As part of the culture wars of the 1980s and early 1990s, these texts and others like them depicted institutions of higher learning as captive to the dark forces of political correctness and identity politics, embroiled in speech codes and sexual harassment guidelines, and extorted by those who want to gut the Great Books tradition. Alarmist and overly reliant on anecdotal evidence, such texts foretold the downfall not only of America but of the West in general.[83]

The more particular arguments proffered by women and minority conservatives are variations on these themes, with the major difference that they are being offered by insiders. Books such as Shelby Steele's *The Content of Our Character* and Christina Hoff Sommers's *Who Stole Feminism* chide black studies and women's studies, respectively, for engaging in "group think" and for producing scholarship of questionable merit. Both argue that such programs, in seeking to provide a safe haven for women and minority students, actually encourage escapist fantasies and self-segregation. Conservatives and fellow travelers, on the whole, celebrate the reasonable exploration of the histories and contributions of African Americans, Latinos, women, and homosexuals. But they are fiercely opposed to such efforts if they threaten notions of our common heritage in favor of attacking "dead white men" of the past and white heterosexual men of the present.

The same position is promulgated by organizations such as the National Association of Scholars (NAS), which has grown since 1987 to nearly two thousand members, with affiliate chapters in twenty-five states. The NAS opposes "trendy methodologies," gender and ethnic studies devoid of "genuinely scholarly content" and courses that serve as little more than "vehicles of political harangue or recruitment." The NAS also stands against preferential treatment in hiring, retention, and admissions, "discriminatory harassment" via speech codes, and "double standards in appropriate intellectual criteria."[84] Above all, as Herbert London, an NAS cofounder and a former dean of New York University's Gallatin School of Individualized Study, put it, "attempts to diversify the curriculum should be opposed because they do not lead us toward our true humanity." Occupying a distinctive niche within the conservative network, the NAS has also offered an additional platform for women and minority conservatives via its quarterly publication, *Academic Questions*, and through its speaker's bureau, placement services, research center, fellowships, and conferences.[85]

These arguments against ethnic chauvinism, cultural difference, oppression, and victim studies extend beyond the walls of academia, however, and are key to an understanding of how conservative ideologies have been mobilized in the public arena. Two members of the California chapter of the NAS, for example, spearheaded the drive against affirmative action in the state university system and helped to compose the text of California's Civil Rights Initiative (Proposition 209). To this extent, Manning Marable was correct when he observed, "By attacking multicultural education and affirmative action, they [conservatives] are deliberately manipulating racial and gender symbols to mobilize their supporters."[86] Any stress on difference and separateness, in classrooms or in public policy debates, inhibits sympathy for individuation and assimilation; while negative cultural messages—the glamorization of rappers and Chicano gangs—encourages negative behavior patterns that impede social advancement. So too with the glamorization of a gay ghetto with a gay subculture. Similarly, presupposing that women are weak and need sexual harassment guidelines, or that motherhood is somehow bad, reinforces the view of women as victims and mothers as losers. Moreover, conservatives charge, inviting the government onto our campuses extends its reach that much further into our private lives and inhibits our ability to assimilate into the public world as individuals.

Conclusion

Dangerously, they romanticize public separateness and they trivialize the dilemma of the socially disadvantaged.   —*Richard Rodriguez*

But today conservative discourse on race has largely been reduced to slo-
ganeering, filled with references to black criminality, illegitimacy and
cultural pathology.   —*Glenn Loury*

There is a certain internal logic that links conservative ideas about culture,
identity, politics, and public policy. The critique of the civil rights establishment in the name of a silent majority, the disparagement of the radicalism of the 1960s, and the assault on multiculturalism and identity politics
are all different facets of the same ideological core. Mainstream and multicultural conservatives are united in arguing that race, ethnicity, gender, and
sexuality are not and cannot be used as an appropriate foundation for
making claims on the state. Simply put, this is the primary problem with
the civil rights establishment.

The CRE's crimes include maintaining a strict orthodoxy that silences
opposition and ignores the real conditions that affect the constituencies it
claims to serve, indulging in special-interest group power brokering, and
supporting a vision of identity that emphasizes the group over the individual and thereby fosters an ideology of separateness, differentiation, and balkanization. Instead of traveling any further down the dead-end road of government interference and ineffective political solutions, we should, conservatives aver, focus our attention more forcefully on the private realms of
culture and behavior. Yet, a more critical reading of how conservatives invoke
culture and identity, especially in relation to the promise of individualism and
the free market, reveals a variety of problems and paradoxes.

First and foremost, the conservative agenda rests on bypassing the road-
block of the establishment New Class, a process that entails a detour away
from politics per se and toward culture and behavior. As we have seen, a
major component of multicultural conservatism is the insistence that it is
not historical and contemporary modes of discrimination that impede inclusion but deviant patterns of behavior and distorted understandings of
values. Hence, gay conservatives (or at least those who are not libertarians)
have stressed the importance of "upright" behavior, especially in the face
of the AIDS crisis, and have pressed for homosexual marriage, in part because of its moral implications. Katherine Kersten's conservative feminist,
likewise, is careful not to pursue exclusively political strategies for what
she feels are largely cultural ills. And uprooting the culture of poverty is as,
if not more, important than dismantling what Robert Woodson calls the
Poverty Pentagon. Indeed, arguments about a culture of poverty are indicative of the concern over the connections between cultural values and

behavior found in the writings of those multicultural and mainstream conservatives who have struggled to present an alternative to state-based initiatives and the establishment.

"Black success and social acceptance now are both tied to rebuilding the African American community," Dinesh D'Souza writes. "If blacks can achieve such a cultural renaissance, they will teach other Americans a valuable lesson in civilizational restoration." By raising their own level of civilization, African Americans will finally heal the schizophrenia "between their racial and American identities" and "become the truest and noblest exemplars of Western civilization."[87] Not all conservatives are willing to state the matter as boldly and brashly as D'Souza. Glenn Loury and Robert Woodson terminated their affiliation with the American Enterprise Institute after it funded D'Souza's work and called a press conference to denounce the tome in the interest of "self-defense." "It strikes me as a book," agreed columnist William Raspberry (who, along with Loury and Woodson, is mentioned favorably in the text), "that only a racist could cheer."

Still, D'Souza's heavy-handed demarcation of the proper versus the improper meaning and function of culture is widely shared, albeit often more diplomatically phrased. He praises culture and cultural strategies for racial uplift, but only those that advance assimilation and acculturation. "What blacks need to do," lectures D'Souza, "is to 'act white,'" by adopting professedly white, middle-class standards, "so that they can effectively compete with other groups." This good (and white) vision of culture is juxtaposed to a bad (and black) one. Hence, black culture is presented "as a vicious, self-defeating and repellent underside that is no longer possible to ignore or euphemize."[88] Expressed in more neutral terms, whereas good culture works to destroy the necessity of a hyphenated identity, bad culture functions to preserve difference, separateness, and pathology.

Similar arguments, in equally extreme language, have been produced within the debate among conservatives about immigration. While some conservatives (such as Linda Chavez, William Bennett, and William Kristol) have emphasized the positive dimensions of legal immigration and have opposed the more draconian proposals (e.g., California's Proposition 187) to deal with illegal immigrants, others have indulged in nativist warnings against the "browning of America." In works such as Peter Brimelow's *Alien Nation*, Lawrence Auster's *The Path to National Suicide*, and John Tanton and Wayne Lutton's *The Immigration Invasion*, "our common culture" is presented as endangered by a host of Third World and other immigrants of color who cannot be assimilated. This debate about the ability of immigrants to assimilate, however, is carried on under the assumption that full assimilation, as opposed to cultural pluralism, is the only goal worth pursuing. Here, too, the desire to preserve a distinct cultural heritage and a hyphenated identity is viewed with suspicion at best and with horror at worst.

In all fairness, many conservatives, even those who do suppose the existence of a culture of poverty and negative pathologies rooted in subcultures, do not descend to the depths reached by D'Souza, Brimelow, and Tanton. In fleshing out a more positive vision of culture, a number of conservatives, including Woodson, have been influenced by the idea of "mediating structures" popularized by Peter Berger and Richard John Neuhaus via the American Enterprise Institute's Project on Mediating Structures in the 1970s.[89]

Berger and Neuhaus defined mediating structures as indigenous institutions, such as churches and community centers, voluntary associations, grass-roots organizations, and other nongovernmental instruments for encouraging civic virtue, cohesion, mutual respect, and community standards. Such structures are positioned between the large and impersonal "megastructures" of public life—government, political parties, unions, corporations—and the private lives of individuals. Arguing against any public policy that threatens these structures or circumscribes their activities, Berger and Neuhaus defended vouchers for public education to increase parental choice and oversight of schools, community-based environmental activism, greater autonomy for local political units, family support programs, job training, and resident management of housing projects, among other initiatives.

While none of these ideas is by any means exclusively conservative (they echo the ideas of figures from Alexis de Tocqueville to Saul Alinksy and even some of the objectives of community-based Great Society programs), they are presented in the context of a forceful critique of liberalism and the ravages of modernity. "Liberalism has no real message for private life," wrote Berger.

> Its attitude toward private life is, essentially, that it should be left alone, for the individual to manage as best he can. While this attitude has of late been in some tension with the "statist" trend, it is still quite vital. Liberals continue to have a serious commitment to the protection of private freedoms against encroachment by large public institutions. Now, this laissez-faire attitude works well as long as private life is given structure and

meaning from other sources—religion, the family folk or ethnic subcultures, and the like. The crises of modernity, however, is precisely the fact that these other sources are in danger of drying up.[90]

Berger's insights into the necessity of mediating structures, coupled with his sensitivity to cultural integrity within racial, ethnic, and immigrant neighborhoods and communities, is ideally suited to some of the ideas advanced by multicultural conservatives. Uniting leftist and rightist criticism of components of modern life, it preserves a special role, albeit a private one, for the development of ethnic subcultures guided by their own standards and practices.

In this it offers a kinder, more compassionate conservatism than is sometimes found within the New Right and allows women and minority conservatives to reaffirm their commitments to reaching and assisting others. The idea of mediating structures also has the added benefit of softening the suggestion, made by D'Souza and others, that African Americans, in particular, are insufficiently civilized. Unfortunately, pragmatic attempts to use a host of mediating structures to improve the lives of minorities and to empower communities of color, such as Woodson's work with his Neighborhood Enterprise Center, has met with little real and sustained interest among far too many within the conservative movement and the New Right.

Berger himself, it should be noted, turned away from his original complex vision of mediating structures, a vision comfortable with neither unregulated market forces or a highly individualistic ethic, in favor of exploring a "Third Way" within a capitalistic and corporatist framework.[91] Robert Woodson and others, while attempting to maintain the initial promise of Berger's ideas as an alternative to state-backed and funded programs, have also come to embrace the free market—a move that seems to induce a series of paradoxes.[92] Like that of many women and minority conservatives, Woodson's perspective rests on the character issues, with character defined in terms of Judeo-Christian values, civic virtues, responsibility, and middle-class respectability. The merit of this approach is that it is nearly impossible to argue against character, civic responsibility, and moral fiber, even though conservative arguments about the centrality of culture and behavior tend to be premised on an odd sort of myopia.

Part of this myopia has to do with the uneasy relationship many conservatives have with the idea of subcultures and, in general, with the notion of cultural difference. Take, for example, Linda Chavez's extraordinary claim that "the entitlements of the civil rights era" were directly responsible for the desire among Latinos to "maintain their language and culture, their separate identity." Here, culture has negative connotations precisely because it is separate and, by implication, anti-American. To this extent, culture (and mediating structures) is valuable only if it serves the larger goals of assimilation, self-help, and "proper" modes of behavior.

A similar understanding of culture is echoed in the way conservatives tend to talk about the concept of the underclass—a group of persons said to constitute a separate class literally *underneath* the class structure and thus *outside* the market and its fluctuations. In such an approach, it is culture and its ability to generate negative individual modes of behavior that takes precedence over the nature of the economic structure itself. If there is a culture of poverty that traps and circumscribes the underclass (and this point has been subjected to much debate),[93] then there is also its obverse, a "culture of virtue," that accounts for drive, determination, and success. But are these two cultures as distinct and mutually exclusive as they are often portrayed? Surely, there are important survival strategies among the poor and the underclass that are different from those typically regarded as middle-class virtues, but they are no less appropriate for that. Alternatively, some of the much-prized middle-class standards that are said to produce success, particularly those that serve the logic of free-market capitalism, are equally embedded in, say, rap music and Chicano gang culture. As Mario Puzo suggests in his *Godfather* series, the criminal underworld, Wall Street, and Capitol Hill share not a few tendencies. What it really means to "act white" and whether this is always advisable are therefore much more complicated than conservatives are generally willing to allow.

In the writings of many conservatives, however, this culture of virtue (and its "healthy" mediating structures) is portrayed as oddly autonomous from the particularly workings of race, ethnicity, and sexuality. It is ideally American, nonhyphenated, and, more problematic, capitalistic. Linking the culture of virtue with the demands of the free market, conservatives unaccountably assume that capitalism itself plays a role in generating positive values—despite a system driven by consumption, immediate gratification, and materialism. To what extent, then, must the logic of capitalist accumulation be viewed as a contributing factor to the very social and cultural conditions conservatives bemoan? Can the cure and the disease emanate from the same source? As Gary Dorrien so aptly frames the matter in his book on neoconservatism, the "moral corruption and narcissism that neoconservatives condemn in American society thus owed more to commercial impetus then to the failures of some fictionally autonomous 'culture.'"[94]

This paradox about cultural (and class) values, individual behavior, and the free market is also reflected in the riddle of how class-based government initiatives are more just than ones based on race, ethnicity, or gender. Richard Rodriguez takes the civil rights establishment to task for ignoring the lessons of the classical Left in its disregard for the importance of class and for "assuming that the disadvantages of the lower classes would necessarily be ameliorated by the creation of an elite society." This statement is factually inaccurate. Affirmative action and race and gender set-asides were designed not as antipoverty programs but to increase opportunities and access for qualified individuals. The point was to transform an institutionalized system in education and employment premised historically on a series of exclusions and discriminatory practices. The critical race theorist Cheryl Harris argues that affirmative action was always more than a program: "it is a principle, internationally recognized, based on a theory of rights and equality." In contrast to formal or procedural equality, which "overlooks structural disadvantage," affirmative action calls for "*equalizing treatment* by redistributing power and resources in order to rectify inequities and achieve real equality."[95]

Performing this type of structural critique offers a far more fruitful discussion of groups and structures as opposed to simply individuals; it also allows us to talk in terms of broader societal benefits and goals. In rethinking his earlier opposition to affirmative action and other programs that are cognizant of race, Nathan Glazer appeals to a broad notion of the common good, the fairness of American institutions, and the viability of American democracy. While Glazer remains uncomfortable with preferences, he has come to believe that some limited form of affirmative action is a necessary evil. "To admit blacks under affirmative action no doubt undermines the American meritocracy, but to exclude blacks . . . by abolishing affirmative action would undermine the legitimacy of American democracy."[96] Glazer bases his defense of preferences on the history of exclusion, legal segregation, and discrimination and on the history of the past thirty years. In the early 1970s, when Glazer first denounced affirmative action, he did so in the faith that tearing down the legal barriers to integration would finally solve the race problem. Thirty years later, he concedes that such has not been the case, at least not to the degree that one would have hoped.

Despite its flaws, affirmative action programs have been successful in enlarging the middle classes (hardly an elite society) in minority communities and in opening up institutions and occupations to women. If, as many conservatives believe, joining the middle class is an indication of probable achievement, then by this standard alone affirmative action has in fact worked.[97] Further, eliminating a consciousness of color from public policy may render us blind (and deaf and dumb) to differences based on race, gender, and ethnicity, but it also leaves us blind to the sorts of claims to democratization and inclusion detailed by Glazer. Conservatives would do well to move in the direction urged by Glazer and by Glenn Loury, who advocates "a morally astute, politically aware conservatism that acknowledges personal responsibility as one part of the social contract but also understands the importance of collective responsibility."[98]

The idea of cleansing our public life of race, ethnicity, and gender, along with sexual orientation and class, by embracing an autonomous and "American" culture of virtue is optimistic at best. It is unlikely that the ideologies that once sustained the idea of America as a melting pot *could* be revived, even if we came to believe they should. In 1973, during the (re)emergence of ethnic assertiveness, Michael Novak published *The Rise of the Unmeltable Ethnic*. In this autobiographical and sociological text, he addressed the adverse effects of "Americanization" on PIGS (Polish, Italians, Greeks, and Slavs). "You are catechized, cajoled, and condescended to by the guardians of good Anglo-Protestant attitudes. . . . The entire experience of becoming Americans is summarized in the experience of being made to feel guilty."[99] Having come so far in the pursuit of a truly multicultural society, surely few would want to take steps backward.

Moreover, a strict bifurcation of the public self and the private self is overtly abstract and difficult to police, given the porous nature of the distinction. All identities are shaped by individual attributes and by collectivities—race, gender, ethnicity, sexuality, religion, class, region, and so forth—that we carry with us as we move through the world as citizens, members of groups, and private, unique human beings. Besides, public blindness to difference is never in reality as blind as it promises. As the philosopher Charles A. Taylor points out:

The claim is that the supposedly neutral set of difference-blind principles of the politics of equal dignity is in fact a reflection of one hegemonic culture. As it turns out, then, only the minority or suppressed cultures are being forced to take an alien form. Consequently, the supposedly fair and difference-blind society is not only inhuman (because suppressing identities) but also, in a subtle and unconscious way, itself being highly discriminatory.[100]

Public assimilation via an official blindness to difference also forestalls what might be a necessary recognition of difference, especially for differences once (and still) defined as inferior or unnatural.

When gay and lesbian activists adopted the powerful slogan "Silence = Death" to encourage homosexuals to come out of the private closet and into the public light, they expressed something crucial about the politics of recognition. For public recognition makes demands beyond mere tolerance or a form of minimal acceptance that regulates such matters to the private sphere. "My being an African American, among other things, shapes the authentic self that I seek to express," writes K. Anthony Appiah in his commentary on Taylor's essay "The Politics of Recognition." He continues: "And it is, in part, because I seek to express my self that I seek recognition of an African American identity."[101] Conservatives seem to imply that individual liberty and freedom can be bought at the price of discarding claims to difference in public policy and public life; the price might be said to lay in the abandonment of the desire for recognition. But is the cost, to be borne disproportionately by some and only to a lesser extent by others, too high?

Appiah also reminds us that identity and recognition are bound up with survival. Survival in this context extends beyond a concern for the ability of a culture (even, some might argue, a gay culture) to give meaning to the lives of the present generation but stretches indefinitely into the future. Woodson implicitly recognizes the connections between culture and survival in his practical and theoretical applications of the theory of mediating structures. Unlike D'Souza's facile demand for black acculturation by "acting white," Woodson (along with Elizabeth Wright and Walter Williams) charges that forms of forced desegregation, especially through busing, have weakened organic ties in black neighborhoods. Moreover, in formulating a "pragmatic" approach to black empowerment, he has adopted a perspective that necessarily contains elements of liberalism, conservatism, black nationalism and American patriotism.

Regardless of his stress on Americanization, even Woodson (not to mention D'Souza and Brimelow, among others) maintains a distinction, as strict as it is artificial, between private expressions of collective identities and public ones. It is as potentially false to proclaim that the personal is always the political as it is to argue the opposite. Finally, to insist that we base our demands for justice on procedural liberalism with its universal claims, uniform standards, and suspicion of collective goals and identities, not only among African Americans and Latinos but also among women, homosexuals and recent immigrants, rejects the responsibility the nation bears for a legacy of group-based exclusions. From this perspective, history, including the history of the civil rights establishment and the political struggles that produced it, is not something we can afford to sweep neatly underneath the rug, as much as we may desire to do so. For history has become too significant a part of our lived reality as individuals, as members of groups, classes, and cultures, and as a nation.

There is no other way but autobiography by which
to cure oneself of too much objectivity.

—*Michael Novak,* Confessions of a
White Ethnic *(1973)*

The man is only half himself, the other half is his
expression.   —*Ralph Waldo Emerson, "The Poet"*

CHAPTER 3

"I Write Myself, Therefore I Am"

Multicultural Conservatism and the
Political Art of Autobiography

History surrounded the nomination and con-
firmation of Clarence Thomas to the Supreme Court. President George
Bush's decision to put Thomas forth was described as historic, while
Thomas's detractors and supporters vigorously debated his appropriateness
as a replacement for Justice Thurgood Marshall and the high court's
"black" seat. Thomas was also adept at packaging his personal history for
public consumption. Throughout the controversy Thomas told—and others retold—the story of his personal struggle up from poverty. The tale was
in many ways a conventional one and thus resonated with Americans, especially African Americans.

Born in rural Georgia, Thomas was rescued from a life of hardship and
limited opportunities by his paternal grandfather, a noble and ennobling figure who schooled young Clarence in the rigors of discipline, hard work,
thrift, and responsibility. Having absorbed and duly internalized these lessons, Thomas set out on the road of success. Receiving ample assistance and
support along the way, he became, in essence, a self-made man. What was and

remains so intriguing about this story is not so much the facts it relates, or that Thomas felt compelled to tell it in such a public manner. Far more revealing was the dramatic extent to which it was accepted as a plausible, even reasonable explanation of his conservative politics and judicial philosophy. Indeed, the story became a sort of metonym for his conservatism. As the historian Christine Stansell notes, given Thomas's refusal to engage with questions about his legal, political, and philosophic positions, "this restrained account [of his life] expanded to fill the void and eventually came to dominate popular discussions of the nominee."[1] In this case, the personal became the political to the exclusion of other, more pressing concerns.

Thomas, of course, is hardly alone in exploring political identities through the prism of personal narratives; therefore, his story should be viewed as indicative of a broader phenomenon. The art of autobiography, or the shaping of a public self in and through language, has often been linked to the desire to "testify," to "witness," and to give voice to those who have been marginalized by history and society. This writing of the self, moreover, has often been viewed in a decidedly political light. As Henry Louis Gates writes in his introduction to a collection of African American autobiographies, "scholars have long registered the relation in the African American tradition between the declaration of selfhood and the public act of publication." He continues:

Deprived of formal recognition of their subjectivity in Western arts and letters, in jurisprudence, and in all the signals of full citizenship, African Americans sought out the permanence of the book to write a rhetorical self into the nonexistence of language. "I write myself, therefore I am" could very well be taken as the motto of "the race" in this country.[2]

Gates's observations have been echoed repeatedly in the assessments of other theorists who have returned again and again to the study of how the production of personal narratives among members of minority groups has served a greater social, political, and collective purpose, one that incorporates the distinctive voice of the individual but that ultimately transcends him or her.[3] If this is true among authors aligned with liberal or leftist causes and tendencies, then it should be equally true for conservatives.

While I have touched briefly on the use of autobiographical appeals to experience and authenticity in the preceding chapters, herein I take a representative sample of autobiographies written by minority conservatives as my primary object of analysis. Although conservatives are not generally included in the anthologies and critical studies of minority cultures, their desire to "write themselves" into existence and recognition has emerged as a pronounced tendency—one that is also, as the example of Thomas illustrates, highly serviceable in public and political arenas. It is my contention that the various ways African American, Latino, and gay conservatives choose to narrate their lives and to present their public selves tells us something crucially important about their political and ideological commitments. Because so many minority conservatives have been denounced as "traitors" to their race, ethnicity, or sexual orientation, their attempts to root their politics in their experiences are particularly striking.

In my efforts to listen attentively to the voices of minority conservatives, I have been greatly influenced by a number of scholars who find profound insight in the conjunction of experience and narrative in the process of storytelling. In essence, autobiographies are narratives, or stories, about experience. Among poststructuralists, feminists, critical legal theorists, and critical race theorists, storytelling, especially by those who occupy marginalized positions in society, is an inherently oppositional act. Because stories are always fragmentary and particularist in nature, they have the power to dispute and disrupt *any* claim to authority and universality.[4] From this perspective, experience becomes an epistemological foundation in its own right and ensures the possibility of competing truth claims. While many conservatives would, I expect, be uncomfortable with such skeptical and relativistic theories, their logic insists we take all appeals to experience seriously, even those (or perhaps precisely those) that serve to justify conservative political identities.

Since they have not always been accepted by liberals or leftists or by mainstream conservatives, minority conservatives are uniquely placed to destabilize common assumptions about the connections that link race, ethnicity, sexuality, and ideology on both the Left and the Right sides of the political spectrum. The very existence of a Latino conservative forces us to rethink any facile presumptions that one's identity somehow dictates one's politics. In the autobiographies and semiautobiographical texts of Bruce Bawer and his fellow gay conservative Marvin Liebman, or of African American conservatives George Schuyler and Glenn Loury, or of Latino fellow traveler Richard Rodriguez, what emerges are political identities that do not fit comfortably into any preexisting categories.

These authors differ in terms of race, ethnicity, sexuality, age, religious orientation, and political opinion, yet each has produced an autobiographical text in which the personal is the political and in which experience becomes a foundation for political and moral reasoning as the author retells the story of his life from childhood to manhood. I want to acknowledge that manhood and the social construction of masculinity through race, ethnicity, and sexuality plays a commanding role in the following analysis, as I have consciously chosen to focus primarily on texts produced by male authors.

Discourses of masculinity are key to deciphering how these authors situate their desire for individuality, freedom, and autonomy despite their having social identities defined, both internally and externally, by social groups. Returning briefly to Clarence Thomas's story, one is immediately struck by its American-ness, its African American-ness, and its gendered quality. The story's central action, Thomas's movement, both literally and metaphorically, through the world, is linked to his gender in understated but inexorable ways. Once again, Christine Stansell's reading of Thomas's narrative performance is pertinent here. "Less noted," she writes, "was the story of growing up male, linked to the theme of uplift through the figure of Thomas's grandfather":

> Indeed, reading the story through a feminist lens, you notice that it turns upon the moment Thomas left his downtrodden mother to live with his grandfather. The breakup of his nuclear family released him and his brother from the downward pull of his mother's poverty and his tiny little Georgia town and propelled him into the orbit of his grandfather's high expectations and hard-edged racial pride.[5]

Thomas's escape from feminized poverty stands in stark contrast to his sister's relative confinement in the role of dutiful daughter and family caretaker. While Thomas is able to present himself as a heroic self-made man, he transforms his sister, Emma Mae Martin, into an irresponsible, dependent welfare cheat.

Justice Thomas's derogatory use of his sister's predicament was surely one of the darker moments in his career as a public figure and as an advocate of conservative ideologies. In omitting pertinent facts of his sister's life—her resourcefulness as a minimum-wage-earning mother of four; her temporary stint on welfare as she cared for a sick aunt—Thomas portrayed her in an exceedingly negative and manipulative manner. This episode not only demonstrated the power of negative stereotyping but also spoke to the realities of class and gender in determining and, at times, delimiting an individual's access to opportunity.

This is not to suggest that Thomas's sister could not also have come to adopt conservative politics; many women from all social classes and circumstances have certainly done so. In fact, one black conservative woman, Star Parker, limns a series of experiences and misadventures—numerous abortions, drugs, blatant welfare fraud—consonant with almost every stereotypical portrayal of the black "welfare queen": that specter that has haunted the American political consciousness since the Reagan years. Parker, however, managed to work her way off welfare and into the circuit of conservative spokespersons for self-reliance, family values, and moral reform. What I do want to suggest is that when we shift our perspective from men to women, as I attempt to demonstrate in my reading of Star Parker's autobiography in a later section of this chapter, the story must be reformulated to take gender differences into account. And yet, what multicultural conservatives such as Schuyler, Loury, Rodriguez, Thomas, Liebman, Bawer, and Parker share, despite differences in race, ethnicity, sexuality, and gender, is a desire to justify their political choices in light of their personal experiences. If they fashion themselves as jeremiahs bringing a message of hope and redemption to the nation, then it is reasonable to inquire into what sorts of experiences make a successful conservative prophet.

The Making of a Conservative

What is immediately noticeable about the autobiographies of minority conservatives is the degree of effusiveness concerning their political and ideological motivations. Perhaps because they are forced to justify political identities many regard and dismiss as inherently oxymoronic, a number of minority conservatives have chosen to preface their autobiographies with provocative statements of their own philosophies. Leaving aside Booker T. Washington's *Up from Slavery* and the debates that surround both the man and the text, the first autobiography of any note by a self-styled African American conservative is George Schuyler's *Black and Conservative*. Published in 1966, Schuyler's autobiography is a reflection on his early childhood in New England and a meditation on his nearly four decades of public life as a journalist and an activist. Adhering to the conventions of the genre, Schuyler's text begins with his family and the environment of his youth. But before the reader is introduced to him with the traditional "I was born . . ." formulation, Schuyler inserts the following declaration:

"A Black person learns very early that his color is a disadvantage in a world of white folks," he writes. "This being an unalterable circumstance, one learns very early to make the best of it. So the lifetime endeavor of the intelligent Negro is how to be reasonably happy though colored."[6]

This "intelligent" attitude toward the ways in which race functions in American society is also, Schuyler suggests, what molds the African American into an "outstanding example of American conservatism." Schuyler grounds his racial philosophy of adaptation, restraint, and stoicism—a philosophy he adopted "not consistently but most of the time"—in the circumstances that shaped his childhood. Having learned "very early in the life that I was colored," Schuyler writes, "this fact of life did not distress, restrain or overburden me."

> One takes things as they are, lives with them, and tries to turn them to one's advantage or seeks another locale where the opportunities are more favorable. This was the conservative viewpoint of my parents and family.[7]

Richard Rodriguez was equally shaped by his childhood, but more so by his movement away from his close-knit family and its Mexican-immigrant culture. "Once upon a time," writes Rodriguez, inserting a playfully ironic tone into the first page of his story, "I was a socially disadvantaged child." Like Schuyler, he prefaces his narrative with a statement of his philosophy, which transformed him into a "middle-class American man. Assimilated."[8] Rodriguez writes as an assimilated man, marked by "indelible color" but very much changed by education and social mobility. "My book is necessarily political," he adds, "in the conventional sense, for public issues—editorials and ballot stubs, petitions and placards, faceless formulations of greater and lesser good by greater and lesser minds—have bisected my life and changed its course."

> And, in some broad sense, my writing is political because it concerns my movement away from the company of family and into the city. This was my coming of age: I became a man by becoming a public man.[9]

Rodriguez's autobiographical narrative is also political to the extent that he chooses to employ his own life experiences to question and denounce programs such as affirmative action and bilingual education, both of which he views as creating barriers to assimilation for himself and others.

This desire for assimilation and acceptance by the wider society through an embrace of individuation is a common theme that runs through each of the texts, as does a longing to transcend the confines of difference. For Marvin Liebman, who as a closeted gay man has been one of the leading conservative activists in the United States for nearly four decades, the problems of identity and ideology result not so much from assimilation as from differentiation. "Coming Out Conservative" not only is the title of Liebman's autobiography but also names a process shared by other gay conservatives such as Bawer. Uniting sexual identity and political ideology, their autobiographies constitute a double coming out. Liebman begins his narrative with the experience of outing himself in an open letter published in the *National Review* in 1990. "In my letter," he writes, "I said how I regretted all those years of compliant silence. I continue to regret them, but they are over and unsalvageable. I will never be silent again."

But Liebman's autobiography is not only a testament to the virtue and necessity of coming out; it is also an attempt to rescue his political cause (defined more in terms of conservative politics than of homosexual politics) from "the bigots hovering in the distance, waiting to take over a rudderless conservative movement that had lost its focus."[10] These dangerous "bigots" are by and large various "far-right groups" associated with the Religious Right and family-values organizations that use gay bashing techniques to raise funds and to disseminate their views. "They were able to promote fear and hatred of gay and lesbian Americans," he writes,

And at the same time, provide themselves with a *raison d'etre* for their money-raising beating the drums for 'traditional American (white Christian) family values' under attack by the vanguard of the homosexual menace. Their effort to impose a New Morality had begun. I feared that there would be no stop to the bigotry and hatred that would sweep America. This was my political motive in writing my letter to Buckley and coming out so publicly.[11]

Bruce Bawer also gives a decidedly political motive for writing in a semiautobiographical style, and he shares a number of Liebman's fears about the Religious Right and the demonization of homosexuals. In his "Author's Note," which prefaces the text, he states that his book is "a reflection of the theme of homosexuality," composed and published because "the current debate on homosexuality has generated more heat than light." He says his text is autobiographical to the extent that "my sense of what it means to be gay derives largely from my own experiences."[12] Like Liebman, he wants to bring his own experiences and analysis of contemporary political developments to bear on the debates over homosexuality. Whereas Liebman targets the bigotry of the Right, Bawer is far more concerned with the liberatory project of the gay Left, bolstered by the idea of a gay subculture and intellectual trends such as queer theory. Along with Rodriguez and other minority conservatives, Bawer is opposed to any political-intellectual project that risks elevating the group over the individual or that threatens to confine the individual within the boundaries of race, ethnicity, or sexuality.

Ultimately, coming out, which has such a particular meaning for Bawer and Leibman, becomes a metaphor for other politically conservative minorities. Among homosexual activists, coming out has always implied both an assertion of one's identity and voice in a public forum and an acceptance of and pride in oneself. Each of the texts under consideration begins with a coming out of sorts, in the form of a declaration of political sensibilities in which conventional notions of identity are challenged or at least problematized. The political and philosophical statements that preface each of these autobiographies, then, function as a framework that organizes the author's subsequent life stories.

Remembering the Past

Memory teaches me what I know of these matters; the boy reminds the man.   —*Richard Rodriguez*

Both Schuyler, in his *Black and Conservative*, and Richard Rodriguez, in *Hunger of Memory*, draw a strong connection between formative childhood experiences and the articulation of their later philosophies. In the early chapters of his text, Schuyler is particularly interested in explaining how his knowledge of "being colored" did not become a source of constraint or restriction. Judging by the manner in which he delineates his childhood experiences with the dynamics of race and family, he would have almost certainly agreed with his contemporary and fellow political conservative Zora Neale Hurston. Hurston maintained that she was not "tragically colored"; that she did not belong to "the sobbing school of Negrohood who hold that nature somehow has given them a lowdown dirty deal."[13] While Schuyler certainly had an affinity for such a position (he wrote elsewhere that race was nothing more than a superstition), race and racial consciousness permeates Schuyler's text.

Schuyler was born in Providence, Rhode Island, on February 25, 1895, and was raised primarily in Syracuse, New York, by parents and grandparents who were uncomfortable with some of the more negative aspects of history, especially slavery. As he relates his family lineage on the maternal and the paternal sides, he is careful to distance his family from the tragic legacy of slavery, noting that if "any of the family were ever slaves, it must have been before the Revolutionary War." Instead, his family boasted of having been free persons of color as far back as anyone could or cared to remember, and they "haughtily looked down upon those who had been in servitude."[14] Not only did his family tend to erect barriers between themselves and those who were supposedly tainted by a history of bondage, but they also chose to reside in an area where they were the only black family on their block in Syracuse, where African Americans constituted less than 1 percent of the population.

Class privilege was also a structuring factor in Schuyler's relatively happy and comfortable childhood. As a chef in a local hotel, his father was part of the elite of the small colored community, and the family lived in surroundings befitting what Schuyler calls "our class." The death of his father and his mother's remarriage to a transplanted black southerner did not affect the family's class status in any dramatic way, though his stepfather's background and their relocation to a more integrated neighborhood did introduce Schuyler to the strictures of intraracial regional difference. In their new neighborhood, Schuyler's family lived among three black families who had recently migrated from the South. Although his mother was married to an "industrious" southern migrant, she refused to associate with these families, judging them to be uncouth and without standards.

Racial politics, or indeed political activism of any stripe, does not appear to have intruded into the Schuyler home. In fact, the first political event Schuyler says he recalls was the assassination of President William McKinley by an anarchist. "Great indignation was expressed by the adults," he writes.

I was told that an anarchist was one of those foreigners who believed in no government at all. This seemed incredible. To me, government represented the genial cop on the corner, the jangling fire engines with their galloping horses, the even tenor of the way of life in our neighborhood. These were things one wanted to conserve.[15]

What strikes most contemporary readers as incredible is that Schuyler chooses to recall, retell, and perhaps to rewrite this event in these terms. Unlike the majority of autobiographies produced by African Americans, Schuyler's presents his first encounter with politics, and even race, in astoundingly benign terms.

In this regard, Booker T. Washington's *Up from Slavery* offers a better comparative text than, say, Richard Wright's *Black Boy*, with its vivid depiction of racism and brutality. Washington introduces himself and draws the reader into his narrative through a deceptively happy tale of plantation life. Naturally, Washington does not disguise the fact of being born a slave or having lived in "the midst of the most miserable, desolate, and discouraging surroundings." But, a quarter of the way into the first chapter, he relates the following anecdote: "One of my earliest recollections is that my of my mother cooking a chicken late at night, and awakening her children for the purpose of feeding them. How or where she got it I do not know. I presume, however, it was procured from our owner's farm."[16] As the African American literary theorist Houston A. Baker argues, Washington's outrageous invocation of one of the minstrel tradition's stock stereotypes—a "chicken-stealing darky"—was a particularly soothing and reassuring image for white readers. Indeed, Baker praises Washington's masterful manipulation of the "mask" of the minstrel and his strategic use of stereotypical "Negro behavior." It is Washington's mastery of the Afro-American *sound* and his deftness in crafting a story with immediate appeal to a white southern audience that Baker finds so remarkable.[17]

In the context of Washington's narrative, as well as of his broader political project, the story is designed to function as an illustration of the sorts of values, such as thrift, ingenuity, and the ability to make a virtue of necessity, that Washington learned from his mother. The same type of racial softening is found in Schuyler's text, as is a characterization of the maternal figure as the source of values. Of his mother, Schuyler writes: "A true conservative, she was an apostle of the possible, a strong believer in preserving the values of society, and firm advocate of reasonable change."[18] For Schuyler and Washington, their mothers become, in a sense, the idealized Mothers of the Race: the fonts of virtues, the progenitors of strong (male) children, and the anchor of the family. Weaving in this strong emphasis on female virtue, before the conclusion of the first chapter of his autobiography, Schuyler provides a fairly rich and suggestive description of how his early experiences of race, family, gender, class, and status shaped his life and the course of his myriad political engagements. What the auto-

biographies of Washington and Schuyler share is a need to present conservatism as a natural aspect of African American culture and their own personal development. The presentation of conservatism as a set of attributes
emanating from the womb of mothers and Mothers serves to legitimate it
as a philosophy of life. Conservatism is not something that one discovers
late in life, they suggest, but something that is remembered from one's
early years.

If Schuyler's (and Washington's) is a story of what one carries through
time and circumstances, Richard Rodriguez's *Hunger of Memory* is a story
of what must be left behind. Rodriguez presents a picture of family life
that is as cohesive as Schuyler's, but where Schuyler focuses primarily on
tensions between his family and others, Rodriguez focuses on tensions
within the family unit itself. Like other narrative explorations of the lives
of children of working-class immigrants in the United States, Rodriguez's
memoir offers up the painful details of his growing sense of alienation
from his parents. "At last, seven years old," Rodriguez recalls, "I came to
believe what had been technically true since my birth: I was an American
citizen. But the special feeling of closeness at home was diminished by
then."[19] His determination to master the English language, his drive to
succeed in school, and his desire for acceptance in the world beyond
home all led to the sorts of generational fissures chronicled in countless
narratives of ethnic assimilation in America. And yet, Rodriguez grounds
his account of his experiences, especially in terms of his education, not so
much in ethnicity or culture as in a much-fought-for and prized class status, class mobility, and individuation.

While the narrative structure of *Hunger of Memory* shares a number of tendencies with the rich genre created by first- and second-generation immigrants, Rodriguez distinguishes himself by not appealing to this American
literary tradition. The model he selects to conceptualize his personal struggle is in fact neither ethnic nor American. Instead, he chooses to view his
childhood and adolescence through the lens of the British author Richard
Hoggart's *The Uses of Literacy*. Rodriguez tells us that he happened upon
Hoggart's text in a moment of distraction from his studies in the British Museum and found himself in the Englishman's sensitive description of the
scholarship boy. "For the first time," Rodriguez writes, "I realized that there
were other students like me, and so I was able to frame the meaning of my
academic success, its consequent price—the loss."[20] Hoggart's scholarship
boy is of working-class origin. Confronted with the disjuncture between the
rigors and expectations of school, with its demands for order and discipline,

and the noisy gregariousness of family life, with its communal (and feminine) ethos of the hearth, the boy determines that he must divorce himself from the latter if he is to "get on" in the world. "He is a child," Rodriguez surmises, "who cannot forget that his academic success distances him from a life he loved, even from his own memory of himself."[21] It is, Rodriguez suggests, this distance that eventually makes him free, whole, individual, and, of course, upwardly socially mobile.

This stark contrast between the private world of family and the public world of freedom also plays a role in structuring the texts of gay conservatives. For both Bawer and Liebman, early childhood experiences are presented as stories of self-discovery done mostly in private (and in secret) within the context of family lives in which their sexual identities are problematic. Both men frame their childhood experiences in terms of self-acceptance despite negative stereotypes of and attitudes toward homosexuality. For Liebman, his budding sense of sexual preference was a marker of difference, separating him from his family, especially his father, to whom he was "a disappointment." "I knew that my mother loved me," Liebman writes, "but she could never understand or accept me. She knew I was 'different.'"[22] Knowledge of his difference and a desire for acceptance pulled Liebman away from the world of his Jewish immigrant family and toward the social world of radical politics in the late 1930s, including a brief stint in the Young Communist League and other communist groups. In these groups he met other "bohemian" (gay) men and (lesbian) women, although his liaisons with men were carried on in secret.

Liebman's account of these years of young adulthood are dotted with references to his ambiguity over his sexual desires for men and his need for recognition in the male world. He even greeted the news of his induction into the army with elation since "now I could be one of the boys," although his service in the army was cut short when his identity as a "New York Jew faggot" was discovered.

I became a pariah, bitterly lonely and desperately unhappy. I was shunned by everyone. Not one single word of greeting or compassion or understanding or even desultory conversation was uttered. I was also upset that I had been publicly called "Jew." This increased my difference—a Jew faggot.[23]

Dishonorably discharged, he sought to re-enter his old life, only to find it increasingly drained of meaning. He recalls, "I was desperately looking for something to give my life purpose and meaning as the Communist Party had done." Struggling to maintain his leftist credentials, he joined the left-wing orbit of the Zionist movement and for a time worked to assist Jewish refugees and to ensure a free Palestine.

His conversion to anticommunism as a way of life came after hearing the story of Elinor Lipper, a German-Jewish, ex-Communist refugee forced to endure the hardships of a labor camp in the Soviet Union. His conversion may seem quick, he notes, "but it was really the culmination of five years of internal intellectual conflict I had hidden from myself."[24] Disillusioned by the Left, by the Communist Party, and by the Soviet Union, he embraced the Right. Liebman's entrance into the disorganized and largely ignored world of conservative politics in the 1950s was also mediated by sexual desire on the one hand and the fear of difference and alienation on the other. After his discharge from the army, Liebman's dedication to remaining safely in the closet intensified; convinced now of the merits of anticommunism, he put all of his energies into organizing political groups such as the Young Americans for Freedom, the Committee of One Million, and the American Conservative Union. He was always content, he tells us, to remain behind the scenes and out of the limelight.

Liebman, like Rodriguez and Schuyler, provides vivid descriptions of leaving home and meeting the world. For Liebman and Schuyler, this experience was mediated through army life. Although Schuyler's time in the army (during the era of World War I and with the challenges of racism) was dramatically different from Liebman's (during World War II and with the conflicts over anti-Semitism and homophobia), it was also a turning point in his life. During adolescence it became increasingly clear to Schuyler that "the Negro had his place in Syracuse, and it was no where near the top, nor would it be, no matter his schooling." After dropping out of high school, he was convinced there was no future for him in his hometown and no real point in pursuing a college degree. Fortunately, military service opened an avenue of escape.

Years before he had witnessed army maneuvers at a local base and was impressed by the vision of Negro soldiers in positions of authority. These soldiers, he recalls, "were clean, upstanding, orderly and polite."

They talked of far-off places where they had served—the Philippines, Cuba, the Indian Territory, and the expanses of Texas, Arizona, and New Mexico. These were the inheritors of the tradition of conflict in the

Revolutionary War, the War of 1812, the Civil War, and the Indian Wars
in the West. How they contrasted with our uninviting lot in Syracuse![25]

Schuyler's association of military heroism with wars of conquest and U.S.
imperialism, particularly against peoples of color, is suggestive and even
slightly horrifying. At the same time, military service was, in his mind, a path
to dignity and freedom. His mother agreed, believing the army would "make
a man" out of him. Hence, in 1912, full of dreams of seeing the world and
hoping to find a chance for advancement, Schuyler enlisted.

While Schuyler takes it for granted in his autobiography, this road to
freedom and respectability was almost wholly contingent on his gender.
Generations of African American men have served in the armed forces
not only in hopes of proving their loyalty and securing their rights as
Americans but also out of a desire to prove their manhood. In Schuyler's
case, his gender, coupled with his willingness to enlist, allowed him access into a world beyond the confines of Syracuse and the immediate
bonds of family life. Although racial discrimination remained an ever
present fixture in his life, military service took him to fairly "exotic" locations—Hawaii, Japan, the Philippines, China—and afforded him the
opportunity to develop and hone his skills as a creative writer and a
journalist. Serving from 1912 to 1919 as part of the Twenty-fifth Infantry,
a segregated unit, Schuyler prided himself on being a soldier's soldier,
able to gamble, swear, fight, and hustle officers with the best of them.
Army life also provided Schuyler with the raw materials of some of his
most endearing literary efforts.

After his discharge, Schuyler headed for New York and Harlem—the
Black Mecca—whose magnetic charm was attracting African American
intellectuals, artists, writers, and political advocates from across the country. Neither Rodriguez nor Bawer had the experience of military service, but both rushed to meet the world in different venues. For Rodriguez, the nature of his education and institutions of higher learning,
including his experiences at the British Museum, preformed this role,
while Bawer's path led him into the arena of poetry and, eventually,
journalism. While each author devotes different amounts of space to
chronicling personal relationships with friends and family, intimate moments of sexual discovery, and private thoughts and feelings, the world
beyond hearth and home emerges as far more decisive than the clois-
tered world of the family. For the world beyond the home is also the
world of politics.

The Politics of Conversion: Making a Home in the World

I have moved from place to place, from idea to idea, from person to person, from left to right, from Jew to Catholic, from middle class to bohemian and back again . . . looking for a family, a place, a home where I
could be me.

> —*Marvin Liebman,* Coming Out Conservative

The often difficult and even painful search for self-awareness, identity, and
a home is a common motif in the genre of autobiography, and it plays an
overt, politically charged role for conservative authors. For circumstances
dictate that they engage in an apologetics of their political choices. Many
of these narratives highlight the often high cost of individualism and individuation, while simultaneously emphasizing their value. Liebman's search
for a home in the world—a search that led him from Left to Right, engendered his conversion to Catholicism late in life, and eventually made it
possible for him to come out as a gay conservative—is atypical but in-
formative. For Liebman, and for Schuyler, Rodriguez, and Bawer, this
search involved not only various forms of assimilation but also a political,
philosophical, and an emotional conversion to conservatism and Christianity. Individual assimilation and political conservatism are certainly not
coterminous, yet these authors often treat them as if they were, especially
when invoking (and praising) freedom from group consciousness.

While each defines assimilation in a slightly different way, each employs
the language of individualism in his attempt to isolate and describe the
moment when he found, and began to adhere to, political positions that
coincided with his emergent identity. None of their conversion narratives
is as dramatic as Paul's spiritual experience on the road to Damascus or
Saint Augustine's redemption from sin, but a species of political conversion is nonetheless portrayed as a central aspect of their paths to freedom
and authenticity.

Richard Rodriguez tells us that he truly found himself during the campus turmoil of the late 1960s and early 1970s, when he began to publicly
critique programs such as affirmative action and bilingual education. He
did so not so much out of an affinity for right-wing politics but out of a
loyalty to having become "a public man. Assimilated."

> Slowly, slowly, the term *minority* became a source of unease. It would re-
> mind me of those boyhood years when I had felt myself alienated from

public (majority) society. . . . The terms sounded in public to remind me in private of the truth: I was not—in a *cultural* sense—a minority, an alien from public life.[26]

In 1973, two of his essays on being educated away from the culture of his family were published, and in 1974 and again in 1977 he published denunciations of affirmative action, with the basis of each essay being his realization that he was "no longer like socially disadvantaged Hispanic-Americans." These essays were also his ticket to wider public recognition, leading eventually to speaking engagements. As a writer and a public speaker, he put forth the now conventional argument that programs such as affirmative action, and any other measure that "unduly" ties the individual to the group, are ipso facto damaging to the persons who are said to have benefited from them. This he knows because he benefited from such programs, but came to feel regret about it later. Having wandered into sin, he can now see the light. By the 1990s, this had become among the most important and successful critiques of race and ethnic-based programs.

It is in the very nature of such critiques that they can be performed only through direct reference to personal experience and private pain. Consider, for instance, the highly effective use of such a critique in Stephen Carter's *Reflection of an Affirmative Action Baby*. Although a professor of law at Yale University and by all objective measures a talented and successful scholar, Carter remains, because of affirmative action and the image of incompetence that unjustly surrounds it, beset by personal doubts about his ability and his place in the world. "For many, perhaps most, black professionals of my generation," Carter writes, "the matter of who got where and how is left in a studied and, I think, purposeful ambiguity."

Most of us, perhaps nearly all of us, have learned to bury the matter far back in our minds. . . . Those of us who have graduated professional schools over the past fifteen to twenty years, and are not white, travel career paths that are frequently bumpy with suspicions that we did not earn the right to be where we are. We bristle when others raise what might be called the qualification question—"Did you get into school or get hired because of a special program?"—and that prickly sensitivity is the best evidence, if any is needed, of one of the principal costs of racial preferences.[27]

This critique of collective group-based efforts is not exactly a new phenomenon, however, regardless of its increasing centrality in contemporary conservative thought. While Rodriguez lays much of the blame for these developments at the feet of the New Left,[28] George Schuyler takes on the older generation. But, whereas Rodriguez is careful to distinguish the civil rights movement of the 1950s and early 1960s from the "distortions" that came after, Schuyler attacked even the early years of the movement as overtly collectivist and communist-dominated. Schuyler (like Liebman) was part of the post–World War II growth of American conservatism in which anticommunism was a driving force. As with many others of that generation, he had been condemning communism and communists since the 1930s, although in his case he was particularly worried about the damage communism would inflict upon Africans and African Americans.[29]

Schuyler's conversion to the conservative cause was a long and slow one. Although he joined the Socialist Party in 1922 during a brief return to Syracuse, he did so not out of a true ideological commitment but because the SP offered one of the few venues for stimulating intellectual life. During the years of the Harlem Renaissance and the rise and fall of Garveyism, he worked at odd jobs and landed a position in the office of A. Philip Randolph's *Messenger* magazine. By the 1930s he had become one of the foremost black journalistic opponents of communism and the Communist Party, not only in the United States but in Africa and Latin America as well.[30] "This did not come to me suddenly," he writes:

> I had read the work of these men and women, attended their meetings and lectures. . . . It took some time to sense the proportions of what seemed to me to be a conspiracy to plant collectivism in America and nourish it to the final harvest. . . . In their suspicion and hatred of free enterprise capitalism, they were working toward the same ant-heap slavery inherent in collectivism.[31]

During this period he also garnered a reputation for ruthlessly critiquing almost any form of cultural nationalism, lampooning, in articles such as "The Negro Art Hokum" (published in *The Nation*), the attempts of black artists to create a distinctively African American style. In perhaps the most famous of Schuyler's essays, he casts aspersions at the very notion of "Negro art" and "Negro artists" (as opposed to artists and writers who happen to be Negroes) as distinct from American art. Holding that it is "sheer nonsense" to talk about racial differences in terms of American arts and letters, Schuyler goes as far as to proclaim the "Aframerican is merely a lampblack Anglo-Saxon." Prefiguring positions later adopted by critics such as Stanley Crouch, he insisted that the Negro American is nothing more or less than simply American, with the additional proviso that claiming otherwise inadvertently buys into the white supremist doctrines of men such as Madison Grant and Lothrop Stoddard.[32]

By the 1950s, his political ideology had become so deeply embedded in anticommunist discourses on the one hand, and in assimilationist discourses on the other, that he could see precious little merit in the post–World War II civil rights movement, which he denounced for engaging in "Red techniques" and ideologies of collectivism. It was not, I think, until this point in his life that Schuyler became an actual political conservative as opposed to a fairly liberal anticommunist or a contrarian iconoclast. During the turmoil over the civil rights movement, Schuyler clearly aligned himself with the conservative movement. Not only did he help to organize the Conservative Political Union in New York; in 1946 he ran on its ticket, opposing Adam Clayton Powell for a congressional seat in the Eighteenth District in Manhattan (Harlem). Schuyler's loss was decisive. He received only 0.06 percent of the vote to Powell's 84.6 percent. His defeat may have been yet another factor in his rightward drift, pushing him ultimately into the John Birch Society.[33]

Having finally lost his position with the *Pittsburgh Courier* and after the tragic deaths of his daughter, Phillipa, in 1967 (she died in a plane crash while covering the Vietnam War for the *Union Leader*), and of his wife, Josephine, in 1969, Schuyler appears to have sought and found solace within a predominately white and conservative environment. His final break with the editorial staff of the *Courier* came in 1964 after Schuyler gave a radio interview during which he expressed his support for then presidential nominee Barry Goldwater ("a fine man, a good conservative") and for Goldwater's condemnation of the Civil Rights Act on constitutional grounds. As if this were not enough, Schuyler deepened the growing chasm between himself and his employers by submitting a column in which he judged Martin Luther King an unfit and unworthy recipient of the Nobel Peace Prize. The *Courier* refused to print it, but it did find a place in New Hampshire's *Union Leader*, edited by his friend William Loeb. Subsequently the article was reprinted in many parts of the country, though largely in conservative newspapers.

But Schuyler not only moved to the Right; he moved to the far Right, joining the John Birch Society "sometime in the early 1960s" and writing for the Society's *American Opinion* as well as for its weekly *Review of the News*. More and more conservative Republican groups, Schuyler relates, "mostly white, asked me to speak to them during the winter and spring of 1965."[34] Thereafter, his writings and speeches continued to meet with acclaim in the white conservative press and with silence in African American circles, until the NAACP's *Crisis* finally wrote him off publicly as a mere iconoclast.[35] His publishing career virtually ceased, however, after his wife's suicide—an event that took place years after the publication of *Black and Conservative*. "But I doubt that I shall be here very long," Schuyler wrote to his friend William Loeb days after discovering his wife's dead body. "I have tried to fight the good fight for what I have considered right, but now the long battle has worn me down. It is hard to hold one's head high and to carry on under crushing burdens of responsibility."[36] Schuyler died, alone, in a New York hospital in August 1977.

Marvin Liebman also converted to conservatism via anticommunism. In fact it is highly probable that his path crossed Schuyler's in various organizations, ranging from the American Committee for Cultural Freedom, to the New York State Political Conservative Union, to the campaigns of Barry Goldwater, whom both men supported. For Liebman, homosexuality played as large a role in his conversion as did race and ethnicity for Schuyler and Rodriguez. "From the time I quit the Communist Party," Liebman writes, "I have been a firm believer in the importance of the individual over any state, political party, or religious hierarchy."

> To me, the individual is all, subservient only to God. With my belief in the individual comes a belief in the sanctity of privacy and the freedom of silence. At first, this belief was vital to my hiding as a homosexual. As I grew older, it became an integral part of what I believe—the right to privacy, to "do your own thing" as long as you don't hurt anyone else. The less regulation, the less interference in one's life—the better.[37]

As Liebman implies, conservatism embodied the potential to function as a safe haven from pressures to conform to widely accepted notions of group identity, and much the same could be said, I suspect, of other minority conservatives. Still, Liebman's conversion did not alleviate his pain. His place in the history of the New Right is undeniable; along with Buckley and William Rusher, James Burnham (an ex-communist), Whittaker Chambers (ditto), Frank Meyer, and Brent Bozell, he constituted something of a bridge between an older, moribund conservatism and a new brand of conservative activism. Liebman was by all accounts one of the premier organizers and fund-raisers of the movement.[38] His life as a

Jewish conservative in a predominantly Christian, Protestant movement and as a closeted gay man was not without its stressful moments, however. To take just one example, in the early years of the Young Americans for Freedom (YAF)—organized out of the youth movement for Goldwater after the 1960 Republican National Convention failed to select Goldwater as Nixon's running mate—Liebman was forced to wage a protracted battle to keep YAF out of the orbit of the John Birch Society (JBS). As far-Right extremists, the Birchers represented everything Liebman and his circle detested about the old style of American conservatism, especially its unthinking bigotry. "It was during this struggle," he relates, "that I began to see again the latent bigotry in the American Right and once again became its target." Scott Stanley, Jr., a YAF director and protegee of the JBS's Robert Welch, pulled the organization in one direction, while Liebman and his supporters worked to strengthen the influence of the *National Review* circle. In the midst of this internal war, Liebman brought in Richard Viguerie, who would go on to perfect the use of direct-mail campaigns so crucial to the growth of the New Right in the 1970s and 1980s, as YAF's executive director.[39]

Tensions within the Young Americans for Freedom finally boiled over during its Second Annual Awards rally in March 1962 at Madison Square Garden. Senators Goldwater and John Tower were scheduled as featured speakers, but disputes erupted over the other honorees. John Dos Passos, Charles Edison, and M. Stanton Evans were slated to receive awards, as were Herbert Hoover, John Wayne, Liebman, and General Edwin A. Walker, a Korean war hero and committed Bircher. Because the extreme views of the JBS "(including the belief that Eisenhower was a lifelong agent of the Soviet Union) put it outside of the kind of movement we were all working toward," the YAF board decided to withdraw General Walker's invitation. The JBS retaliated with an anti-Semitic smear campaign against Liebman (and Goldwater), publishing a story in the boldly racist and anti-Semitic *Liberty Lobby* on "Kosher Konservatives." "The most influential single individual in YAF holds no office," read a subsequent report issued by the Birch-controlled National Patriotic Research Association. Focusing on Liebman's enigmatic record and recent conversion to the cause, it continued: "Liebman, a fanatical Zionist, hates Arabs. His background includes a mysterious trip to Israel, which he steadfastly refuses to explain. . . . Perhaps his strong Zionist sentiments explain the fact that most of his office staff . . . is Jewish or Negro."[40] With such virulence in the air over one aspect of his identity, it is little wonder he struggled to keep the other, more explosive dimension, under wraps.

Bawer also came to have personal and political difficulties within the mainstream of the conservative movement that Liebman helped to create. A poet and a devotee of "New Formalism," in 1985 he sent an unsolicited article on writing to the conservative *American Spectator*. A person Bawer refers to only as one of the magazine's "second-rung" editors took an interest, and thus began Bawer's four-year stint as the *Spectator's* movie reviewer. He was painfully aware of the magazine's homophobia but had adopted a "don't ask, don't tell" policy toward acknowledging his sexual orientation. When the humorist J. P. O'Rourke contributed a piece, "Manhattan Swish," on New York City's law prohibiting housing discrimination against homosexuals, that compared rights for gays and lesbians with rights for alcoholics, Bawer maintained his silence, as he did on other occasions. When the magazine ran an article by the British journalist Christopher Monckton on "The Myth of Heterosexual AIDS," in which he urged the adoption of universal AIDS virus testing and the quarantine of anyone who tested positive, Bawer felt obligated to issue a denunciation in the letter-to-the-editor column, as did *Spectator's* editor-in-chief, Andrew Ferguson.

"If I continued my association with the *American Spectator* despite its publication of such articles as Monckton's it was because I felt that as long as I was allowed to write about what I wanted," Bawer explains, "I could hardly complain that other writers were granted the same privilege."[41] Bawer *did* complain when one of his reviews was rejected for supposedly condoning (that is, not forcefully condemning) homosexuality. He fought for the integrity of the review, issuing a "furious jeremiad against homophobia," but to no avail. Bawer was faced with a choice between omitting the offending line about "our common humanity" regardless of sexual orientation and having the piece rejected. "We have a conservative readership," he was told. "There are a lot of gay conservatives in Washington, but they keep to themselves because they understand that other conservatives don't want to hear about it."[42] Bawer refused to alter his review, and his association with the *American Spectator* came to an end. His autobiography is sprinkled with stories of other gay conservatives who maintain their silence on matters of sexuality and homophobia. Indeed, many have experienced this form of forced suppression of difference in the name of "political correctness" concerning what other conservatives do not want to hear or acknowledge.

While they have vastly different experiences and trajectories, Liebman, Schuyler, Bawer, and Rodriguez share a disdain for what Schuyler calls collectivism, and for what a later generation of American conservatives has come to derisively label identity politics and political correctness: In each case the individual is viewed as being sacrificed to the orthodoxies of the group. Reading these texts, one is immediately struck by the weight and burden of difference in these men's lives. While their gender, class status, and notoriety arguably provide them with a fairly large sphere of freedom and choice, they nonetheless have crafted tales of the oppressive nature of group identity and difference. Although it would be unfair to view the entirety of their political positions through such a personal and psychological prism, these aspects of their autobiographies do seem to shed some light on the connections between their personal and political struggles.

It is hardly surprising that a number of multicultural conservatives have come to prize their antiorthodox views and to compose personal narratives that explain and celebrate their choices in the face of often hostile opposition. Glenn Loury's recent collection of essays, *One by One from the Inside Out*, opens and closes with autobiographical sketches that frame the more analytical portions of the text. In the opening sketch, Loury tells us a bit about his personal search for an authentic sense of identity. Authenticity, he suggests, cannot be found in "our collective experience of racism," nor in the "empathetic exchange of survivor's tales among 'brothers,'" nor even in the "collective struggle against the clear wrong of racism."

> I am so much more than the one wronged, misunderstood, underestimated, derided, or ignored by whites. I am more than the one who has struggled against this oppression and indifference; more than the descendant of slaves now claiming freedom; more, that is, than either a "colored person" (as seen by the racist) or a "person of color" (as seen by the anti-racist).[43]

If we link personal identity only or primarily to race, we fall tragically short of recognizing our potential for individuality, argues Loury. Forced to choose between "intellectual integrity" and the "collective consciousness of racial violation and shared struggle," Loury selected the former. Cut off for political and intellectual reasons from the group, with his "racial bona fides in question," he experienced a sense of loss and an uncertainty about "who I really was."[44]

Loury prefaces these personal musings with the story of a childhood friend named Woody, who "looked to all the world like your typical white boy." Although Woody claimed Negro ancestry and fully identified with blackness as a social and political reality, he found his status challenged when he and Loury attended a black political rally. Woody was rebuffed, his claim "I'm a brother, too" falling on suspicious and hostile ears unless someone else was willing to vouch for his racial credentials. "To my eternal disgrace," Loury writes, "I refused to speak up for him."[45] Woody's story becomes for Loury a metaphor for self-definition, acceptance, and recognition, as well as for the ambiguity that surrounds notions of authenticity and race in America. Having gotten a taste in adulthood of what Woody experienced in adolescence, Loury, through this story, also focuses our attention on the difficulties of defining just who and what is authentic. To what extent, we might appropriately inquire, do Loury's complex views of race and identity serve as a means of reaching back and redeeming that long-ago moment when he chose the strictures of racial group belonging over the feelings of a close friend?

Loury's second story, which serves as an epilogue to his book, takes the reader deeper into his personal life as an adult; it is also about redemption. Having reached the pinnacle of his professional life, Loury nonetheless found his private life a shambles. Drug abuse, drinking, marital infidelity, and selfishness had left him depressed and spiritually bereft. Herein, Loury chronicles not his racial journey, or his political conversion to conservatism, but his awakening to Christ. The process was a slow one. "There was not one moment where the skies opened up and something dramatic happened," he writes. "There was not a particular instant where I can definitely say I was reborn."[46] But reborn he was, over months of prayer and reflection. Through the power of faith, Loury comes to redefine his understanding of freedom, moving away from personal gratification and a selfish conception of liberty and toward an understanding of mutual obligation and self-love as intrinsic dimensions of the love of others.

In many respects, it is a moving soliloquy, as Loury seeks to bring his hard-won spiritual insights to bear on matters of cultural and racial reconciliation, economics, and social justice. On this note, Loury closes: "To paraphrase slightly a currently popular cry: no Jesus, no peace." I would suggest, tentatively and carefully, that Loury's religious rebirth helps to explain the apparent softening of his views on issues such as affirmative action and our collective responsibility to confront the realities of racism and racial inequality.

Spiritual experiences and religious commitments have been as important in the autobiographies of a number of minority conservatives as has their search for individualism and freedom. This is certainly true for

Loury, as it is for Marvin Liebman, Bawer, and Rodriguez. Of course, for Bawer and Liebman, their spiritual quests have been problematized by their sexual orientation. Liebman has had the unique experience of being not only a Jew but an ex-Jewish Catholic and a gay conservative. Even Mel White, the gay Christian conservative who was once the ghostwriter for Jerry Falwell, among others, and who has recently come out in the pages of an autobiography (*Strangers at the Gate*), cannot top Liebman's diverse positionality. With the rise of the Religious Right, this aspect of their identities has become increasingly problematic, externally if not internally. On this score they are engaged in a three-way battle to be accepted as gay Christian conservatives, despite the exclusionary rhetoric and practices of the gay and lesbian Left, the Christian (and Jewish) Right, and the institutions and organizations aligned with the mainstream of the conservative movement.

Their stories remind us of the highly charged nature of some claims to identity and how they conflict with others. Turning on themes of coming out, recognition, and acceptance by self and others, along with disputes over morality that continue to structure and divide American political culture, these stories also touch upon debates over the proper relationship between individuals, groups, the public sphere, and the state.

Pariahs or Parvenus? The Public World and the Private Self

What Liebman, Schuyler, Bawer, and Rodriguez share is a faith that one's struggles with difference can be solved by relegating them to the private sphere. Given their painful experiences and their disillusionment with the Left, there is little wonder that they would be drawn to movements emphasizing, as Liebman put it, the primacy of the individual over the state and the social group. In this they tie themselves to a tradition in political thought—from Theodore Adorno and Christopher Lasch on the Left, to Gertrud Himmelfarb and Irving Kristol on the Right, with liberals like Ronald Dworkin and John Rawls straddling the middle—that erecting boundaries between the public and the private spheres is essential to preserving human freedom. Such a view was also adopted by Hannah Arendt, a German-Jewish émigré and political theorist. While she has driven some feminist critics to the brink of madness with her seeming reliance on "male-oriented" doctrines of impartiality and universality, her work on the status of the pariah, totalitarianism, and revolution offers a number of insights into the positions commonly advocated by minority and women conservatives. Moreover, Arendt has the added virtue of being equally difficult to label, ideologically. When asked where she would place herself along the political spectrum, she replied: "I don't know and I've never known. . . . You know the left think that I am conservative, and the conservatives sometimes think I am left or I am a maverick or God knows what. And I must say I couldn't care less."[47]

In her major theoretical work, *The Human Condition*, Arendt ruminates on the "rise of the social," that is, the introduction of the shadowy realm of the household into the public sphere. Deriving her inspiration from ancient Greek philosophy, she depicts the public realm as the space of moral homogeneity and political egalitarianism where citizens (in the Greek context, native-born male heads of households) conducted the political affairs of the *polis*, guided by a respect for the law. The public sphere was also the region of deliberative speech and oration, political and moral greatness, honor, heroism, display, and meaningful actions in concert. She writes: "Thought was secondary to speech, but speech and action were considered to be coeval and coequal, of the same rank and of the same kind: and this originally meant not only that most political action, insofar as it remains outside the sphere of violence, is indeed transacted in words, but more fundamentally that finding the right words at the right moment, quite apart from the information or communication they may convey, is action."[48]

The private sphere, in contrast, was the realm of the body, labor, private economic interest, and household maintenance—all those aspects necessary for social reproduction. While Arendt is careful not to place mind/body, public/private, and male/female into a calcified binary system with all the positive ("masculine") values assigned to the first terms and all the negative ("feminine") values assigned to the second, she comes perilously close to doing just that from time to time. More important, the collusion of these separate spheres, she believes, ignored the "original meaning of politics" and paved the way for the rise of the modern totalitarian state. In *On Revolution*, Arendt locates the genesis of this destructive tendency around the era of the French Revolution, when the masses (the poor, working classes, women) appeared on the scene for the first time as mass political actors, spurred on by the dictates of necessity, that is, social and economic concerns. "When they appeared on the scene of politics, necessity appeared with them, and the result was that the power of the old regime became impotent and the new republic was stillborn; freedom had to be surrendered to necessity, to the urgency of the life process itself."[49]

Robespierre's desire to embody the will of the people led to a politics of compassion and pity, a politics premised on need. Unlike the American Revolution, which Arendt applauds for lacking pity and securing freedom by creating lasting institutions governed by the rule of law, the French Revolution "was defeated almost from its beginning from this course of foundation through the immediacy of suffering."[50]

Since the introduction of private concerns (necessity) into the public realm leads inevitably, Arendt argues, to a repressive political regime, reaffirmation of the public/private split is essential for the preservation of a truly democratic politics and a vibrant public sphere. Politics, for Arendt, always involves the process of negotiation, deliberation, and, as the contemporary political theorist Lisa Disch maintains, storytelling.[51] According to Arendt, modern life no longer affords us the dangerous luxury of objective or Archimedean standpoints somewhere outside or above politics; we can come to political decisions only by meeting together, each of us bringing our own particular perspectives. Further, her perspective on the efficacy of public identities destabilizes the conservative critique of group consciousness in fairly complex ways. For Arendt did not believe that a vibrant public sphere is devoid of group identities and difference. While her ideal (and idealized) public sphere would police itself of bodily necessity and private concerns, such was not in her view coterminous with the absence of a public recognition of difference.

Indeed, Arendt's concern for the status of the pariah—the outsider, the outcast, the marginal—is intimately bound up with group identities and motivated much of her thinking about politics and freedom. And here she speaks most directly to the issues most relevant to multicultural conservatives. Of her own identity Arendt once remarked: "I have always regarded my Jewishness as one of the indispensable factual data of my life."[52] In one of her most engaging works, her biography of Rahel Varnhagen, a late-eighteenth/early-nineteenth-century German-Jewish woman, she puts her skills as a teller of tales to good effect, using Rahel's life to explore the distinctions between accepting life as a pariah and rejecting the status of a parvenu. In Arendt's telling, Varnhagen's life becomes a parable of the failures of German-Jewish assimilation and the dire consequences of seeking to be "emancipated from one's Jewishness." Rahel's tragedy lies in her strenuous efforts to escape life as an outcast by transforming herself into an "exceptional" Jew, a Jew who apes the mannerisms of the majority culture in order to be accepted. For Arendt this form of assimilation, entailing distance from one's origins, is an active and aggressive process that inevitably obscures political realities. It is damaging not only to the individual but also to the group or culture the individual seeks to escape.

In a remarkable, if lengthy, passage, Arendt writes:

> No assimilation could be achieved merely by surrendering one's past but ignoring the alien past. In a society on the whole hostile to the Jews— and that situation obtained in all countries in which Jews lived, down to the twentieth century—it is possible to assimilate *only by assimilating to anti-Semitism also*. If one wishes to be a normal person precisely like everybody else, there is scarcely any alternative to exchanging old prejudices for new ones. If that is not done, one involuntarily becomes a rebel—"But I am a rebel after all!"—and remains a Jew. And if one really assimilates, taking all the consequences of denial of one's own origin and cutting oneself off from those who have not or have not yet done it, one becomes a scoundrel.[53]

Arendt does not countenance the "senseless freedom of the individual" at the expense of the group, since this involves not only infiltrating the dominant culture but reinforcing its prejudices as well. Moreover, in declaiming assimilation as "politically naive" (and here we know Arendt is thinking of and with the realities of the Holocaust), she draws a sharp distinction between legal emancipation and political emancipation. The former appeals to abstract notions of the individual and to universalistic doctrines; the latter embraces a politics of public recognition of meaningful forms of difference and cultural diversity. According to Arendt, when one is attacked as a Jew, one must defend onself as a Jew, not as a "German, not as a world-citizen, not as an upholder of the Rights of Man."[54] What's more, a truly democratic culture would allow for such claims to be made.

Arguing in the same vein, Arendt also differentiates between liberty and freedom. Recognizing that liberty always has a negative impetus, as in liberty *from* an infringement on one's rights, freedom incorporates liberty but makes more strenuous demands. True freedom embodies positive aspects and is produced, in Arendt's terms, only when human beings act in concert to create public spaces where genuine politics flourish. In service to this ideal, a true critic rejects the path of the individual parvenu and embraces the life of what Arendt calls the "conscious pariah"—the rebel, the independent thinker bound by neither authority, tradition, nor ideology. The conscious pariah is a critic who operates inside a society, yet at a healthy distance from the center of power.

In rejecting assimilation, she does not wallow in alienated silence and despair; nor does she assent to abstract individualism. Instead, the conscious pariah remains a distinct person, rooted in a particular time and place and in a particular culture with its own history. This groundedness and acceptance that all knowledge is partial is necessary, in her view, since the sort of public anonymity that suppresses difference is ranked among the most dangerous tendencies of the modern age. In the end, both flooding the public sphere with private concerns *and* the draconian cleansing of the public sphere of difference and group identity lead to tyranny and repression. Conceptualizing diversity as a safeguard against political repression presents a direct challenge to the negative depictions of balkanization so common among adversaries of multiculturalism.

The challenge Arendt leaves us, then, is how to find an appropriate balance that allows for increased public participation as citizens and appropriate public recognition of group identities. Where many multicultural and mainstream conservatives err, I think, is assuming that such a balance is not in fact possible. While Arendt's work is far from flawless (she assumes, for instance, the category of Jewishness without ever fully teasing out its foundations), it does give us a place to begin rethinking the connections between identity and politics, the individual and the group, in a more dynamic manner.

Black, Female, and Conservative

Arendt's conscious pariah is also willing to be ranked as an outsider among her own people. Although she believed in the importance of claiming a relationship to one's culture in a decidedly partisan fashion, Arendt did not urge that we do so in an uncritical way. She was no apostle of group think or essentialism. In fact, her views accord nicely with the dual nature of the Afro-American jeremiad in its ability to speak critically to the nation on the one hand and to the masses of African Americans on the other. It is this aspect of Arendt's philosophies that adds nuance to the reading of multicultural conservative ideology, even as other aspects raise serious questions about some conservative positions. Her idea of a conscious pariah as a minority within a minority names the space that many black, homosexual, and Latino conservatives seek to inhabit. Arendt also helps to establish a framework for an exploration of how gender does and does not matter to the conscious pariah. It was in fact Arendt's desire to seek recognition for all parts of her self, including her gender. "I am, as you know, a Jew," Arendt once said, "*femini generis*, as you can see, born and educated in Germany, no doubt, you can hear, and formed to a certain extent by eight long and rather happy years in France."[55]

If we take her position on the necessity of acknowledging that all positions are finite, nonabsolute, and grounded in the particular, then one's gender would be important but not definitive. While Arendt often links the concerns of the private sphere with women, she by no means suggests that women must become nongendered in order to have a public voice. Star Parker, it seems to me, walks the fine line set up by Arendt in this regard. As Parker tells her story as the foundation for her politics, her voice is structured by both race and gender; her female gender shapes the narrative in countless ways, even as themes of family, community, movement, freedom, individuality, faith, and political commitment remain as important in her autobiography as they are in the autobiographies of Liebman, Schuyler, Bawer, and Rodriguez.

True to form, Parker begins with a political declaration (after a laudatory introduction written by Rush Limbaugh[56]). She prefaces her autobiography with a description of how she, "a political outsider with no formal party affiliation," came to give a speech at the New Conservatives conference organized by Pat Buchanan and his sister Bay Buchanan. Initially Parker was reluctant to attend, but she was finally persuaded by Bay Buchanan's solicitousness. "I knew my personal politics coincided with Republican values, but I wasn't anxious to court the GOP's inner circle," she explains.

> I had to wonder whether the good old boy's club would really want to listen to a brash and outspoken black woman, especially a conservative one like myself. As for a past? Whoa—boy, did I have a *big* one.[57]

Instead of hiding her big past, she chose to make it the centerpiece of her speech, excerpts from which are reproduced in the first chapter of her autobiography. An explication of her past is threaded throughout the speech and throughout her nonlinear narrative, moving backward and forward in time. At every point, the message is that bad choices and irresponsible acts continuously shaped her life.

In her New Conservatives speech (November 1993), she draws on her personal experiences with drugs, criminal activity, sexual promiscuousness, and welfare to urge her listeners to fight the culture wars in order to rescue people (who are as she was) from government paternalism, broken homes, bad environments, and, finally, themselves. Parker is quick to recognize the differences between herself and her audience, but she is just as quick to stress points of commonality. "You can eat your lox while I'm enjoying my ham hocks, but we gotta work together to win this culture war," she tells them. "You talk about new conservatives, and to you, I probably sound like one of the old ones. Well, not exactly. You all went through Georgetown and I went through the 'hood!" Thus, Parker preforms what passes for an authentic ethnic identity for the consumption of a white audience while simultaneously making it safe and amusing. She also, it seems, aims at out-conservative-ing the conservatives, or at least suggests that her credentials are more appropriately grounded in material reality and experience.

There is something almost titillating and voyeuristic about Parker's performance and the autobiography that follows. The reader is invited to travel down the dark corridors of her life, to walk the proverbial mile in her shoes, assured, all the while, that her Christian redemption lies just around the next corner. In this sense, her book is less an autobiography than a confession in the tradition of St. Augustine. (In these tell-all times, however, perhaps this distinction no longer obtains.) This tension gives the work a strange quality. Parker was born November 25, 1956, in Moses Lake, Washington. Her father, James Irby, was a noncommissioned officer in the air force, while her mother, Essie Doris, worked as a beautician for most of her life. Parker was the third of five children in what appears to have been a relatively happy family during her childhood, despite having to move from place to place because of her father's profession.

Life changed for the Irby family when they moved from an air force base in Japan to one in Belleville, Illinois. Setting up house in East St. Louis, "one of the worst ghettos in the country," precipitated the family's decline and the beginnings of Parker's downward spiral. In East St. Louis, Parker not only discovered the face of urban poverty; she discovered race and racism. "I spent my adolescence," she writes, "blaming most of my troubles on white people."[58] Unlike Schuyler's 1966 autobiography, which downplays the dynamics of race and racism, Parker's wallows in its self-destructive aspects. During her teens, she was beset with difficulties. She was a middle child who struggled to find an identity within the family unit; she was forced to navigate a foreign and hostile environment with inadequate school facilities, armed teachers, incompetent counselors, and a family coming apart at the seams under the pressure.

My family was drifting apart and increasingly, I got into even more trouble. I hung out with older kids and started learning about militant black culture. My parents knew I was up to no good because I stayed out late, vandalizing school buildings and storefronts. They never asked me what I was doing and I guess they didn't really want to know.[59]

Suggestively, she chooses to narrate her education about "race" in almost wholly negative terms. Race is substantially reduced to militant black culture—a phrase invoked but not explained—and the hatred of others. In such a formula, race becomes something defined externally and in a reactionary defensive manner.

Another move, in 1970, to Mount Holly, New Jersey, did not increase the family's fortunes; Parker drifted even further away from her parents. "My parents weren't there," she recalls, "so I made my own decisions—but I had no moral foundation to base them on."[60] Among the "horrible choices" she made was to get involved with an older white military man, "White Rob," who committed an act of sexual molestation shortly before her seventeenth birthday. Sickened by his actions, "I soon began to hate all white people even more for what had happened"; she told no one. While Parker later came to realize there were people—both black and white—who cared for her and tried to render assistance, at the same time she was blinded by rage. "What I really needed," she summarizes, "was some tough love."

Trained in irresponsibility and little else, she left home for Philadelphia, hoping to eventually save enough money to move to California to pursue a career as a *Soul Train* dancer or perhaps a movie star. Following a series of bad experiences, including robbery, and negative relationships with men, Parker did eventually go west—the destination of generations of Americans seeking to re-create themselves and improve their lives. Here, her decadence, materialism, and hedonistic desires plunged her to a new low. She became, in her words, "a welfare brat," using Medi-Cal stickers sold on the informal black market and wages from jobs paid under the table to supplement her "alternative lifestyle." Seven years, four abortions, numerous parties, and a full-term pregnancy later, she decided it was time "to earn an honest living."

Thanks to a California state grant, she managed to finish college and to pursue gainful employment to make a better life for her and her daughter, Angel. Equally important, and ultimately decisive, she began to attend church services. As Parker describes the circumstances leading to this critical turning point in her life:

In 1982 I was still jobless, living off welfare, and partying occasionally with the old crowd from Venice. The difference was I was going to church on a regular basis. Pastor Fred Price was a very articulate black man who often spoke of the future. Sometimes I felt his sermons were directed at the possibilities of my own future. He became the most influential person in my life.[61]

Price preached on the necessity of parental obligation and of abstinence from sex before marriage as an absolute standard and against drugs and all forms of dependency, including welfare. He also preached against "racism and reverse racism." "From his pulpit, he would say that white people weren't the enemy—the devil was the enemy."

After Parker's spiritual awakening, she began to reach back and retrieve other examples of how to live a moral life, although apparently nothing from her seven years in California had any redeemable qualities. With great affection she recalls the lessons of her grandmother, lessons taught less through words than deeds, and lessons she was just beginning to fully appreciate. While her grandmother lived in an ugly, rundown house without indoor plumbing and was by all objective standards poor, she was also, Parker began to realize, rich in self-reliance, independence, and satisfaction. "If you were poor, she felt you should be content," Parker explains. "Now I understand why poor people who aren't counting on a government check are some of the happiest people I know."[62] Yet her grandmother's day-to-day life in rural South Carolina was not attractive to Parker. She was determined to be happy but certainly not poor.

Benefiting from sliding-scale payments for Angel's day care, she decided to go into business for herself; she started a magazine for young, black Christian singles. Parker's tale of the difficulties facing small entrepreneurs constitutes a harrowing chronicle of poor financing, dishonest contractors, and yards of bureaucratic red tape, but also the joys of watching one's bank account grow. With the assistance of Rosey Grier (yes, Rosey Grier), the ex-football player turned Christian minister, she met and married her husband, Peter Parker, a deeply religious (and white) man involved in outreach ministries. Married, self-employed, and with a second child on the way, Parker was on the verge of living the American Dream; the family had even moved to a nice suburban location. Although they still struggled to make ends meet, all was well until the 1992 L.A. riots destroyed the majority of her magazine's advertisers' businesses.

The riots and their aftermath mark a break in Parker's text. Here the autobiography proper ends and the conservative Christian advocacy begins in a more forthright manner. "Someday," she writes, "I hope to resurrect my magazine."

> I believe it's my calling and it provides a service for the black community—a conservative voice emphasizing self-initiative and morality. I have always viewed the magazine as a link between the neighborhoods, the churches, and the businesses in the area, and would like to see it grow so I can offer job training opportunities to young men and women who need that first break.[63]

Parker's calling has led her to embrace much of Peter Berger's and Robert Woodson's perspectives on "mediating structures," although this is not articulated as such in the text. It has led her to stand against the federal government's efforts and those who support them. Thus, the "pimps" of the book's title—*Pimps, Whores and Welfare Brats*—are "government socialists who believe man is basically good, but has a few character flaws that can be corrected with a little help from Big Brother." Correspondingly, the "whores" are primarily African American liberals who serve as the government's foot soldiers. Both pimps and their whores are engaged in a conspiracy of ignorance to produce as many welfare brats as possible.

The "lewd left" offers no real solutions, Parker insists. Not only has it prostituted itself to the highest bidder, but as secular humanists its members have "edged God away from the center of our national moral compass." Having severed our relationship with God, we are left, as individuals and as a society, spiritually adrift, numb to violence and indulgent toward perverted behavior. The ACLU (an organization rooted, Parker believes, in the hatred of religion and capitalism) bears some responsibility for our current condition, as do media elites, black politicians, the Democratic Party, and feminists. Interestingly, feminism is mentioned only once in Parker's texts, and then only in relation to reproductive rights. Linking the right to abortion to the right to own slaves, she chides feminists for conceiving of a property right in one's own body. Finally, Parker urges others with whom her experiences resonate to break the code of silence maintained by the civil rights establishment: "I know breaking the code of silence can be frightening. I am a female black conservative—a minority within a minority—and it hasn't been easy."[64]

Liebman, Bawer, Schuyler, Loury, and Rodriguez would no doubt agree with Parker; most minority conservatives present themselves as a minority within a minority. Yet, the gendered quality of Parker's text makes it distinctive from these others. Because she privileges the ability of most women to bear children, she cannot conceive of freedom and nonconformity in a singular sense. For her, freedom seems to always carry responsibility to self and others, especially during pregnancy. Further, Parker appears to reserve a special role for women, one that resurrects older notions of (white) republican motherhood and the need for strong (black) mothers of the race.[65] While Parker may be equally desirous of escape from the confines of narrow definitions of race, she heralds a decidedly female responsibility to be mothers and caregivers and prophets. Such a proposition entails women entering the public sphere as women, in Parker's case as a black and conservative woman.

Conclusion

Black conservatives are few in number, with few exceptions have no name recognition in the African American community, have little to no institutional base in our community, have no significant Black following, and have no Black constituency. Indeed Black conservatives' highest visibility is in the white, not the Black community.

—*Deborah Toler, "Black Conservatives"*

I think there is more going on here than any simple gesture of conforming to a Horatio Alger script. Revealing the degree to which ideology can cut across demarcations of race, ethnicity, and sexuality, minority conservatives also present a troubling challenge to what has been termed the politics of experience as well as to notions of cultural authenticity. In the end, it is precisely because they can lay claim to experience and authenticity, in their autobiographies and elsewhere, that they are able to issue powerful, conservative-accented critiques from the inside out. And it is on this level, among others, that they should be understood and addressed. Such an approach necessarily problematizes any charge that minority conservatives do not understand the "real experiences" of the groups to which they belong.

Critics of multicultural conservatism tend to dismiss its adherents as misguided (which may arguably be the case), as duplicitous, as self-aggrandizing, and as woefully detached from the communities they profess to represent. Yet, varying percentages of women and minorities identify themselves as either conservative or Republican or both. Unfortunately, the charge of "false consciousness" looms large. As the British cultural theorist Stuart Hall has pointed out, it is a "highly unstable theory about the world which has to assume that vast numbers of ordinary people, mentally equipped in much the same way as you or I, can simply be thoroughly and systematically duped into misrecognizing entirely where their real interests lie."[66] Moreover, it is hard to espouse, as many leftist and liberal theorists do, the idea that the social constructions of race, ethnicity, gender, and sexuality are remarkably fluid and that experience can serve as an epistemological ground and not include the existence of black, Latino/a, women, and homosexuals within such sophisticated intellectual paradigms. Instead of judging the messenger, I propose we simply judge the message.

The message is less than stirring. While I support the necessity of telling and listening to stories—how else is real communication possible?—Liebman, Bawer, Schuyler, Loury, Rodriguez, and Parker jump too quickly from the particular to the universal; the "I" slides too easily into the "we." Further, to the extent that their positions are tied to a highly individualistic understanding of assimilation, their message fails to meet the challenges put forth by Hannah Arendt, among others. Stretching Arendt's argument against parvenus to its logical conclusions forces us to ask whether assimilation in the views of Parker, Loury, Schuyler, Bawer, and Rodriguez is implicated in the taint of assimilation into racism and antiblack ideologies, into anti-ethnic sentiments, and into homophobia. For Arendt's suggestion that assimilation as an individual "exceptional" Jew is in reality an acceptance of anti-Semitism is echoed by other scholars who have raised similar questions. On this score one thinks immediately of Toni Morrison's evocative reading of assimilation and Americanization throughout American history.

Morrison's excavation of how the distancing of "Africanism"—the imagined alien black presence—was essential for an "operative mode of new cultural hegemony" after the inception of America parallels Arendt's concern for the Jewish other and the relationship between Jewishness and nationalism, as does Morrison's reading of assimilation as, historically, the assimilation into codes of whiteness that exist at the expense of blacks. And Morrison means this quite literally. For generations of ethnic others, becoming American has entailed, in her view, adopting a hostile posture toward blacks, a racialized estrangement from their presence, and an acceptance of antiblack stereotypes and ideologies. Further, Morrison argues that the drive to distance, silence, and repress blackness as a metaphor for that which is not American is never fully successful but reemerges and seeps through in unconscious, subtle, and often encoded ways.

Blackness, then, is a form of irreducible difference, always simultaneously absent and present. Connecting her extended essay on blackness as the foundation of whiteness in the American literary imagination to its similar function in the creation and maintenance of the national consciousness, she writes:

There is still much solace in continuing dreams of democratic egalitarianism available by hiding class conflict, rage, and impotence in figurations of race. And there is still a lot of juice to be extracted from plummy reminiscences of "individualism" and "freedom" if the tree upon which the fruit hangs is a black population forced to serve as freedom's polar opposite: individualism is foregrounded (and believed in) when its background is stereotypified, enforced dependency. Freedom (to move, to earn, to learn, to be allied with a powerful center, to narrate the world) can be relished more deeply in a cheek-by-jowl existence with the bound and unfree, the economically oppressed, the marginalized, the silenced.[67]

Multicultural conservatives are, I think, trapped within this tension, or paradox, of American identity—one produced by a series of exclusions in the nation's history. From my own vantage point, I cannot judge them guilty of a conscious complicity with racist, ethnocentric, and homophobic ideologies. Indeed, Morrison's attempt to do just that in her harsh characterization of Clarence Thomas through the lens of Robinson Crusoe's Friday ("Both Friday and Clarence Thomas accompany their rescuers into the world of power and salvation"[68]) is frankly offensive. It strips Thomas and people like him of all critical agency and self-consciousness.

At the same time, I do believe we should take Morrison's and Arendt's warnings against the dangers of parvenus seriously. Individuals such as Liebman, Schuyler, Bawer, Parker, and Loury may have solved their own problems with identity by embracing conservatism and assimilation, but they do not necessarily offer the rest of us an appropriate alternative. In critiquing an easy, though illusory, striving for acceptance through assimilation, Arendt and Morrison provide us a far richer model of public life and democratic politics than is currently available from conservatives.

Arendt and Morrison are hardly alone in this venture. Others have pursued this line of inquiry and taken it in new directions, focusing on what Bruce Bobbins describes as the "unresolved as perhaps unresolvable tensions" within the very concept of a public sphere between the universal collective subject, the national "we," on the one hand and a more relaxed, decentered plurality of subjects "spread liberally through many irreducibly different collectivities" on the other.[69] What much of this scholarship shares is a concern for a public sphere (or spheres) that are not desanitized and cleansed of race, ethnicity, sexuality, and other forms of difference and identity but substantially enriched by them.

If there is a way out of this tension over individualism, identity, assimilation, and nationalism, conservatives, many of whom are committed to the singularity of bourgeois values and universalism, have yet to discover it. Nor has their work fully addressed the crumbling of the public sphere itself in the age of late capitalism. In practice, the public sphere has undergone shrinkage and decline under the combined pressures of corporatization, mass media, concentration of industry and new technologies, PACs, and lobbies. The citizen participant is being progressively replaced by the citizen consumer. Given this situation, now is the time to open up new avenues of public participation, speech acts, and dialogue—even those that may be judged subversive, disruptive, discontinuitous, partial, and partisan. Listening to the stories of conscious pariahs and rejecting the comfort of generalized consensus is, I think, the very essence of a radically democratic pluralism that recognizes both culture and individuality as inherently valuable.

In the end, the conservative desire to silence irreducibly different collectivities in the name of a constrictive and artificially singular American identity offers no real solution. The very simplicity of this idea should make us all nervous. So, too, as I attempt to demonstrate in the following chapter, should the differential treatment of race, ethnicity, sexuality, and gender on the one hand and religion on the other. For, while many conservatives rail against the dangers of identity politics in the first instance, others have sought to secure a highly politicized role for religion and religious identities.

Segments of the conservative movement have even pushed to declare the United States a Christian nation, despite the plurality of religious beliefs and institutions that are non-Christian and antifundamentalist, and have raised questions about the validity of our current interpretation of the antiestablishment clause in the Constitution. Such notions have caused not only numerous disagreements within the national life of the country and its local communities. They have also caused cracks and fissures within the conservative movement itself. Judging homosexuality as sinful, homosexual marriage as unnatural, abortion as a sin, and feminism as an unmitigated disaster, one finds little willingness—apart from the libertarian wing of the movement—to allow such matters to reside in the private sphere or in the hands of the parties directly involved.

Indeed, some have egregiously violated the spirit of the public sphere as a space of freedom and rational deliberation by directly invoking the power of the state pressed into the service of fundamentalist Christian reform. As the movement continues to diversify and expand, the internal fissures created around the so-called social and cultural issues, which touch on some of the most private matters in our lives, have taken on a new meaning. At the same time, the history of the Religious Right and its present efforts to gain power over both the private and the public spheres present us with a host of dangers. As Marvin Liebman warns: "Political gay bashing, racism and anti-Semitism survive even in this golden period of conservatism's great triumphs: but they are for the most part hidden in the closet. I think they are waiting to be let out once again."[70]

Conservatives face a choice: having fought the leftists politics of gay liberation, do they now fight the
conservative instinct to form families? The right may
choose to act as if all gays belong to Queer Nation.
But if they do so, they will alienate the vast majority
of gays who seek to join the mainstream.

—*James Pinkerton*

CHAPTER 4

Strange Bedfellows

Gender, Sexuality, and "Family Values"

For the generation of Americans that wit-
nessed, in concentric succession, the rise and decline of the New Left and
the counterculture, the contentious struggle for civil rights and Black
Power, and the scores of urban rebellions in the late 1960s, as well as the
growth of vocal movements for women's liberation, reproductive rights,
and sexual freedom in the 1970s, these developments reinforced the idea
that America was teetering on the brink of political and moral chaos.
Seizing the opportunity to capitalize on widespread anxieties over the
shifting terrain of race, gender, and sexuality, as well as on the continuing
economic uncertainties unleashed by the end of the postwar boom, conservatives began to forge a new social agenda to return the nation to its
cherished values and traditions. In retrospect, it is clear that the ability of
politicians such as George Wallace and Barry Goldwater to draw unex-
pected levels of support (not only in the South and the West but in the
urban North as well) by railing against permissive liberalism and big government was indicative of long-range trends that would produce the Reagan Revolution of the 1980s.[1]

Those traits that Hannah Arendt identified as the "rise of the social," or the inappropriate introduction of private social issues into the public sphere, also marked the emergence of the New Right in the 1970s and early 1980s. If there was anything truly new about this brand of conservatism, it was the level of attention accorded social issues—abortion, busing, pornography, school prayer, homosexuality—framed in terms of both religious doctrine and populist rhetoric. As Jerome L. Himmelstein notes in his study of the transformation of American conservatism, the 1970s provided conservatives with a cornucopia of issues on which to build a coalition attractive to blue-collar workers, middle-class professionals, women, and evangelical Christians. As conservatives incorporated basic traditionalist themes drawn from the conservatism of the 1950s and 1960s, the new centrality of social issues precipitated an "ideological division of labor" within the emergent movement "that directed the traditional emphasis on moral order, community, and constraint to the social issues while the discussion of economic issues stressed mainly libertarian themes of individualism and freedom."[2]

This ideological division was accompanied and informed by a concomitant gender division between the male world of work and libertarian rhetoric on the one hand and female-oriented themes of family and community on the other. Whereas individual liberty and freedom of choice were invoked to argue against minimum wage legislation, labor unions, and big government, conservatives argued *against* choice when it came to abortion rights, reproductive freedom, and women's liberation. Thus, libertarian arguments stopped short when confronted with the female body, perceived threats to patriarchal authority, the welfare of children, and the traditional family. In the first instance conservatives adhered to the liberal philosophical tradition (as represented by John Locke and social contract theory) by privileging the individual as the basic unit of society. In the second instance they retreated to alternative paradigms that presuppose the family, or household, as the foundation of the political community.

The tensions produced by this ideological and gendered divide also pervaded conservative positions on homosexuality. The aggregate of social issues spawned in response to a more militant gay and lesbian rights movement were rooted, that is to say, in the tensions between individual liberty and the common good that underlay the New Right. Does being a conservative necessitate defending the common good by condemning homosexuality as aberrant and immoral, as social and religious conservatives claim? Or does it mean that homosexuality is a wholly private matter, an aspect of an individual's identity and behavior that should not be a target of legal discrimination and social bigotry? Is the desire among gays and lesbians to marry and form families a truly conservative one, as James Pinkerton has recently argued, or a profound threat to the very institution of marriage and thereby to the social fabric of American life? These questions, and others like them, have been and remain a prime source of dissension within the ranks of the New Right. While emphasis on social issues and moral reform once helped to generate a new political coalition on the Right, the contentious nature of such questions now threatens to rip that coalition apart at the seams.

The preceding three chapters explored parallels and similarities among women and minority conservatives as well as their conjunctive attempts to broaden the mainstream of the conservative movement and to alter American political culture. In the present chapter I want to turn my attention to the equally important matter of fissures and rifts within the movement. While disagreements over the proper role of women in society, along with issues of race, ethnicity, immigration, and language, have precipitated significant debates among conservatives, the most open ruptures in the frequently unstable coalition that constitutes the New Right have been induced by homosexuality and the supposed threat posed by the drive for gay and lesbian rights. Women and minority conservatives are, naturally, to be found on all sides of these debates. Representatives of the Religious Right have been pitted against libertarians, and political moderates against "movement conservatives," extending arguments beyond religious interpretation and social philosophy to encompass overall political strategy. A dimension of these debates was on display in the poignant public exchange between Marvin Liebman and William F. Buckley, Jr., in the pages of the *National Review*. It was a small yet significant milestone in the history of the modern conservative movement. Decades ago Buckley dreamed of making conservatism "shoe" (a Yalie term for respectable), and Liebman has devoted much of his adult life to placing a new, intellectually rigorous, and politically savvy conservatism on a solid financial and organizational foundation. More important, the two men were close friends.

In his letter, Liebman appeals directly to their shared history and urges Buckley and the *Review* to live up to their principles of tolerance and antibigotry. He reminds Buckley of the *Review's* stance over the years against racism and, especially, anti-Semitism. "Anti-Semitism is something that, happily for the history of the last three decades, *National Review* helped to banish at least from the public behavior of conservatives," Liebman wrote.

"*National Review* lifted conservatism to a more enlightened place, away from a tendency to engage in the manipulation of base motives, prejudices, and desires: activity which in my view tended to be a major base for conservatism's national constituency back then." Now, Liebman insists, the *Review* must take a public position against the homophobia and political gay bashing that emanate not only from the Religious Right but from the mainstream of the conservative movement as well.

Agreeing in principle with the political and moral dictates of tolerance, Buckley responds with a series of rather evasive questions: "How, exercising tolerance and charity, ought the traditional community treat the minority? Ought considerations of charity entirely swamp us, causing us to submerge convictions having to do with that which we deem to be normal and healthy?" Buckley denounces bigotry and the pain inflicted "sometime unintentionally, sometimes sadistically," yet refuses to make the leap into an indifference toward a way of life rejected by the Judeo-Christian religions. We must, Buckley counters, "be true to ourselves in maintaining convictions rooted, in our opinion, in the theological and moral truths."[3] Thus, Buckley's response to Liebman, and by extension to other gay and lesbian conservatives attempting to rid the movement of homophobia, boils down to disavowing nefarious uses of political gay bashing and intolerance *and* condemning homosexuality on the grounds of Christian theology, morality, and conviction.

The conflicting nature of this position is indicative of the snare that entraps sympathetic movement conservatives, such as Buckley and Pink-erton, and gay conservatives, such as Liebman. Believing homosexuality to be a choice and a lifestyle, a sin against God and an offense against nature, the majority of mainstream conservatives and nearly all of the Religious Right have been on a collision course with libertarians and the movement's homosexual minority for the past three decades. Chief among the so-called social issues animating the rise of the Religious Right and strengthening the conservative movement overall, homosexuality, along with reproductive rights and feminism, has, since the mid-1970s, become a prominent foundation for coalition building and political activism. The AIDS epidemic, which came to light in the early 1980s, did not significantly alter the traditionalist conservative assault on homosexuality. AIDS merely added more fuel to the white-hot flames. At the same time, homosexuality represents one of the major fault lines on which efforts to diversify the movement may founder. Once utterly divisive for the Old Left, homophobia has emerged as equally problematic within the New Right.[4]

This chapter considers the historical and contemporary importance of homophobia in the construction of the New Right, as well as the relationships among the antigay, antifeminist, and anti-abortion movements from the 1970s to the present. These are not, I argue, single-issue movements; they have become inexorably linked under the banner of family values, with homosexuality at its very core. From this perspective, Liebman's portrayal of homosexuality as performing a function today similar to that played by racism and anti-Semitism in the past is accurate. In the post–Cold War environment, homosexuality, particularly when linked to a highly moralistic interpretation of AIDS as God's punishment against gays, has emerged as one of the most significant enemies within that must be defeated. This is not to suggest that racism, often expressed in subtle or encoded ways, has not been and does not continue to be a crucial component of conservative reasoning. Nor is it meant to ignore the ways in which conservative positions on family values, gender, and sexuality are informed by racial presuppositions.

I suggest, however, that there is a much greater consensus around race in the New Right than around homosexuality, that as openly racist rhetoric became increasingly unacceptable socially, traditional notions of gender and sexuality have been more overt fixtures in the ideological glue of the movement. While race can be masked by rhetorical commitments to color blindness, there is no similar articulation of a blindness to sexual orientation. Moreover, since political gay and lesbian bashing have proved to be a more flexible strategy for coalition building than either racism or anti-Semitism, this chapter also explores attempts, many successful, at using homophobia as a basis for outreach into Black and Latino communities. Organizations such as the Christian Coalition and the Traditional Values Coalition have been especially diligent in using homosexuality to recruit within African American Baptist churches and among Latino Catholics. This strategy also inspires the push for "racial reconciliation" by the Christian Coalition and groups such as Promise Keepers, an organization that brings thousands of men together and urges them to reclaim authority from their wives. In this regard, the similarities between the Promise Keepers rallies and the Million Man March, sponsored in part by the Nation of Islam, are striking.

Deploying the language of shared commitments to Christian values and the common good, the Religious Right has sought to mobilize minorities around fears of gay-friendly school curricula and openly gay and lesbian teachers; against secular humanism and sex education; and for school prayer and vouchers to augment the growth of private and religious schools. In 1993, for instance, the Christian Coalition used the specter of homosexuality to erect a grass-roots coalition among evangelicals, Catholics, Jews, Muslims, and other concerned parents to discredit New York City's multicultural Rainbow Curriculum and to seize control of local school boards in the name of parental rights. Their efforts led to the temporary suspension of schools Chancellor Joseph Fernandez and to bitterly fought contests in the subsequent elections for school board seats in the city's five boroughs and thirty-two school districts. With the support of Cardinal John O'Connor, head of the New York Archdiocese, Roy Innis, director of the Congress of Racial Equality, and Rabbi Shea Hecht of the National Committee for the Furtherance of Jewish Education, more than half of the 130 profamily/anti–Rainbow Curriculum candidates won seats. Pointing to the success of this effort, Ralph Reed, then executive director of the Christian Coalition, urged social and religious conservatives to step up efforts to build a multiracial, multiethnic, and ecumenical movement. "The pro-family movement's inroads into the African American, Hispanic, Catholic and Jewish communities," Reed wrote, "may be the most significant development since its emergence in the late 1970s."[5]

Before leaving his position with the Coalition, Reed also endeavored to propel the movement beyond abortion and homosexuality as organizing tools. Both issues have, nonetheless, become entrenched in the movement's outreach efforts. Specifically targeting African American communities, the Coalition and other groups have warned blacks that homosexuals are out to distort and denigrate the historical legacy of the civil rights movement by using its symbols to press for a host of so-called special rights. While some minority conservatives, such as black conservative Ward Connerly, have welcomed homosexual conservatives into political alliances, others, such as Elizabeth Wright, have greeted their homosexual counterparts with hostility and invective. Engaging in homophobic attacks is, for some minority conservatives, a means to prove their conservative credentials and yet another method of distinguishing themselves from leftists and the civil rights establishment.

Finally, focusing on the question of homosexual marriage, this chapter considers the efforts of Marvin Liebman and other gay and lesbian conservatives, especially Andrew Sullivan, to fight for a place within the conservative movement and for greater tolerance and acceptance. This crusade has been most successful in heightening the raucous dissension within the Republican Party and has prodded the party's religious wing to redouble its homophobic retaliation. Still, the revolt of the moderate Republicans (fiscally conservative, socially moderate to liberal) is and promises to remain an unavoidable fact inside the party. The degree to which an acceptance, if not an active embrace, of homosexuals and moderates is or is not possible reflects the overall potential for a truly inclusive and diverse conservative movement—one open not only to homosexuals but to other minorities as well.

Building a Moral Majority: Sex, Race, Gender, and the New Right

Of all the factions that make up the New Right coalition, the most explosive segment has been the Religious Right, organized around such groups as the Moral Majority (later renamed the Liberty Federation), the Christian Coalition, Concerned Women for America, Focus on the Family, Eagle Forum, and the Traditional Values Coalition. It enjoys the support of religious institutions ranging from the Southern Baptists Convention to the Roman Catholic Church and incorporates televangelists, including Jerry Falwell and Pat Robertson.[6] While some organizations and activists aligned with the Religious Right are Catholic, Jewish, or Mormon, the core constituency tends to be Protestant, specifically Baptist; fundamentalist (believing in the literal truth of the Bible); evangelical (dedicated to the proselytization of the Gospel); and "born again" (having accepted Christ as one's personal savior). They also tend to be disproportionately southern and are more likely to be women. In general, core supporters of the Religious Right score slightly lower on measures of income, education, and occupational status, although a number of activists and supporters are middle-class professionals.[7]

The social class of evangelicals and fundamentalists has led many observers, in both scholarly and popular texts, to characterize their activism in terms of status anxiety and Nietzschean notions of resentment. Appealing to earlier studies by the sociologists Seymour Martin Lipset and Talcott Parsons and by the historian Richard Hofstadter—social scientists who had in the 1950s and 1960s cast a critical eye on the right-wing extremism of Nazism, the Coughlinites, McCarthyism, the KKK, and the John Birch Society—a new generation of commentators also pointed to status and resentment to account for a new wave of what Hofstadter famously called the conspiratorial or paranoid style in American politics.[8] Overall, these older studies provided valuable intellectual insights and established an analytic framework for understanding the emergent Religious Right. They pointed most consistently to the depths of isolation and frustration of those left behind in a shifting economy and an increasingly secular culture.

Separating out movements based in economic vicissitude and unemployment, Lipset developed the thesis of status politics to frame political movements whose chief appeal is to individuals and groups that desire to improve or maintain their social status. The groups most receptive are, he argued, not only those that "have risen in the economic structure and who may be frustrated in the desire to be accepted socially by those who already hold status, but also those groups already possessing status who feel that rapid social change threatens their own high social position, or enables previously lower status groups to claim equal status with them."[9] Of particular interest in the present context, Lipset fleshed out the processes by which conservative movements exploit status anxiety in building coalitions across traditional demarcations of class. His central point was that to attract lower-class voters, whose initial enfranchisement is normally accompanied by a shift to the left in voting patterns, conservative parties operating in political democracies must actively reduce the saliency of class. "These efforts," he notes, "may take the form of . . . stressing non-economic bases of cleavages such as religious and ethnic differences or issues of morality."[10]

Unfortunately, the dominant tone of such assessments, particularly those included in the edited volume *The Radical Right* (published originally in 1955 and expanded and revised in 1962), was set by the stress on mephitic irrationality in thought and behavior. In general, the contributing authors failed to take religion and a religious perspective on the human condition seriously. A Manichaean view of the world that takes the eternal struggle between good and evil as an article of faith and that accepts sin as a definable reality may fly in the face of a secular and modernist orientation, but it is hardly ipso facto irrational. "At its worst," as the black theologian and activist Cornel West maintains, religion "serves as an ideological means of preserving and perpetuating prevailing social and historical realities," but at its best it has the potential to yield "moralistic condemnations of and utopian visions beyond present social and historical realities."[11] Yet, secular-minded scholars too often fail to pay adequate attention to nuance when subjecting religious doctrines, practices, and individuals to study and critique. As Garry Wills points out in his text on the 1988 presidential campaign, "most political commentators show acute discomfort when faced with expressions of religious values in the political arena," even though the revivalist spirit has been remarkably consistent in American life. Evangelicalism is, arguably, *the* mainstream religion in the country and certainly not an odd set of recondite beliefs.[12]

Regardless how one chooses to view the phenomenon, the collusion of fundamentalism and politics that created the Religious Right began to take shape in the mid-1970s. While calls for a Protestant reawakening were issued in the 1950s and 1960s, the enormous *political* potential of this constituency was brought into focus in the wake of the *Roe v. Wade* decision and with even greater precision during the 1976 presidential campaign of Jimmy Carter. Both events helped to break down the barriers between religion and political activism. The majority of fundamentalist ministers had traditionally maintained, at least since the early twentieth century (post-Scopes), a strict separation between religion and politics, church and state. Politics belonged to the temporal world and was depicted as venal, materialistic, and unconcerned with other-worldly salvation. Falwell himself had once denounced Martin L. King, Jr., and the Southern Christian Leadership Conference as members of the clergy who engaged in inappropriate political activities. "Believing in the Bible as I do, I would find it impossible to stop preaching the pure saving gospel of Jesus Christ and begin doing anything else—including fighting communism or participating in civil rights reform," Falwell proclaimed. "I believe that if we spent enough effort trying to clean up our churches, rather than trying to clean up state and national government, we would do well."[13]

If the civil rights movement revealed the irresistible power of religion and churches to organize believers for political goals and to press for social reform, then the crusade by the National Council of Catholic Bishops against abortion brought this message home in a more sustained fashion. The origins of the right-to-life movement lay in the creation of the Family Life division of the NCCB, the chief governing body of the Catholic Church in America. Their immediate response to the *Roe* decision was to reject the ruling of the high court and to call for a major legal and educational battle against abortion. In its 1975 "Pastoral Plan for Pro-Life Activity," the NCCB urged pastors to exploit the institutional framework of the Church and to establish a network of "prolife committees" based in parishes. The purpose of this network was to monitor the stand on abortion of elected officials and to support the drive for a constitutional amendment to ban abortion. From the very beginning, then, the NCCB placed religious doctrine—life begins at conception; hence, abortion is murder, and the law sanctions genocide—and religious institutions in the service of politics. In so doing, they reaffirmed the tensions between individual liberty (of the mothers) and communal obligations (to protect the unborn).

The feminist scholar Rosalind Pollack Petchesky argues that the Catholic prolife movement was in fact a model for the entire Religious Right in particular and the New Right in general. By building a mass, grass-roots, and well-coordinated movement linked by a network of shared resources, Catholic prolifers demonstrated the viability of operating outside the two-party system while bringing pressure to bear on both parties. On this point (and on few others) Petchesky and Paul Weyrich find themselves in complete agreement. "What the right-to-life movement has managed to put together on the abortion issue," Weyrich wrote in his 1979 blueprint for building a moral majority, "is only a sample of what is to come when the full range of family and educational issues become the focus of debate in the 1980s."[14]

The idea that political activism was a legitimate activity for fundamentalists was also strengthened by the presidential campaign of Jimmy Carter. Carter made his "born-again" Christian identity a prominent note in his election strategy, while politicians and analysts rediscovered fundamentalism as Gallup poll surveys revealed that one-quarter to one-third of the American population identified themselves as born-again. (No matter that all Christians are by virtue of baptism "born again"; for evangelicals the concept carries an extra psychological and cultural resonance.)[15] Analyzing election results and exit poll data, conservative strategists were not slow to understand the importance of strong evangelical support to Carter's victory. With Carter seated in the White House, conservatives redoubled their efforts to appeal to fundamentalists and evangelicals. They were particularly cognizant of the increase in evangelical congregations even as membership in liberal and mainstream denominations was shrinking yearly.[16]

Surveying the turmoil of the late 1970s, conservative strategists came to understand the potential of bringing evangelicals into their political fold via a series of interlocking social issues, from abortion to busing. Increasingly willing to engage in social battles, the nascent evangelical political movement began to wage campaigns to restore Christian, Bible-based morality to an increasingly decadent and sinful nation. They joined Catholics in the fight against the legalization of abortion; founded coalitions against the growing gay and lesbian rights movement; lobbied against the threat to the tax-exempt status of private and religious schools; and campaigned against the Equal Rights Amendment. Each cause, especially the efforts to stop the ratification of the ERA, brought new leaders to the public's attention and added to the ranks of what would become the Religious Right.

When Congress passed the ERA in 1972 Phyllis Schlafly, who would lead the STOP-ERA forces, was a minor, semipublic figure; her Eagle Forum was an obscure little political group based in Illinois and catering largely to housewives such as herself. Although Catholic, she nonetheless led a massive, heavily evangelical ten-year effort to defeat ratification. Because the Amendment guaranteed equal rights but left the particulars vague, Schlafly was able to launch a crusade of vilification and exaggeration against feminists and other ERA supporters. She warned that the ERA would destroy families, abolish a husband's duty to care for his wife and children, force women away from the home and into the workforce, lead to the conscription of women in the armed services, require men and women to share unisex showers, and, if ratified, mandate state-funded abortions.[17]

The central problem, according to Schlafly and other spokespersons, was that the Amendment threatened the right of women to be protected. The ERA would, Schlafly wrote, "take away the marvelous legal right of a woman to be a full-time wife and mother in the house supported by her husband." Schlafly and others supported their position not only in terms of pragmatic concerns and the biological realities of gender but in terms of religious doctrine as well. "The woman who is truly spirit-filled will want to be totally submissive to her husband," writes Beverly LaHaye, who founded the Concerned Women for America in 1969 as an alternative to NOW. "This is a truly liberated woman. Submission is God's design for women."[18] Female submission is also the design promulgated by fundamentalist ministers and other male antifeminists whose ideas inform the political positions adopted by the Religious Right. For the movement's male spokespersons, feminism and the ERA represented a direct and unvarnished assault on male privilege and authority. The weakening of male authority and the rise of ungovernable women would lead, by extension, to the crumbling of society. Falwell, just to give one prominent example of this widely shared line of reasoning, cursed feminists for launching a "satanic attack on the home," which "strikes at the foundation of an entire social structure."[19]

Feminism, in the words of LaHaye, whose husband Tim holds as exalted a position in the hierarchy of the Religious Right as hers, is "a philosophy of death." This view is not, I hasten to add, confined to the extreme regions of the Religious Right. Using slightly more secular terminology, George Gilder and Michael Levin have both argued for the moral superiority and natural amenity of patriarchal gender relations.[20] Women are valued first and foremost for performing a civilizing function on the male character; thus, their work has been used against feminism, single-parent female-headed households, and gay marriage—since two men cannot civilize each other, they remain a threat to themselves and society. Gilder's most frequently quoted observation is that, while single men are only 13 percent of the population, they make up 40 percent of all criminal offenders and commit 90 percent of all violent crimes. Hence, he advocates marriage to women in order to civilize men and constrain their dangerous impulses, thereby extending protection not only to women but to society as a whole.

In an early, often compelling, and surprisingly sympathetic attempt to understand the women of the New Right, the feminist theorist Andrea Dworkin argues that such ideas, whether expressed by men or by women, make certain "metaphysical and material promises to women that both exploit and quiet some of women's deepest fears." The Right promises, by turns, to place restraints on male violence and aggression toward women; to endow women with a "simple, fixed, predetermined, social, biological and sexual order"; to supply women with the comfort of established rules and a circumscribed sphere of freedom through submission; to provide women with shelter and the love of husband, Christ, and child. Dworkin grasps the attractive qualities in the traditionalist view of the role of women in society and recognizes its indebtedness to aspects of Christian theology but nonetheless critiques it for preventing women from being free, authentic, and independent agents in the world.[21] As her forceful defense of women's liberty bears out, the disagreements between socially conservative women and feminists revolve around the very meaning of gender, identity, freedom, and liberation.

Thus, by privileging the family and the common good over individual liberty, broadly construed, the anti-ERA movement galvanized conservative and evangelical women and became an important foundation for conservative politics.[22] The conservative reading of liberation for women was embodied in the 1972 platform of the American Party, the party that nominated the southern segregationist and Alabama governor George Wallace for president in 1968, and echoed most of these themes:

The deceit is planned to "liberate" women from their families, homes, and property, and as in Communist countries, they would share the hard labor alongside men. Women of the American Party say "No" to this insidious socialistic plan to destroy the home, make women slaves of the government, and their children wards of the state. We urge people to notify their state legislators to resist adoption of the so-called "Equal Rights Amendment" commonly known as "Women's Lib."[23]

Along with Schlafly's gendered appeal to women as wives and mothers, the American Party, the John Birch Society, the National Council of Catholic Women, the Daughters of the American Revolution, and various ad hoc groups joined the STOP-ERA movement in order to preserve the sanctity of marriage and the American family.

The family had to be protected not only from women bent on destroying it as an institution and sacrificing innocent lives in the service of their own careers and freedom but also from homosexuals. The anti-ERA movement established links with the early prolife movement and simultaneously branched out to target the drive for civil rights for homosexuals. Among other things, Schlafly and the anti-ERA forces charged, the Amendment would eventually result in the legalization of gay and lesbian marriage and the right of homosexuals to adopt children. (Falwell admitted later that he would have supported a measure like the ERA if it specifically had prohibited homosexual marriage and adoption as well as the drafting of women into the armed services.)[24] In 1977, with the ERA ratified in thirty-five out of fifty-five states, the opposition received a boost to its ability to tie the ERA to homosexual rights. With the anti-abortion movement well on its way, the momentum of STOP-ERA was augmented by local grass-roots efforts to oppose ordinances that prohibited discrimination based on sexual orientation.

For religious conservatives the initially sporadic drive to secure civil rights and greater social acceptance for gays and lesbians was yet another indication of the nation's decline into a moral morass. Characterizing homosexuality as a perverse *choice* clearly prohibited by the Bible, evangelical Christians began to found political organizations, such as Anita Bryant's Save Our Children, Inc., to counter the gay and lesbian "lobby" and to warn parents against homosexual recruitment. In a tortured bit of logic, they reasoned that, since homosexuals can not procreate as a group, they must increase their numbers by preying on the young and the unsuspecting. In a word, homosexual miscreants recruit.

With an eye toward protecting children, in 1976 Bryant, along with her husband, Bob Green, launched the first religiously based campaign against gay rights, opposing a vote by the Dade County Commissioners to prohibit bias in housing, employment, and public accommodations. A 1977 fund-raising letter read:

> Dear Friend: I don't hate homosexuals! But as a mother, I must protect my children from their evil influence. When the homosexuals burn the Holy Bible in public, how can I stand by silently.[25]

Never mind that there are no accounts of marauding bands of homosexuals burning Bibles. The point was to portray the homosexual as a dangerous and subversive presence. Neither fully male or female, homosexuals were deemed outside the moral order and therefore excommunicate. Homosexuals, in another word, are *ethnic*, whose etymological root means literally "against the faith." Like feminists who supported abortion rights and the ERA, homosexuals were cast as a terrifying satanic force.

Bryant's success in using such tactics to inflame the prejudices and fears of the public did in fact force a referendum to repeal the Commissioners' vote. Moreover, the Dade County victory encouraged similar forms of antigay activism in other locations, including the 1978 "California Defend Our Children Initiative." Led by state senator John Briggs, who had worked with Bryant in Florida, the initiative provided for charges to be brought against school teachers and others who advocated, encouraged, or publicly and indiscreetly engaged in homosexual behavior. It also allowed school boards not to hire and to fire homosexuals deemed unfit. The initiative failed by more than a million votes and, ironically, received a blow when Ronald Reagan publicly denounced it from a libertarian perspective.[26] Bryant's own efforts to take Save Our Children, Inc., national collapsed under the combined pressures of lack of political sophistication, her much publicized divorce, and the national boycott against the Florida orange juice industry for which Bryant had served as spokesperson.

In an interesting turn of events, after her public disgrace Bryant was forced to rethink her nearly three years in the national limelight as a gay basher. Divorced and unemployed, Bryant also raised questions about the strictures of her faith. In a 1980 interview she claimed to "better understand the gays and feminists' anger and frustration." "Fundamentalists," she continued, have their heads in the sand. The church is sick right now and I have to say I'm even part of that sickness. I often have had to stay in pastors' homes and their wives talk to me. Some pastors are so hard-nosed about submission and insensitive to their wives' needs that they don't recognize the frustration—even hatred—within their own households.[27]

But others, such as the Reverend Louis Sheldon, who worked with Briggs in California and who now heads the Anaheim-based Traditional Values Coalition, went on to found new antigay organizations and to continue to mobilize around the homosexual "menace."

In conjunction with the early anti-abortion movement, the antigay and lesbian initiatives, and STOP-ERA, the groups that would come to form the core of the Religious Right also saw their influence increase with the successful efforts to block a move on the part of the federal government to revoke the tax-exempt status of private and religious educational institutions. Many observers had noted the increase in such schools at the primary, secondary, and college levels in the wake of the 1954 *Brown* decision. The independent school movement grew slowly after 1954 and gained momentum in the 1970s during the busing controversy. Between 1970 and 1980 alone the number of Christian schools grew by some 95 percent, even though overall school enrollment in primary and secondary schools decreased by 13 percent.[28] While proponents of independent schools publicly explained this dramatic increase as a response to secularization, there was little doubt that the more proximate cause was integration and busing. In their opposition to the IRS, and to school desegregation in general, conservative evangelicals typically articulated their opposition in moralistic terms as a stance against secular humanism and not in terms of race. The central problem, they claimed, had less to do with fears of interracial classroom (which may lead to interracial dating, marriage, and sex) than with an educational system that shuns fundamentalist (and indeed any) religious beliefs.

Liberals and leftists tended to find this supposed race-neutral argument uncompelling. The IRS Commission, in response to the demands from civil rights groups, agreed and submitted a proposal that would have denied tax exemptions to some of these private schools, particularly those created in districts under desegregation rulings. When the proposal was announced, fundamentalist activists, including Jerry Falwell, a prominent leader in the Christian school movement in Virginia, initiated a letter-writing campaign and deluged IRS offices. The matter was effectively

dropped after an emotional four-day hearing. Within a year, fundamentalist activists successfully urged Congress to enact legislation to prevent the
IRS from resurrecting the idea.[29]

All of these movements and causes convinced evangelicals and religious
conservatives that they could in fact work together to effect concrete
moral reform while flexing their new-found political muscles. What these
movements and their participants seemed to share, moreover, was a belief
that the federal government was not only ungodly but also clearly be-
holden to radical feminists, homosexuals, civil rights activists, and secular
humanists. Bloated and unresponsive to average (read heterosexual, white)
Americans, the government emerged as a chief antagonist to Christian
values. In victory and defeat, evangelical Christians, orthodox Catholics,
and Jews were increasingly coming to believe that they could be a force in
American politics—a belief amply shared by politically savvy conservative
strategists.

The vision of the federal government as a tool of evil and a facilitator of
sin came increasingly to coincide with the antistatist (and anti–New Class)
rhetoric of the Republican Party, with its call for a revolt against taxes, social spending, and the welfare state. The real turning point came in 1979 as
disparate yet interrelated single-issue campaigns (against abortion, against
homosexual rights, in defense of religious schools, against the ERA) were
coalescing more fully around a shared perspective on traditional family
and American values. A new umbrella organization—the Moral Majority—was founded.

The Moral Majority was the direct result of a series of extensive discussions between Jerry Falwell and conservative strategists Paul Weyrich
(who first suggested the name "Moral Majority"), Richard Viguerie, and
Howard Phillips, founder of the Conservative Caucus. Of the three,
Viguerie had the skills that would prove to be decisive. Having honed his
talents as a direct-mail guru working for the Young Americans for Freedom and other conservative groups, Viguerie pooled the mailing lists of
various religious and secular organizations and created a grass-roots data-
base of impressive size and scope. Thus, he brought a new level of political
sophistication to evangelical activists and provided a national framework
for organizing and lobbying.[30] It was, to be sure, a mutually beneficial relationship, erecting the foundation of the budding coalition among politically engaged evangelicals and movement conservatives.

In helping to construct the Religious Right, conservative strategists also
created a base of support for the election (and reelection) of Ronald Rea-

gan and the rightward drift in American political culture. Registering millions of voters and getting them to the polls, evangelicals accounted for two-thirds of Reagan's ten-point lead over Carter in 1980. Reagan received 63 percent of the white, born-again vote in 1980, a strong but less than astounding showing. In 1984, however, he captured 80 percent of that vote—the largest shift of any identified social category and twice the shift for the electorate as a whole.[31]

Yet, the coalition that rode to prominence and power on Reagan's coattails was never completely stable. Reagan himself was less than the conservative Christian savior of the Religious Right's dreams and was in some ways a disappointment to far-Right movement conservatives. Reagan embraced the language of the free market and supply-side economics, but he increased the federal deficit, the budget, and the size of government. Joining the chorus of neoconservatives, he railed against affirmative action and welfare entitlements but did little to dismantle the federal programs he publicly claimed to despise. Reagan was, at heart, a libertarian, fond of quoting Thomas Paine; he made only largely symbolic gestures to the evangelical forces within the Republican Party and the conservative movement.

For example, when the IRS resurrected the issue of federal funding for schools clearly in violation of Congress's antisegregation laws, the Reagan administration acquiesced to strong liberal support for withholding state financing for institutions such as Bob Jones University, which prohibited interracial dating.[32] Moreover, he invested few political resources in a proposed anti-abortion amendment to the Constitution and devoted even less political capital to the proposed amendment to restore school prayer. While Reagan reportedly thought homosexuality "a sad thing" and feared that his son might be gay, he had little personal antipathy toward gays and lesbians.[33] Despite such disappointments, the Religious Right was nonetheless well placed to expand its constituency and its influence.

Indeed, by the mid-1980s the "profamily" movement, as the chief umbrella for a series of interlocking causes and concerns, had captured much of the conservative movement, along with a growing segment of the Republican Party. To the horror of many moderate Republicans and libertarians, the ideological division of labor between economic and free-market conservatives on the one hand and social and religious conservatives on the other deepened into a gaping chasm by the end of the 1980s. With the upswing in the economy, social conservatives mounted a full-blown campaign for ascendancy within the party and American political culture overall. In 1987, Paul Weyrich, as head of the Free Congress Foundation, commissioned a study, *Cultural Conservatism: Toward a New National Agenda*, which argued that social and cultural issues, informed by a religious perspective, offered a more effective platform for conservatives than economic ones. *Cultural Conservatism: Theory and Practice*, edited by William S. Lind and William Marshner and including essays by Russell Kirk, William Bennett, and Weyrich, followed in 1991. Both texts functioned as handbooks for the Free Congress's Center for Cultural Conservatism.

Weyrich and the Free Congress's role in rehabilitating the Religious Right should not be underestimated. In 1986 Falwell disbanded the Moral Majority, claiming that its work was done. It was subsumed by the broader, more frankly political Liberty Federation, which collapsed in 1989. After a series of scandals that discredited televangelists and Pat Robertson's defeat in the 1988 presidential primaries, the evangelical movement temporarily lost its moorings.[34] The movement was revitalized and strengthened, however, by Robertson and his Christian Coalition, founded in 1989 with the support of Weyrich and the Free Congress Foundation, which continues to serve as the Coalition's chief think tank. While the Christian Coalition is certainly an extension of the efforts that had animated the Religious Right since the mid-1970s, it helped to push the movement in slightly new directions.[35]

Robertson would prove to be the bridge between the first iteration of the Religious Right and the second. Falwell and the Moral Majority dominated the first phase of organizing, but by the late 1980s Falwell himself aspired to move from the fringes to the center. He even endorsed the candidacy of moderate Republican George Bush, a move that signaled his growing affinity for the mainstream of the Party and the conservative movement.[36] Robertson, who switched his party affiliation from Democratic (he campaigned heavily for Carter in 1976) to Republican in 1984 was unwilling to be placated by timorous movement conservatives. Already dismayed by Reagan's failure to deliver on the agenda of the Religious Right, he opposed Bush in the Republican primaries. His campaign, launched from the stoop of a brownstone in the Bedford-Stuyvesant section of Brooklyn, where he had briefly ministered to a predominantly black population as a young man of God, revolved around his staunch opposition to homosexuality and abortion under any circumstances.[37]

Although he received strong support in the early phases of the campaign season (he placed second in the key Iowa caucus), he was dogged by his fundamentalist credentials and his lengthy record of ill-advised and intemperate remarks on African Americans, Jews, and secular Americans. He did try to downplay his evangelicalism, his belief in faith healing, and his other charismatic tendencies. He emphasized instead his lineage as the son of a former senator, his law degree from Yale, and his business acumen in building the Christian Broadcasting Network and Regent's University.[38] But he could not outdistance his past. In his bid for legitimacy, Robertson repeatedly accused the national media of religious bigotry for its harsh treatment of his views, and the media in return pointed to Robertson's duplicity. There is some basis in fact to substantiate both charges. The press *was* clearly hostile to Robertson and not above taking snipes at his religiosity. He was depicted as a dangerous lunatic, and on more than one occasion the press portrayed his evangelical supporters as a pachydermal crowd of somnambulant supplicants.[39]

Robertson actually encouraged the media's derogatory treatment, however. To the mainstream media Robertson represented himself as nothing more than a moderate, reserving his theocratic views for the audience for his "700 Club" and other outlets of the Religious Right. In these venues he characterized the separation of church and state as an "atheistic communist" ideal and promised to govern the nation in accordance to biblical precepts. In the mainstream press Robertson spoke the language of tolerance and inclusion, while promising the faithful that a person who is not born again "cannot enter into Heaven."

> We're talking about millions of people! And you say, "Well, you shouldn't interfere with their lifestyle. They're going to do their thing." Well, maybe they're going to do their thing, but their thing is a broadway to destruction. That's what Jesus Christ told us. And he came to give us a Christian country.[40]

Such views were frightening not only to secular voters but to many religious voters as well.

Robertson's efforts to mask his fundamentalism notwithstanding, he was forced to withdraw from the race. Turning certain defeat into possible victory, Robertson joined the mailing lists generated by his campaign and his new-found public prominence to create the Christian Coalition. He saw the need for a new grass-roots organization strong enough to dominate the Republican Party and to force action on the social agenda of the Religious Right.[41] Learning from his past mistakes, Robertson also realized the depth of his image problem. To solve this dilemma, he ceded public relations duties to Ralph Reed, Jr., young, photogenic, well educated (he had earned a Ph.D. in history from Emory), and much more diplomatic, while maintaining undisputed control of the organization behind the scenes. Reed's talents lay in softening the image of the Coalition, broadening its language (i.e., "creation science" was substituted for "creationism") and establishing stronger connections with nonevangelical Christians, Catholics, and Jews. With Reed's savvy approach, the Christian Coalition became, arguably, the most important organization within the Religious Right.

During Reed's tenure as executive director, the Coalition's outreach efforts did enjoy marked success. Despite Robertson's best-selling treatise *New World Order*, in which he linked Jews with a Zionist conspiracy to rule the world, the National Jewish Coalition, founded in 1985 to establish a Jewish presence in the Republican Party, sees more areas of agreement than disagreement with the Coalition, according to Matthew Brooks, the executive director of the NJC. Brooks customarily glosses over the tensions over school prayer, homosexuality, and the desire of some fundamentalists to make America "a Christian nation," though the NJC has supported Jesse Helms, who used antigay hysteria as fodder in his war on the National Endowment for the Arts and none too subtly coded racist messages in his campaign reelection advertisements. Indeed, Brooks insists, "you can have within the party the National Jewish Coalition and the Christian Coalition and both feel very much at home."[42]

Going on the offensive, Brooks has argued that the Democrats "demonize the Christian conservatives because it's the only wedge issue they have" to keep Jews from leaving the Democratic Party. Despite evidence of anti-Semitism in the party's Religious Right, Brooks concludes: "There's a greater social acceptability for Jews to be Republicans and support the Republican Party."[43] The Coalition has also attempted to establish closer ties with Catholics, but its move to create and sustain the Catholic Alliance as a division of the Coalition has met with lukewarm response, especially from segments of the Catholic hierarchy. While Reed was careful to note that a Catholic-evangelical alliance is based on more than political expediency, he clearly recognized the potential represented by the Catholic Alliance.

"If Catholics and evangelicals can unite, there is no person who cannot run for office in any city and state in America that cannot be elected," Reed gushes. "There is no bill that cannot be passed in either house of Congress or any state legislative chamber in America."[44] The Alliance was founded in October 1995, the week after Robertson met with Pope John

Paul II during the pontiff's visit to the United States. It received support from New York's Cardinal John O'Connor and from Bishop Pilla, the president of the U.S. Bishop's Conference, as well as from lay Catholics, including theologian Michael Novak, George Weigel of the Ethics and Public Policy Center, and Pat Fagan of the Heritage Foundation. In terms of long-range strategy, the Alliance could also function as a bridge linking evangelicals, white ethnics, and Latino communities.[45]

In branching out beyond diehard evangelicals, the Christian Coalition not only dominated the profamily movement in the early 1990s but also came to wield enormous power inside the Republican Party.[46] The platform construction at the 1992 Republican National Convention and the shocking display of intolerance as speaker after speaker—most notably Patrick Buchanan—rose to urge the party faithful on in the culture wars, owes a good deal to the ascendancy of the Religious Right within the Republican Party. Although Buchanan, a conservative Catholic and staunch isolationist, drew no more than 37 percent of the vote in any Republican primary, he and his supporters, many of whom issue from the religious wing of the party, forced their way onto center stage during the Houston convention. The platform President Bush was required to accept promised that the GOP would defend the nation's "Judeo-Christian heritage" in the face of a Democratic Party bent on waging a "guerrilla war against American values." Robertson spoke at Houston, accusing the Democrats of plotting to destroy the American family by "transfer[ing] its functions to the federal government"; Marilyn Quayle, the wife of Vice President Dan Quayle, tied Bill and Hillary Clinton to the 1960s counterculture of sex, drugs, and draft dodging. Buchanan, however, stole the show, inflaming the passions of supporters and detractors alike. Displaying his fondness for militaristic language, he proclaimed in ululant tones:

> My friends, this election is about more than who gets what. It's about who we are. It's about what we believe and what we stand for as Americans. There is a religious war going on in this country for the soul of America. It's a cultural war as critical to the kind of nation we shall be as the Cold War itself.[47]

In his speech, Buchanan blasted feminists, abortion rights advocates, black criminals, the federal government, secular humanists, the Democratic Party, and, of course, homosexuals for threatening American society. While the speech was extreme on a number of counts, it revealed and indeed reveled in the ongoing usefulness of political gay bashing. Despite Reed's labors to expand the social agenda of the Religious Right to encompass taxes, immigration, school choice, crime, and welfare, the real basis for the expansion of the profamily movement remained firmly rooted in abortion, feminism, and, as the decade wore on, homosexuality.

Reaching Out: Abortion, Homosexuality, and the Culture Wars

The use of military metaphors by Buchanan and other religious conservatives is not incidental. Orthodox religion has a long association with the concept of holy war; in the contemporary context it functions as yet another manifestation of what the political theorist Michael Rogin has called the "countersubversive tradition" of "political demonology" in American politics. These terms point to the "creation of monsters as a continuing feature of American politics by inflation, stigmatization, and dehumanization of political foes," from the savage Indian cannibal to the bomb-throwing anarchists to the Evil Empire and, more recently, to the agents of international terrorism. The demonologist, Rogin writes, splits the world in two, "attributing magical, pervasive power to a conspiratorial center of evil." The catch, as Rogin sees it, is that the demonologist actually needs the monsters "to give shape to his anxieties and to permit him to indulge his forbidden desires." In the end, the process of demonization allows the "countersubversive, in the name of battling the subversive, to imitate his enemy."[48]

From this perspective Buchanan's call for a "guerrilla war" of the righteous against the "guerrilla war" being waged by the Democratic Party and other subversives, as well as his call for a domestic Cold/Culture War, makes sense. The enemy is within. Ralph Reed has also indulged in militaristic language, as in his oft-quoted appeal for the "stealth approach" in local political campaigns. "It's better to move quietly," Reed said, "with stealth, under cover of night"—a statement from which he later backed away, blaming leftist conspiracy thinking for creating a false impression.[49]

With the rhetoric of Buchanan and Reed very much in mind, I agree with Chris Bull's and Peter Gallagher's depiction of the Religious Right and the gay Left as "perfect enemies" in the 1990s.[50] I want to stress the idea that homosexuality constituted a much more flexible foundation for coalition building and outreach than racism, ethnocentrism, or anti-Semitism. While moderate Republicans, some movement conservatives, and groups such as the National Jewish Coalition may prefer that homosexuality not dominate so much of the profamily movement's agenda, they can by and large make their peace with it. The NJC, for instance, was staunchly opposed to the 1996 attempt to make a candidate's stance on partial-birth abortion into a litmus test for party support.[51] But it has been relatively quiet on the matter of homophobia. And silence, as the old saying goes, implies consent. The only internal dissent on the use of homophobia and gay bashing has issued from the Log Cabin Republicans and from a small but periodically vocal group that, like James Pinkerton, fears that gay bashing only intensifies the image of conservative Republicans as intolerant and hateful.

For Pinkerton, the explosive antigay rhetoric of Jesse Helms and others does more harm than good. He points to Helms's opposition to the confirmation of Roberta Achtenberg as assistant secretary of Housing and Urban Development because she is a "damn lesbian." She was confirmed and is now free, Pinkerton asserts, to pursue her agenda and to slough off future criticism as merely more lesbian bashing. Moreover, Helms's behavior reinforces the GOP's image as the party of homophobia. "Other Republicans of a more live-and-let-live bent had better speak up," Pinkerton warns, "lest Helms be seen as speaking for the party."

> Gays aren't going away. They are organizing, fund-raising and voting. And they have friends and family. If the issue is abetting intolerance, silence equals death for the GOP.[52]

Above all, Pinkerton aspires to return the party to the principles of Lincoln, who understood that you "conquer your political opponents by making them your friends."

This runs counter, however, to the techniques of subversive demonology that seek to make one's opponents the monsters hiding under every bed, an evil presence to be exorcized. Moreover, homosexuality supplies opportunities for fund-raising and coalition building too good to pass up. By the early 1980s, the scope of the AIDS epidemic was becoming increasingly clear and terrifying. The toll of the disease on the gay community gave more shape and substance to the political gay bashing that animated so much of the Religious Right. In a sad and ironic twist, AIDS created a more coherent and structured movement among homosexuals, who banded together for mutual support, fund-raising, and lobbying,

while simultaneously engendering an even more virulent antigay movement. The fear of AIDS also rendered homophobia and gay bashing more
acceptable to a more diverse constituency. As one theorist put it, AIDS
provided "a pretext to reinsert homosexuality within a symbolic drama of
pollution and purity."

> Conservatives have used AIDS to rehabilitate the notion of "the homo-
> sexual" as a polluted figure. AIDS is read as revealing the essence of a
> promiscuous homosexual desire and proof of its dangerous and subver-
> sive nature. The reverse side of this demonization of homosexuality is the
> purity of heterosexuality and valorization of a monogamous marital sex-
> ual ethic.[53]

Prominent spokespersons of the Religious Right have expressed, with
an inordinate amount of pride and satisfaction, their reliance on homophobia and fears of contamination by the polluted bodies of homosexuals.
The Reverend Louis Sheldon, head of the Traditional Values Coalition,
once remarked, "Don [Wildmon] has got pornography; Randy [Terry] has
got abortion; Phyllis [Schlafly] and the Concerned Women for America
have religious liberties; Jim [Dobson] has family values; the Christian
Coalition has candidates; and I've got the homosexuals."[54] But this is not,
strictly speaking, at all true; political gay bashing is an equal-opportunity
tactic, and antigay campaigns are more often than not joint ventures. The
1992–1993 Colorado ballot initiative drive to amend the state constitution
to prohibit antidiscrimination measures based on sexual orientation was,
for instance, a cooperate campaign.

Passed by a majority of Colorado voters (after an enormous media and
grass-roots effort) in November 1992 and slated to take effect on January
15, 1993, the amendment read:

> Neither the State of Colorado, through any of its branches or depart-
> ments, nor any of its agencies, political subdivisions, municipalities or
> school districts, shall enact, adopt or enforce any statute, regulation, ordi-
> nance or policy whereby homosexual, lesbian, or bisexual orientation,
> conduct, practices or relationships shall constitute or otherwise be the
> basis of, or entitle any person or class of persons to have or claim any mi-
> nority status, quota preferences, protected status or claim discrimination.
> This Section of the [Colorado] Constitution shall be self-executing.[55]

Nothing if not thorough, the amendment was sponsored by Colorado for Family Vales (CFV), which received the support of five national organizations: Focus on the Family, Summit Ministries, Concerned Women for America, Eagle Forum, and the Traditional Values Coalition (TVC). Each organization had representatives serving on the executive and advisory boards of the CFV, and, while the Christian Coalition did not, it lent its support in more indirect ways. Two injunctions, one temporary, one permanent, and an appeal to the Supreme Court later, the amendment was judged to be unconstitutional. Although the measure was not enacted, the campaign revealed the skillful manipulation of homophobic sentiments to achieve larger political goals.

Homophobia has been a key issue beyond the confines of the Religious Right, however. Neoconservatives also participate in the discourse on the dangers of homosexuality. Norman Podhoretz, for example, linked homosexuality as a form of decadence to the "culture of appeasement" that he believes is undermining a strong U.S. foreign policy. Drawing an analogy between the corrupting influence of homosexual decadence in Britain after World War I and the intellectual environment in the United States during the 1960s and 1970s, Podhoretz proclaimed: "In war poem after war poem and in memoir after memoir, the emphasis was on the youthful, masculine beauty so wantonly wasted by the war, their bodies meant for embrace by their own kind that were consigned so early to the grave." The literary output of British intellectuals such as W. H. Auden, Harold Acton, and Christopher Isherwood also, Podhoretz argued, evidenced nothing but contempt for middle-class and adult heterosexual life.

As part of the "feminization" of leftist anti-Americanism, this homosexual angst has also found a home in the United States. "Anyone familiar with homosexual apologetics in America today will recognize these attitudes," he continued.

Suitably updated and altered to fit contemporary American realities, they are purveyed by such openly homosexual writers as Allen Ginsberg, James Baldwin, and Gore Vidal—not to mention a host of less distinguished publicists—in whose work we find the same combination of pacifism (with Vietnam naturally standing in for World War I), hostility to one's own country and its putatively middle-class way of life, and derision of the idea that it stands for anything worth defending or that it is threatened by anything but its own stupidity and weakness.[56]

Thus, homosexuality has been linked to the public health crisis, the decline of traditional morality, the endangerment of children and the family, the crippling of the authority of male heads of households, and the nation's weakness in foreign policy—and all before the outcry against President Clinton's proposal to lift the ban against gays and lesbians in the military.

Minority conservatives, especially those numbered among the religious wing of the movement, have also engaged in their own distinctly accented forms of political gay bashing. Black social and religious conservatives share the widespread view among African Americans that homosexuality is essentially a "white thing"; they have labored to portray the "homosexual lobby" as essentially white and economically well off. "Homosexuals are no dummies," proclaims Elizabeth Wright, the editor of *Issues and Views*. Her lengthy article on the subject can serve as a representative text. "From the first, they recognized the advantages of hitching their wagon to the 'civil rights' star. By asserting that their goal is to achieve their rights as citizens, and invoking the rhetoric of the 1960s, they touched a nerve in American society."[57] Their primary goal, she continues, is to become an officially recognized and protected minority group so as to gain power via "America's weird patchwork of ethnic favoritism." Wright is obstinate in not acknowledging the existence of homosexuals who are also black or Latino (or Asian or Native American or poor, for that matter). To do so would lessen the rhetorical power of her characterization of homosexuals as a relatively privileged group. Factoring statistics that claim the average annual income for homosexuals is significantly higher than that of most American ethnic and cultural groups allows her to insist that homosexuals are not oppressed or in need of further legal protections (i.e., special rights). Nor are they or can they be a minority. Homosexuality is a sickness and a disorder, not an unchangeable characteristic such as race. Thus, homosexuals "should not be allowed to equate inborn characteristics of ethnicity with what is nothing more than a behavior pattern—a way of doing sex." While Colin Powell lost points with religious conservatives on the issue of abortion rights (he is prochoice), he gained by agreeing with the nature of Wright's assessment.[58] To allow homosexuals into the minority clubhouse, black conservatives (and nonconservatives alike) claim, would dilute the established categories of race and ethnicity. For homosexuals to demand civil rights and to use the trappings of the black civil rights movement to do so is also viewed as a dilution of history and a perversion of the movement's symbolic power.

This theft of the movement's accouterments is "an affront to many black Americans, who with their strong religious roots and traditional view of family stand against the normativity of homosexuality," writes Joseph E. Broadus, a member of the Virginia Council on Equal Employment Opportunity.[59] Averring a causal link between the sexual revolution in the 1960s and 1970s and the breakup of the African American two-parent family, black conservatives have also pointed to the antifamily impetus behind abortion rights and, by extension, behind greater liberties for women. Abortion, Peter Kirsanow has proclaimed, is "the defining issue for black conservatives, in the same way that slavery was the defining issue for the nascent Republican Party." To question the humanity of the fetus is for him akin to questioning the humanity of slaves; both positions are racist and represent an eugenic assault on African Americans.[60] While black religious and social conservatives view abortion, homosexuality, and feminism as facets of the same antifamily menace and thereby share numerous points of intersection with white evangelicals, the alliance between them has been beset with difficulties. While they may agree in terms of morality and religious ethics, race remains a stumbling block. While the so-called social issues work to unify religious conservatives (often at the expense of homosexuals), race continues to divide.

The Reverend Earl Jackson, the Christian Coalition's national liaison to African American churches, issued a stern rebuke to prominent Republicans associated with the Council of Conservative Citizens, a white supremist group. He urged the party to adopt "a 'zero tolerance' policy toward members who associated themselves with groups touting racial supremacy." If Republicans ever intend to "break the Democratic Party's monopoly on minority voter loyalty," he insisted, "they must unequivocally denounce racist associations."[61] The Reverend Jackson's position with the Christian Coalition stems from Ralph Reed's open acknowledgment that white religious conservatives carry the legacy of racism "like an albatross." As Reed writes in *Politically Incorrect*: "If we flow out of lily-white churches into lily-white political organizations and support only lily-white candidates for elective office, we cannot expect the larger society to take us seriously." In 1995 Reed approximated the Christian Coalition's African American membership at roughly 3 to 4 percent, and he took steps to boost the level of support. Star Parker was at one point Reed's cohost on "Christian Coalition Live," and in 1996 the Reverend Earl Jackson, who is also a Boston-based radio talk-show host, was appointed as the Coalition's national liaison to African American churches.

In this Parker and Jackson join such other prominent black members of the Religious Right as Dr. Mildred Johnson, a founder and former chair of the National Right to Life Committee (NRLC); Alveda Celeste King, a niece of Martin L. King, Jr.; and Kay James, former spokesperson for the NRLC.

The Coalition has also sought to build on its success in electing its own slate of candidates in local school board races by playing up the homosexual threat to young people. And, more dramatically, in the wake of a rash of arsonist attacks on black churches in the South, the Christian Coalition pledged to raise a million dollars to rebuild the structures ($700,000 of which was actually collected and donated). Finally, at the end of 1997, the Christian Coalition unveiled its "Samaritan Project," of which Jackson serves as national chairman. The Project is the cornerstone of the Coalition's efforts to move beyond abortion and homosexuality to attract minorities. Presented to the 105th Congress in January 1997 as part of the Coalition's legislative agenda, it incorporates a hodgepodge of conservative antipoverty initiatives, voucher and school choice proposals, empowerment zones, plans to remove restrictions against state financing of church-based drug treatment programs, and a $500 tax credit for those who do volunteer work to help the poor.[62] Along with their support of other legislative initiatives such as the Defense of Marriage Act, the Coalition is making a bid to enlarge its reach into minority, working-class, and inner-city communities and to press its agenda in the national political arena. While this agenda seeks to move beyond reliance on social issues exclusively, it is nonetheless deeply informed by conservative positions on sex, marriage, morality, and religious doctrine.

As the substantive agreement between religious conservatives and some feminists over matters of pornography and obscenity demonstrates, issues of sex and power often produced strange bedfellows in American political culture. Indeed, both religious conservatives and nonlibertarian feminists have been accused of being antisex and of being overly reliant on the state to regulate behavior. How the state should adjudicate matters of sex and sexuality, privacy and public morality, individual freedom and the demands of a common culture have all been deeply involved in debates among conservatives and others on the question of legalizing gay and lesbian marriage. The case for homosexual marriage revolves around a mixture of individual liberty and the common good and offers a tenuous balance between the two. It is on this uneasy middle ground, I suggest, that the possibilities for a diverse and inclusive coalition on the Right, one that includes both religious and social conservatives on the one hand and moderates, libertarians, and homosexuals on the other, will grow or founder.

Individual Liberty and the Common Good: Religious Conservatives, Republican Moderates, and the Gay Conservative Case for Homosexual Marriage

In making a case for the legalization of gay and lesbian marriage and fighting to support basic antidiscrimination laws against them, homosexual conservatives have confronted the campaign of vilification and demonology head on. In so doing, they have joined forces with other moderates and libertarians in a battle against the Religious Right and for control of the Republican Party. As Liebman's trajectory suggests, coming out has meant for some gay conservatives denouncing the influence of the Religious Right. It has also involved working against what the Log Cabin Republican's Rich Tafel calls a sexualized variation of the "southern strategy," or, as Nixon called it, "positive polarization." The idea of building a new majority around conservative populism in the South and West and garnering support among disaffected white working-class Democrats in the North and East was premised on the negative technique of engendering the polarization (i.e., backlash) of the electorate against liberals, minorities, the poor, and feminists.[63]

In an analysis of Goldwater's use of this technique in 1964, columnist Robert Novak (who later converted to the conservative cause) describes it as "stopping short of actually endorsing racial segregation" but dismissing "all the sentimental tradition of the party of Lincoln."

> Because the Negro and the Jewish votes are irrevocably tied to the Democrats anyway, this agnostic racial policy won't lose votes among the groups most sensitive to Negro rights. But it might work wonders in attracting white southerners into the Republican Party, joining white Protestants in other sections of the country as hard-core Republicans.[64]

This tactic did, of course, work wonders. It became the standard operating procedure for the Republicans in their expanded efforts to bypass the traditional base of the Democratic Party and to siphon off anxious and angry white voters.

Gay and lesbian conservatives, who are also the victims of positive polarization, have entered into coalitions with moderate Republicans who seek to return the party to its "Lincoln-Theodore Roosevelt-Eisenhower" tradition with its emphasis on individual liberty in order to "contest the growing influence of ideologies on the right, [to] broaden our Party's base of support, and [to] promote sensible candidates and policies." Hence, while one segment of the conservative movement and the Republican Party aspires to use social issues such as abortion, homosexuality, immigration, and school prayer to broaden its base of support, this other segment hopes to expand its coalition in the opposite direction.

As Republicans who are fiscally conservative and socially moderate to liberal, the Republican Mainstream Committee, founded in 1984 by Representative Jim Leach, former RNC chairman Mary Louise Smith, and former Alabama congressman John Buchanan, Jr., established an action agenda for 1999–2000 that included helping moderate Republicans in the states "undertake new and more effective forms of organized political activism"; bolstering the strength of centrist Republicans in the states "by working cooperatively with nonpartisan and bipartisan mass membership organizations"; building stronger coalitions with other "reform-minded Republican organizations in those instances where common ground exists"; and "rais[ing] the national visibility of mainstream Republican concerns and ideas."[65]

By presenting their views as centrists, mainstream, moderate, and reformist, the Republican Mainstream Committee has positioned itself against the Religious Right. Not only have its members worked to create alliances with prochoice Republicans, environmentalists, and racial and ethnic conservatives; they have also welcomed gay and lesbian conservatives into the fold. As such, they have engaged in spirited debates about what it means to be a conservative and a Republican; they depict themselves as *the* mainstream of both, even though they have been accused of betraying the conservative faith and of being "nothing more than Democrats sent to destroy the Republican Party." As one outraged conservative Republican put it, "If they prevail they will only succeed in ripping the heart out of the party."[66] Moderates counter that they are merely attempting to move the Party away from intolerance and toward inclusion and to establish the sort of broad base necessary for the Party to lead the nation into the twenty-first century. "We have a twenty-five-year history of isolating everyone," says Connecticut Governor John Rowland, echoing the views of James Pinkerton and Rich Tafel. "There is a population out there called the baby boomers who we have totally alienated."[67]

Tafel, the Log Cabin Republicans, and other gay and lesbian conservatives are hoping that this struggle between the Religious Right and moderate Republicans will allow them enough room to pursue their own agenda. In making a case for the defense of homosexual marriage, Andrew Sullivan has attempted to demonstrate that conservatism and homosexuality are not mutually exclusive. Indeed, Sullivan's defense of homosexual marriage proposes a union of classical liberalism and modern conservatism. Placing a "premium on liberty," he is quick to acknowledge the limits to what politics can manage. Politics and the law cannot and should not be used to legislate or enforce morality. At best, the law can affect culture only indirectly "by its insistence on the equality of all citizens." To achieve this fairly optimistic proposition, the state must remain neutral. In living up to the promise of liberal democracy, the state is obligated only to ensure full public equality in a manner that neither patronizes nor excludes.

On this basis, Sullivan can argue that "all *public* (as opposed to private) discrimination against homosexuals be ended and that every right and responsibility that heterosexuals enjoy as public citizens be extended to those who grow up and find themselves emotionally different."[68] Thus, the state must abolish sodomy laws that apply only to homosexuals; equalize the legal age of consent; include facts about homosexuality in government-funded school curricula; and secure for citizens equal opportunity and recourse to courts to redress discrimination in law enforcement, government bodies, and agencies. The neutral liberal state must also allow, as a matter of principle, gay men and lesbian women to serve openly and honestly in the military and to marry and divorce legally.

Equal opportunity and public equity in the last two realms—marriage and military service—form the core of Sullivan's argument for inclusion and legal recognition of gays and lesbians in the public life of the nation. Since homosexuals are already integrated into the armed services, his position rests on the imperatives of recognition. And Sullivan is careful to stress that his is not a call for extraordinary or "special" rights. Military service, like marriage, is a healthy desire and part of an existing trend that the law should merely ratify. "Burkean conservatives," he argues, "should warm to the idea." In fact, for Sullivan, "one of the strongest arguments for gay marriage is a conservative one." He explains:

More important for conservatives, the concept of domestic partnership chips away at the prestige of traditional relationships and undermines the priority we give them. Society, after all, has good reasons to extend legal advantages to heterosexuals who choose the formal sanction of marriage over simply living together. They make a deeper commitment to one another and to society; in exchange, society extends certain benefits to them. Marriage provides a mechanism for emotional stability and economic security. We rig the law in its favor not because we disparage all forms of relationship other than the nuclear family, but because we recognize that not to promote marriage would be to ask too much of human virtue.[69]

In consenting to homosexual marriage, conservatives, from this perspective, merely reaffirm the virtue of commitment, monogamy, stability, and the inherent value of family life. Finally, Sullivan insists that neither homosexual marriage nor open military service require a change in heterosexual behavior. Neither requires a sacrifice. As private citizens, heterosexuals are free to act and believe in any way they choose, as long as they do not break the law. Sullivan's solution, then, also diverges sharply and consciously from attempts to protect the rights of a minority by circumscribing freedom of contract and expression. His perspective studiously avoids presenting homosexuals as a victimized minority; nor does it advocate educating a "backward majority" away from bigotry to create a tolerant, inclusive culture.[70] To do so would only reinforce the illiberal tendencies of modern liberalism.

Sullivan's argument fits almost seamlessly into the doctrines of public assimilation articulated by many women and other minority conservatives. Yet, in seeking to restrict what he calls the "prohibitionist," homophobic sentiments among religious conservatives and much of the Religious Right to the sphere of private expressions, in effect to cleanse the public sphere of the language of sexual identity *and* religious belief, he renders his "compromise" ineffectual not only for the Religious Right but for a large segment of the gay Left as well. Sullivan can only hope that their respective inability to compromise will make both camps increasingly marginal in and to American political culture.

Whether a majority of conservatives and Republicans will come to adopt the logic of Sullivan's argument remains a matter of much dispute and not a little bit of doubt. Mainstream conservatives, like their counterparts among women and minorities, remain deeply divided on the issue. If anything, there is more reason to believe that this broadening of the conservative movement and the Republican Party, particularly to the extent that it implies the marginalization of the Religious Right, will fail than there is to hope for its success. Even if conservatives managed to lessen internal tensions around race, ethnicity, and gender, the question of homo-sexuality would remain daunting—not that such a failure is necessarily a bad thing. Nonetheless, Republican homosexuals and the emerging coalition among Republican moderates certainly see a window of opportunity. Given the relative failure of the Religious Right on the electoral and legislative fronts as well as its inability to orchestrate the ousting of President Clinton after his impeachment, moderates are launching a bid for ascendency within the party.

Conclusion

There is some evidence that religious conservatives, who feel betrayed by the American people, may be willing to cede the field. Paul Weyrich, a conservative strategist integral to establishing the Moral Majority and to expanding the sphere of influence of the Christian Coalition, may now be leading the way once again. In a widely circulated open letter to cultural conservatives across the nation, Weyrich observed that, while social and religious conservatives had managed to capture the Republican Party and secure the election of their own candidates, they have yet to see their broader agenda embraced and enacted. The reason, he muses, is that "politics itself has failed." Weyrich locates this failure in terms of politics in the midst of our collapsing culture. "The culture we are living in becomes an ever-wider sewer," he writes. "In truth, I think we are caught up in a cultural collapse of historic proportions, a collapse so great that it simply overwhelms politics."[71] The way out of this impasse is not to abandon the political field completely but to devote more time and energy to "re-taking cultural institutions that have been captured by the other side" and to build separate institutions that embody conservative values.

Weyrich's proposal amounts to a call for conservative separatism. The very definition of "holy," he reminds us, is "set apart." Taking a page from ancient history, Weyrich cites, in a follow-up letter clarifying his position, the efforts of early Christians within the Roman Empire. Although not wholly separate—they served in Rome's legions, paid taxes, and aspired to be good citizens—they nonetheless "built their own communities, largely by serving and protecting each other." Weyrich also takes a more recent example of this strategy, ironically the 1960s slogan "Turn on, tune in, drop out." Like radical leftists who found politics too narrow a sphere for creating the level of change they sought, Weyrich urges cultural conservatives to retreat from

America's decaying dominant culture. In this regard, Weyrich sounds less like Pat Buchanan and more like Louis Farrakhan and the Nation of Islam. Yet, Weyrich's long march through alternative institutions is still nebulous and has yet to gain many converts.

The prevailing view among religious and social conservatives could be expressed as "We're down, but not out." "I believe we should fight all the harder to reclaim territory we've lost," says James Dobson, founder and president of Focus on the Family. Carmen Pate, president of the Concerned Women for America, agrees and points to the list of the movement's achievements. Emphasizing that there would have been millions of additional abortions "had not men and women worked to legislate restrictions" and that pornography would exceed its current ability to generate some eight billion dollars per year had "no one fought to establish laws against it," she prefers to see the glass as half full. Moreover, and with specific reference to the gains of socially conservative women, Pate asserts, "No matter what political ideology you ascribe to, you must concede that feminists no longer claim to speak for all American women."[72]

Yet, other long-time leaders of the Religious Right have joined Weyrich in publicly musing over the movement's demise. Among these are Ed Dobson, who along with Weyrich was one of the founding members of the Moral Majority in 1979, and Carl Thomas, whom Jerry Falwell recruited early on to be one of his top lieutenants. Even Pat Robertson has noted the poor showing of the Christian Right in American politics; his recent defense of Texas Governor and GOP presidential candidate George W. Bush's opposition to efforts to overturn *Roe v. Wade* reflects a new awareness of politic's limited ability to transform public morals.[73]

A more generous reading of the current climate of opinion among the Religious Right and its present difficulties would note, however, that the movement faced a similar moment in the late 1980s when Falwell disbanded the original Moral Majority. Even as pundits and politicians heralded, some gleefully, the end of the Religious Right's influence in politics, a period of reorganization and consolidation generated a surprising reemergence. While embattled, the Religious Right, including African American, Latino, and Asian-American supporters, is hardly willing to go quietly into the dark night and to abandon its desire to transform America into a Christian nation. In the meantime, the often heated debates about the meaning of race, ethnicity, sexuality, gender, the individual, and the common good are likely to continue, both within the conservative movement and within American political culture at large.

What would hold this multiracial conservative coalition together? The answer is: (a) conservative social values (shared by many whites, East Asian immigrants and Hispanics); (b) redistribution (the coalition's partisans in Congress would tax the Northeast and subsidize Republican defense contractors and agribusiness in the South and West); (c) a live-and-let-live states'-rights compromise (for example, different affirmative action policies for the white-majority states and the nonwhite-majority states); and, last but not least, (d) a common hostility to the black urban poor, everybody's favorite scapegoat.

—*Michael Lind, "The End of the Rainbow: The Poverty of Racial Politics and the Future of Liberalism" (1997)*

CONCLUSION

A Multicultural Right? Prospects and Pitfalls

Given the nature of the often heated debates within the New Right, the Religious Right, and the Republican Party, it seems fitting to conclude with the question of whether the already diverse coalitions that have emerged on the Right will successfully congeal into a truly multicultural conservative movement. *If* conservatives aspire to fully diversify their movement—and it is far from certain that all conservatives would agree to the efficacy of such a plan—is it actually possible to do so? Can one party, let alone one movement, contain gay men and fundamentalists women, conservative Catholics and moderate Jews, free-market idealists and anti-abortion activists? Further, could such a diverse contingent find the language to attract a black woman worried about liberal immigration policies, a wealthy white businessman who welcomes new immigrants as a source of cheap labor, and a Latino family divided on the questions of affirmative action and bilingual education? Despite frequent false starts, setbacks, paradoxes, and inconsistencies, a number of African American, Latino, Asian-American, women, and homosexual conservatives, along with their allies in the Republican Party, believe they will be able to construct a large enough tent to encompass them all.

If a viable multicultural conservatism is in fact to evolve from faint possibility to concrete reality, a number of troublesome issues will have to be addressed. The first step in realizing the potential of a multicultural Right, particularly within the political arena, requires that mainstream conservatives take this potential seriously. This transition may seem fairly simple and straightforward in theory, but it has proven problematic in practice. For good or ill, the Republican Party remains the central public face of the movement at large. While the Party has made overtures to African Americans, Latinos, Jews, and, more recently, Asian-Americans, it has a track record of sabotaging its own efforts.

The idea of building a "new majority" inclusive of African Americans began in the late 1960s and expanded incrementally throughout the 1970s and 1980s. When Lee Atwater assumed the helm of the Republican National Committee (RNC) in 1989, he confidently declared that "making black voters welcome in the Republican Party is my preeminent goal."[1] But Atwater was probably not the best choice for such an endeavor. Not only had he cut his political teeth in the 1970 Republican senatorial campaign of South Carolina's Strom Thurmond (ex-segregationist, ex-Democrat, ex-Dixiecrat); Atwater was in 1989 fresh from orchestrating the notorious racially encoded Willie Horton ads for George Bush's presidential campaign against Michael Dukakis. Not a propitious start. With little concrete success to show for its efforts, Atwater's Outreach division was subsequently subsumed into the RNC's Office of Political Coalitions, which also sought to establish alliances with Latinos, Asians, Eastern Europeans, and labor.[2]

Given his past, the choice of Atwater to heal the breach between the Party and African Americans is a small but representative indication of the schizophrenic tendency to reach out to communities of color with one hand and slap them in the face with the other. Regardless of this historical tension, the RNC has recently reorganized yet another new effort in this direction. In 1998 it announced, with much fanfare, the creation of the New Majority Council, with plans to spend over 1.2 million dollars a year on recruiting candidates of color and spreading the conservative message to minority communities. On hand and visible for the public launching were Representative Henry Bonilla and Senator Ben Nighthorse Campbell, who, along with Representative J. C. Watts, remain statistical rarities within Republican ranks.[3]

Since the Council appears to have adequate funding, perhaps it will exceed the gains of its predecessors. Indeed, inadequate funding, along with lack of support from the party establishment, has been a key barrier in the past, and minority candidates have frequently chastised the RNC for its shortcomings in this regard.[4] Even when minority candidates do manage to achieve national office, they do so with the support not of minority voters but in majority-white districts. This persistent pattern raises a number of questions as to how "representative" minority Republicans are and may, in fact, impede further efforts to reach out to voters of color. Here, the argument commonly put forth by liberals and leftists that black conservatives in particular have no real organic connection to the majority of African Americans holds up to a certain amount of scrutiny. Not until conservative African American candidates can appeal to African American voters in significant numbers will they be able to overcome their image as "sellouts" and lackeys of powerful whites. The same is true, for the most part, for the relationship between Latino and Asian-American candidates and voters as well; constituencies will translate to credibility.

Second, solidifying a multicultural Right demands the full integration of the organizations, institutions, and voices of multicultural conservatives. Striving to satisfy white voters in the Party's base and among independents while simultaneously reaching out to minorities and women is vexing enough. And the stakes are raised by the party's endemic image problem, both inside and beyond its own ranks. Cumulatively, conservatives are typically perceived to be antiblack, anti-immigrant, antigay, inflexible on abortion, questionable on other gender issues, and just plain mean. This is not a problem merely with the far and the Religious Right. It threads throughout the movement.

Few organizations aligned with the Right's network have escaped the charge that they exclude conservatives of color. In 1998, six black Republican women who are generally sympathetic to the movement's agenda—Gwen Daye Richardson, editor of *Headway* magazine; Phyllis Berry Myers, founder and chair of Black America's Political Action Committee; Teresa Jeter Chappell, president of the Republican Vanguard of Georgia; Faye M. Anderson, president of the Douglass Policy Institute; Jacqueline Gordon, president of the National Congress of Black Conservatives; and Athena Eisenman, president of the Colorado Black Republican Forum—released an angry statement chastising party leaders for their failure to invite African American conservatives to a two-day Republican Women Leaders Forum. "On the eve of the 21st century, black Republican women are still agitating for inclusion in mainstream activities in the party of Lincoln," they said in a letter subsequently published as a full-page ad in the conservative *Washington Times*.

Echoing the words (falsely) attributed to the nineteenth-century abolitionist Sojourner Truth, they continued: "On behalf of the millions of black women who are voters, taxpayers, wives, soccer moms, caregivers, entrepreneurs, community and civic leaders, we ask the organizers of the Republican Women Leaders Forum and GOP leaders: Are we not women?" Their response to this perceived slight referred not only to the Forum. It also referred to "racial stereotyping" among conservatives and Republicans—a practice, these six black women assert, "at odds with the party's commitment to colorblindness and individual merit."[5] This minor revolt points to the paradoxes of race and identity in which conservatives find themselves trapped. On the one hand, these women have banded together in a collective action *as black women claiming to speak on the behalf of black women* to rectify the party's lack of commitment to racial diversity. On the other hand, the Party's failure to issue them a *special* invitation, under the cloak of color blindness, made the Forum organizers look like bigots. The Forum organizers's insistence that all women were ipso facto invited was insufficient to mullify the six angry women. The conservative Republican doctrine of color blindness cannot, I argue, solve this dilemma.

This dilemma, in turn, speaks to the larger inability of conservatives to woo blacks and other persons of color in large numbers. For, if the Party's black elite meets continuously with such small but significant biases, then what can the rest of the black community hope to find? This feeling of finding, in Clarence Thomas's words, "no room at the inn" has been and will no doubt continue to be an issue for Latinos, Asian-Americans, and homosexuals as well. Deeply rooted in the tension between the universal and the particular, the conservative movement and the Republican Party must seek to negotiate a brand of identity politics suitable to the needs and desires of a diverse coalition. An obstinate blindness to differences in race, ethnicity, gender, and sexuality, that is to say, may not be enough.

A broadening of the Right will also entail more moderate positions on those "social issues" which alienate some (but not all) women, homosexuals, and people of color. This task is the most repellent for social and religious conservatives for whom prochoice and reproductive rights advocates, secular humanists and homosexuals are necessary foes. While organizations aligned with the Religious Right have used such issues in the broadening of its own base—making explicit connections, as with the Christian Coalition, to minority communities—they have failed, as Paul Weyrich concedes, to win much support within American political culture overall. Moreover, even though staunch prolife and antigay ideologies have worked to unite socially conservative men and women across demarcations of class, race, gender, and religious orientation, they have also driven a wedge between the Religious Right and moderate Republicans. Abortion, most notably, is an issue over which little or no compromise seems possible. Hence, prochoice Republican men and women have been marginalized within the Party and the movement, and those Republicans who have attempted to occupy a potentially more attractive moderate center have been rebuked. Queried on what it is like to be a prochoice Republican, one disgruntled GOP woman responded, "Do you like to have things thrown at you?"[6]

Although the question of homosexuality is equally divisive, some winds of change have begun to blow. For instance, in a startling turn of events, the Reverend Jerry Falwell has begun to moderate his views and tone. In October 1999, Falwell's Thomas Road Baptist Church in Lynchburg, Virginia, hosted an antiviolence meeting between two hundred of his flock and two hundred gay rights advocates gathered from across the nation by Soulforce, Mel White's ecumenical group, based in Laguna Beach, California. Since coming out in 1991, White, a former ghostwriter for Falwell and speechwriter for Pat Robertson and Oliver North, has emerged as a critic of his former allies. Agreeing to disagree about whether homosexuality is a biblically prohibited sin, the conference participants focused instead on the Religious Right's "reckless and dangerous language" and "statements that can be construed as sanctioning hate and antagonism." Falwell even conceded that the old canard—love the sinner, hate the sin—has become, unfortunately, "a meaningless cliche."[7]

Moreover, in terms of electoral politics and the Republican Party, Log Cabin Republicans's Rich Tafel sees reason to hope. "What I hear is gay Republicans enthusiastic about the tone being set by the leading candidates [in the 1999–2000 Republican primaries]," he says. "It looks like Republicans for the first time are saying, 'This is a community I'm not going to alienate and maybe I want to reach out to.'"[8] Of course, Republicans have also shown little willingness to risk alienating those fundamentalist Christian voters who continue to regard homosexuality as sinful and aberrant. The additional quagmire for the LCR is that the GOP is not representative of the conservative movement overall. The LCR and its supporters in the party are impressed by the political ramifications of a growing relationship between homosexuals and Republicans. They note that in the 1998 elections "gays outnumbered Jewish and Asian voters and cast more votes for GOP House candidates than any other minority group pulled except Hispanics."[9] Other segments of the movement are fixated on the moral and religious dimensions. Falwell's gestures toward homosexuals aside, the Reverend Louis Sheldon, for one, remains staunchly opposed to the idea of a gay-friendly Republican Party and denies that there has ever been any substantive effort to reach out to gay voters.

Sheldon is among those religious conservatives who seek to use political gay bashing to heal the rifts between conservatives and African Americans and, more recently, between conservatives and Latinos. This tactic of effecting a greater unification, a multiracial *Religious* Right, at the expense of gay and lesbians has been successful in the past and shows no signs of abating. On the contrary, the antigay movement is branching out. La Amistad, for example, a California-based group of Latino evangelical church leaders, operates out of the Anaheim headquarters of Sheldon's Traditional Values Coalition (TVC) and has joined TVC's crusade against homosexual rights. While Republican leaders are not directly involved in La Amistad's efforts, they hope the group, while small, will help usher more Latinos into the fold of the GOP. According to Mike Madrid, a Republican analyst who ran the Party's state Latino outreach before resigning as political director in 1998, La Amistad is a "good harbinger of things to come in California." "The Republican message has historically appealed to an increasingly older white base," he continues. "This is not the future of California."[10]

And the future of California is essential to the future of the Republican Party and perhaps to the conservative movement overall. Throughout the twentieth century, California has played a seminal role in Republican politics and demonstrates the Party's relative successes and failures with minority voters. Under Richard Nixon and, later, Ronald Reagan, Republicans routinely won 30 to 40 percent of the Latino vote and roughly half of the Asian-American vote. More recently, in 1990, Pete Wilson's first gubernatorial campaign garnered almost 45 percent of ballots cast by Latinos and a majority of Asian-American ones. Yet, after California Republicans, following Wilson's lead, began to adopt anti-immigration policies, typically expressed in inflammatory rhetoric, this level of support dropped dramatically. Thus, by 1998, Dan Lungren, the conservative Republican candidate for governor, won fewer than a quarter of Latino voters (by then nearly 15 percent of the total electorate); Asian-Americans (8 percent of the electorate) voted overwhelmingly for the Democratic challenger, Gray Davis. Asian-Americans also cast almost half their ballots for Democratic Senator Barbara Boxer—even though she was defending her seat against Asian-American conservative Matt Fong.[11]

Yet an anti-immigrant stance might appeal to working-class whites and African Americans, whose fears of economic displacement could be tapped and exploited. As far back as 1895 Booker T. Washington urged white southern industrialists to "cast down your buckets where you are," into a pool of black workers who would "stand by you with a devotion that no foreigner can approach." After decades of rising tensions among African Americans, Latinos, and Asians in urban centers from Los Angeles to New York City, even leftists such as Manning Marable concede the growing political relevance of anti-immigrant biases among blacks.[12] Seeking to recruit African Americans at the expense of immigrants, like reaching out to communities of color at the expense of homosexuals and feminists, is, to be sure, a risky and even dangerous tactic, given the far-reaching social implications. Further, as the Republican Party in California discovered, anti-immigrant politics tend to produce a backlash among its victims.

In this regard, the 1998 election merely confirmed trends that had been developing since the early 1990s, trends that point to the difficulties in constructing and solidifying a multicultural Right. Since 1994, some sixty thousand Latinos have registered to vote, many as an angry response to measures such as Proposition 187. The percentage of Latino voters has doubled in the past decade (since 1990 nearly 40 percent of new voters in California are Latino), and their voter turnout rate at the polls has been higher than that for the overall state electorate. As one political strategist put it, "The evidence shows that this sleeping giant is about to wake."[13] Cognizant of this trend, the GOP is actively pursuing the Latino voters in California as well as in Texas and Florida, a state with a crucial Cuban-American vote.

The presidential campaign of Texas Governor George W. Bush provides a window through which to view the convergence of these electoral, demographic, and ideological trends. He stands at the intersection of the Party's conflicting attitudes toward minorities and diversification on the one hand and the internal battles between the Religious Right and Republican moderates on the other. Bush is probusiness and pro-immigration and speaks passable Spanish. Seeking to replicate the governor's relative popularity among African American, Latino, and women voters in Texas, the Bush campaign has made efforts to extend the outreach activities of the party. As Matt Fong, currently an adviser to the Bush campaign, notes, Bush won reelection as governor with "69 percent of the vote, including 65 percent of women voters, 73 percent of independents, 49 percent of Latino voters, and 27 percent of African American voters."[14]

Touting his "compassionate conservatism," Bush has shown signs of rejecting the old southern strategy and positive polarization in order to make a play for the remaining portions of the traditional Democratic Party base. At the same time, during the early months of campaigning, Bush also attempted to downplay the abortion issue. When he did finally confront it head on, he emphasized his willingness to see *Roe v. Wade* overturned, but on constitutional (read: States' Rights) as opposed to moral grounds. The issue dogged him through the primary season as candidates with ties to the Religious Right, including Gary Bauer and Alan Keyes, used the 1999–2000 primaries to attack Bush for his "soft" stance on both abortion and homosexuality. Although Bush attempted early on to bill himself as a moderate, the pressure asserted by Bauer and Keyes, along with the more substantial challenge from Senator John McCain, drove Bush further to the Right than he or his strategists desired.

Whether or not Bush will be able to regain the political center and to successfully triangulate the Democrats on issues such as education, poverty, and outreach to minority communities should reveal a good deal about how serious conservative Republicans are about constructing a multicultural Right. But race, having played such a commanding role in structuring the modern conservative movement and the New Right, will continue to dominate, especially in light of the persistent fervor surrounding affirmative action. As governor of Texas, Bush, who also supports bilingual education, sought to diffuse the turmoil over affirmative action via the 10 percent solution—the top 10 percent of all high school graduates in the state are eligible for spots at the University of Texas—in order to placate angry whites and to preserve access for students of color.

While such measures (successfully adopted in Texas but the center of a political firestorm in Florida, where George W. Bush's brother Jeb is governor) have the potential to give conservatives a more realistic way to talk about race and educational opportunities, and while Bush surely deserves some credit for speaking in a more inclusive manner, the essential problem of race remains. The movement to abolish affirmative action federally or on a state-by-state basis is still viable, and organizations such as the Center for Individual Rights have simultaneously increased the number of cases lodged against individual academic institutions.[15] Further, individual conservatives have also stepped up their efforts to convince Americans that, in the words of Julius Lester, an occasional fellow traveler, America would already be a color-blind society if only blacks would simply stop talking about race and complaining about racism.

In his review of Tamar Jacoby's *Someone Else's House*, a recent addition to a spate of books by "conservabals" (his word for liberals who sound like conservatives), Lester takes on liberals and conservatives who "never sound more racist than when they proclaim their colorblindness." "Now that race is accorded in favor of blacks (as race has always been accorded in favor of whites)," Lester charges, "conservatives ring the bell of meritoc-racy and want blacks to believe that whites are capable of judging blacks on their own individual merits."[16] Lester's critique gets at the heart of the problem with far too much of the conservative discourse on race, espe-cially its overreliance on the dream of color blindness.

In 1898, Justice John Marshall Harlan, once a Kentucky slave owner, dissented from the Supreme Court's majority opinion in *Plessy v. Ferguson*. Denouncing the "arbitrary separation of citizens" as a "badge of servi-tude," Harlan put forth the then novel idea that "our Constitution is color-blind." In so doing, Harlan challenged legal precedents extending as far back as the *Dred Scott* decision, the 1857 high court ruling that all Ne-groes, whether slave or free, had no rights that the white majority was bound to respect. Despite Harlan's dissent, *Plessy* effectively subverted the remaining gains the nation had made during Reconstruction. Nearly sixty years later, the Court began to rectify its mistake through a series of deci-sions beginning with *Brown v. Board of Education*. Half a century later, we remain deeply embroiled in the debates these two ideologically opposed decisions, *Plessy* and *Brown,* helped to generate.[17]

The attempts of contemporary conservatives to revive Harlan's notion of Constitutional color blindness is not without merit. It reminds us of an opportunity sadly lost at the dawn of the twentieth century and holds out possibilities for the future. Yet, the concomitant effort to privatize the real-ities of race and other forms of difference under the convenient cloak of personal responsibility and self-help represents an unconscionable desire to erase the history of both de facto and de jure discrimination in Amer-ica. This radical impulse to escape the past through an ahistorical approach to our present leaves much to be desired. Undaunted, mainstream and multicultural conservatives strive to apply the language of Harlan in a so-cial, political, and economic context where it is unfortunately out of place and premature—a position increasingly untenable to some black conser-vatives and fellow travelers. Conservative policies on crime, drugs, educa-tion, and welfare, Glenn Loury has recently argued, seem not only blind but "tone-deaf on race." "They can't see," he continues, "that our country's moral aspirations—to be a 'city upon a hill,' a beacon of hope and freedom to all the world—seem impossible when one sees the despair of so many of those Americans who descend from slaves."[18]

Noting a study that found that, while only 7 percent of white Americans can attest to being hurt by affirmative action, some 78 percent *believe* blacks make unreasonable demands that adversely affect the white majority, Orlando Patterson has also denounced the dubious embrace of color blindness among conservatives. He views the "angry white male syndrome" as a rebellion against affirmative action and other programs that "bring them [whites] face to face with black anger." While reaffirming the necessity of black self-help and initiative, he is equally insistent that "whites who dominate America's powerful institutions [must] address the roots of black rage by committing to black America's socio-economic advancement."[19]

The mainstream and multicultural conservatives who do not take the perspectives of these black conservatives and fellow travelers seriously run the risk of alienating them and damaging their own movement's ability to attract others. Neither Lester, nor Loury, nor Patterson is complicit with the civil rights establishment; their critiques of the Right cannot be written off by portraying them as manifestations of race obsession, victimology, or power brokering. That intellectuals such as Loury and Patterson currently divide their time between attacking the Left *and* attacking the Right does not bode well for the future of a multiracial Right. Nor does the backlash against conservative Republicans among Latinos over Proposition 209 and especially over Proposition 187. For the difficulties in formulating an appropriate and appealing language of race also extends to and intersects with the problematic relationship some conservatives have with ethnicity and national origin.

As one former GOP Hill aide put the matter, "If the Republicans can convince Latinos that they are not opposed to illegal immigration and they have a message of economic opportunity, they can again become competitive among Latinos. If on the other hand, they side with Pat Buchanan, they're cooked." For the movement overall, the policies and ideologies advocated by activists such as Buchanan and authors such as Peter Brimelow and John Tanton continue to represent a formidable stumbling block. The demographic trends on which Republican moderates as well as segments of the Religious Right want to capitalize are precisely those Brimelow and others want to halt, if not reverse. Unabashedly horrified by the projection that the United States will no longer have a white majority after 2050, Brimelow, in his 1996 book *Alien Nation,* warns that "an Anglo-Cuban society like Greater Miami is going to have little in common with an Anglo-black society like Atlanta or even an Anglo-Mexican society like San Francisco. They will be communities as different from one another as any in the civilized world. They will verge on being separate nations."[20]

With Brimelow arguing vociferously for—and all too few conservatives arguing aggressively against—the idea of America as a white nation under assault by hordes of black, brown, and yellow people, the movement's ability to build a bridge into communities of color is seriously imperiled. But the prominence accorded to Brimelow should remind us that segments of the Right remain inordinately fixated on race. Moreover, the venom expressed in works by conservatives such as Brimelow also impedes the more productive efforts of Latino conservatives such as Linda Chavez and Henry Bonilla to influence the climate of opinion within their communities. They may, like Glenn Loury and Robert Woodson in regard to Dinesh D'Souza's *The End of Racism,* seek to publicly disassociate themselves from extremist and ethnocentric views, but the taint of association lingers. Surely many reasonable people will concede that this "guilt-by-association" scenario is unfair, yet it is nonetheless inevitable.

Perhaps if it can get its own house in order, the conservative movement in America will finally find a language at once inclusive and compassionate. This is a tall order. And, after listening attentively to the voices of a variety of multicultural and mainstream conservatives, I see little likelihood of a deep and lasting success. Perhaps it is simply impossible to alter the conservative discourse to the extent necessary to make it appealing to a truly diverse constituency. Although I am, on the whole, personally delighted by my own grim prognosis, I am left with a lingering sense of regret. The rise of a multicultural conservatism has in fact begun to shake the Left out of its complacency and may in the future pave the way for its revitalization. Or, perhaps, sometime in this new century we will witness a creative fusion between Left and Right, liberal and conservative, as well as, finally, the embrace of a culture at once common, diverse, and plural. As I have attempted to demonstrate in this book, stranger things have certainly happened.

Finally, aside from the question of whether a truly multicultural Right is a possibility now or in the future, one must also ask whether such a development is in fact desirable. Here again, I am forced to respond in the negative. While such a coalition might produce some positive results, there is at least one bleak possibility that must be considered. Even if all the other tensions and pitfalls (over gender, sexuality, immigration, and ideology) are smoothed over, race, or, more pointedly, a politicized representation of "blackness," may, as Michael Lind predicts, prove to be the foundation for the ideological glue able to hold a multicultural Right together. The demonization of black women as overly sexualized and dependent on welfare and of black men through the lens of criminality and rational discrimination (the idea that black men are dangerous and violent and that therefore we are right and eminently rational to fear them), along with the scapegoating of a black (and Puerto Rican) "underclass" as inherently lazy and degenerate, constitutes a powerful if distorted narrative.

As I have argued in the preceding chapters, one point on which Latino, Asian-American, women, and homosexual conservatives seem to agree is the desire, to restate the matter bluntly, not to be like blacks—members of a group that persists in pressing for collective redress from the government rather than pursuing the path of individualism, upward mobility, and assimilation. That some Latino and Asian-American conservatives have engaged in this narrative is troubling. If Toni Morrison is even partially correct in asserting that previous waves of immigrants have embraced a (white, middle-class) American identity "on the backs of blacks," then there is reason to fear that new immigrants will seek to replicate this pattern. In the process, the already tense relationships among African Americans, Latinos, and Asian-American could degenerate. That some African American conservatives, a contingent that remains predominately middle and upper middle class, appear content to follow suit—to assimilate on the backs of the black poor—is doubly disturbing.

The major losers in this shifting discourse about race and identity in America, then, may prove to be poor blacks, who, pathologized and silenced, will continue to be everybody's convenient and favorite scapegoat. The history of the modern conservative movement is, after all, deeply intertwined with race and class. The future may promise more of the same, but with an increasingly multicultural twist. From this perspective, the most pressing question is not whether a multicultural Right *can* be crafted and solidified but at what cost, and at whose expense?

Notes

NOTES TO THE PREFACE

1. The film did well at the box office but took a critical beating. Daniel J. Leab, *From Sambo to Superspade: The Black Experience in Motion Pictures* (Boston: Houghton Mifflin, 1976), 230–232.

2. Louis Hartz, *The Liberal Tradition in America* (New York: Harcourt, Brace & World, 1955). In line with this "consensus school," see also Richard Hofstadter, *The American Political Tradition* (New York: Knopf, 1948), and Daniel J. Boorstin, *The Genius of American Politics* (Chicago: University of Chicago Press, 1953).

3. Russell Kirk, "Introduction," *The Portable Conservative Reader* (New York: Penguin, 1982), xv–xviii.

4. For a good representation of the southern conservative defense of slavery with particularly strong overtones of paternalism, see George Fitzhugh, *Sociology of the South, or the Failures of a Free Society* (Richmond, Va.: A. Morris, 1854), and his *Cannibals All! or Slaves without Masters* (1857; Cambridge, Mass.: Belknap/Harvard University Press, 1960).

5. "The Southern Manifesto: Declaration of Constitutional Principles," *Cong. Rec.*, 84th Congress., 2nd sess. (March 12, 1956). This is not to suggest that all uses of States' Rights are ipso facto racist, only that the doctrine has been put to racist uses from time to time. On the nuances of the doctrine and its relationship to the development of conservative ideologies, see Eugene Genovese, *The Southern Tradition: The Achievement and Limitations of an American Conservatism* (Cambridge, Mass.:

Harvard University Press, 1994); and Dan T. Carter, *From George Wallace to Newt Gingrich: Race in the Conservative Counterrevolution, 1963–1994* (Baton Rouge: Louisiana State University Press, 1996).

6. Susan Au Allen quoted in Lan Nguyen, "An Inconvenient Woman," *A Magazine*, March 31, 1998.

7. A number of texts have dealt with the difficulties of defining neoconservatism. Among the best are James Q. Wilson's foreword to Mark Gerson, ed., *The Essential Neoconservative Reader* (Reading, Mass.: Addison-Wesley, 1996), and Irving Kristol's *Neoconservatism: The Autobiography of an Idea* (New York: Free Press, 1995). On how neocons fit in with the rest of the Right see Ernest Van Den Haag, "The War between Paleos and Neos," *National Review* 41:3 (February 24, 1989): 21–23; Dan Himmelfarb, "Conservative Splits," *Commentary* 85:5 (May 1988): 54–58; and Russell Kirk, *The Neoconservatives: An Endangered Species*, Heritage Foundation Lectures, #178 (Washington, D.C.: Heritage Foundation, 1988): 1–10.

8. David A. Horowitz, *Beyond Left and Right: Insurgency and the Establishment* (Urbana: University of Illinois Press, 1997). For the other side of this debate, see Norberto Bobbio, *Left and Right: The Significance of a Political Distinction*, translated and introduced by Allan Cameron (Chicago: University of Chicago Press, 1996). Bobbio places the distinction in an international context and draws heavily on European (especially Italian) experiences with radicalism, liberalism, and conservatism.

9. Weyrich quoted in Richard A. Viguerie, *The New Right: We're Ready to Lead* (Falls Church, Va.: Viguerie Company, 1980), 59.

NOTES TO THE INTRODUCTION

1. Dan T. Carter, *From George Wallace to Newt Gingrich: Race and the Conservative Counterrevolution, 1963–1994* (Baton Rouge: Louisiana State University Press, 1996), xiv.

2. See for example Arnold Hirsch, "Massive Resistance in the Urban North: Trumbull Park, Chicago, 1953–1966," *Journal of American History* 82 (September 1995): 522–550; Thomas J. Sugrue, "Crabgrass-Roots Politics: Race, Rights and the Reaction against Liberalism in the Urban North, 1940–1964," *Journal of American History* 82 (September 1995): 551–578; Alan Brinkley, "The Problem of American Conservatism," *American Historical Review* 99 (April 1994): 409–429; Michael Kazin, "The Grass-Roots Right: New Histories of U.S. Conservatism," *American Historical Review* 97 (February 1992): 136–155; and Nancy McLean, "White Women and Klan Violence in the 1920s: Agency, Complicity and the Politics of Women's History," *Gender & History* 3 (Autumn 1991): 285–303.

3. While this lack of attention is less surprising with regard to African American, Latino, and gay conservatives, especially in older works, the virtual wall of silence with regard to conservative women is more startling. Even books that do attempt to incorporate women conservatives take a fairly slipshod approach. See, for

example, the paltry offerings by conservative women in Russell Kirk, ed., *The Portable Conservative Reader* (New York: Penguin, 1982), Part 15. Other classic studies, such as Clinton Rossiter, *Conservatism in America: The Thankless Persuasion* (New York: Knopf, 1962), and William F. Buckley, Jr., *American Conservative Thought in the Twentieth Century* (Indianapolis: Bobbs-Merrill, 1970), ignore the contributions of women and minorities. Even Eugene Genovese's *The Southern Tradition* (Cambridge, Mass.: Harvard University Press, 1994) makes no attempt to incorporate African American voices, nor does John Ehrman's *The Rise of Neoconservatism: Intellectuals and Foreign Affairs* (New Haven: Yale University Press, 1995). Other, more recent studies deal better with gender and, at the very least, give a passing nod to Thomas Sowell, including Peter Steinfels, *The Neoconservatives: The Men Who Are Changing America's Politics* (New York: Touchstone, 1979), and Gary J. Dorrien, *The Neoconservative Mind: Politics, Culture and the War of Ideology* (Philadelphia: Temple University Press, 1993). It almost goes without saying that these studies do not attempt to incorporate Latinos, Asian-Americans, or homosexuals.

4. Thomas, "No Room at the Inn," *Policy Review* 58 (Fall 1991): 72–78.

5. Baraka, "Malcolm as Ideology," in Joe Wood, ed., *Malcolm X: In Our Own Image* (New York: St. Martin's Press, 1992), 192.

6. One of the most thorough studies of the infrastructure of the conservative movement and the New Right is Sidney Blumenthal's *The Rise of the Counter-Establishment* (New York: Harper & Row, 1988). Also, John Soloma, *Ominous Politics: The New Conservative Labyrinth* (New York: Hill & Wang, 1984); Alan Crawford, *Thunder on the Right: The "New Right" and the Politics of Resentment* (New York: Pantheon, 1980), and Sara Diamond, *Spiritual Warfare: The Politics of the Christian Right* (Boston: South End Press, 1989).

7. Lionel McPherson, "The Loudest Silence Ever Heard: Black Conservatives in the Media," *Extra!* August–September 1992.

8. Carol Felsenthal, *The Sweetheart of the Silent Majority* (Garden City, N.Y.: Doubleday, 1981), contains a good overview of Schlafly's background and early political career.

9. Information on the founding of the LCR can be found in Richard Tafel's *Party Crasher: A Gay Republican Challenges Politics as Usual* (New York: Simon & Schuster, 1999), 117–122, 142–143; and under "About LCR" at their web site: www.lcr.org; copy in author's possession.

10. Both Parker and Liebman, along with Schlafly, had ties to YAF. Liebman was one of the group's founders but resigned in 1962 amid controversy over whether to put the John Birch Society's Robert Welch on the YAF board. Parker was the only black member of YAF's board. See Gregory L. Schneider, *Cadres for Conservatives: Young Americans for Freedom and the Rise of the Contemporary Right* (New York: New York University Press, 1999).

11. On black conservatives in the late 1970s and early 1980s, see Soloma, *Ominous Politics*, chapter 12; Manning Marable, "Black Reaganism: A Rogue's Gallery,"

Washington, D.C. Afro-American, April 24, 1982; William A. Henry, "Sowell on the Firing Line," *Time,* August 24, 1981; "National Report: Sowell and His Supporters Win Key Posts from Reagan," *Jet,* April 26, 1982; and William Greider and Harold Logan, "Why Blacks Are Turning Conservative," *Conservative Digest* (October 1978): 28–34.

12. Arthur Hu, "Conservative Asian Voters," *Asian Week,* January 3, 1992; "Welfare and Immigrants," *Asian Week,* January 24, 1992; "Republican Stampede," *Asian Week,* December 23, 1994. Hu's views are highlighted in Ramon G. McLeod, "Class-Based Admissions Plan May Not Address Diversity," *San Francisco Chronicle,* March 2, 1998.

13. M. L. Stein, "Newspapers Feuding in San Francisco," *Editor & Publisher,* March 21, 1992; Harre W. Demoro, "Fang Takes Early Lead in BART Race," *San Francisco Chronicle,* November 7, 1990; Steven A. Chin et al., "Fang Purse Wide Open for Jordan," *San Francisco Chronicle,* March 1, 1992. Unfortunately in terms of his chances for a more visible political career, Fang has been beset by charges of campaign finance corruption: Harre W. Domoro, "Fang Admits Unauthorized Deal," *San Francisco Chronicle,* January 17, 1992; Lance Williams, "Fang Resigns as Trade Director," *San Francisco Chronicle,* April 23, 1995.

14. Matt Fong, "APA Roundtable: The Case for George W. Bush," *Asian Week,* July 21, 1999; "When the Going Gets Tough, the Candidates Call on Mother for Help," *Chicago Tribune,* November 1, 1998; William Booth, "California Race Could Signal New Cohesion for Asian Voters," *Washington Post,* November 3, 1998; Tony Perry, "Blood Thicker Than Politics for Fongs," *Los Angeles Times,* October 21, 1998.

15. Lan Nguyen, "An Inconvenient Woman," *A Magazine,* March 31, 1998; William McGurn, "A Hong Kong Girl Who Made It Big in the U.S.," *Far Eastern Economic Review,* December 16, 1993; Susan Au Allen, "A Crime Cure: Shame the Criminals," *USA Today,* October 23, 1993.

16. Lan Nguyen, "An Inconvenient Woman"; Frank Wu and James Carroll, "Anything for the Cause: Susan Au Allen Has Her Own Ideas about Political Empowerment," *Asian Week,* November 26, 1997; Susan Au Allen, "Women and the Affirmative Action Revolution," *Vital Speeches of the Day* (New York: City News, April 1, 1997).

17. In "Promises to Keep: The Christian Men's Movement," *Dignity Report* 3:4 (Fall 1996), Steve L. Gardiner argues that the appeal to racial reconciliation may be genuine but is based on the *idea* of racism and not on the "struggle for real-world equality in economic and political terms"(6). See also Bob Horner et al., *Applying the Seven Promises* (Colorado Springs: Focus on the Family, 1996); Hans Johnson, "Broken Promises," *Church and State* 48 (May 1995): 9; Joe Canason et al., "The Promise Keepers Are Coming: The Third Wave of the Religious Right," *Nation* 263 (October 7, 1996): 12–19; and Russ Bellant, "Mania in the Stadia: The Origins and Goals of the Promise Keepers," *Front Lines Research* 1 (May 1995): 7–9.

18. "Christian Coalition Hires Black Liaison," *Christian Century*, April 24, 1996, 448; D. J. Gribbin, "Bridge Building across Racial Lines," *Christian America* (September 1995): 20–21; Amy Argetsinger, "Christian Coalition Courts Black Churches," *Washington Post*, May 11, 1997; and Justin Watson, *The Christian Coalition: Dreams of Restoration, Demands for Recognition* (New York: St. Martin's Press, 1997), chapter 4.

19. Fred Barnes, "The Minority Minority: Black Conservatives and White Republicans," *New Republic*, September 30, 1991, 22–23; Kay Coles James, *Never Forget* (Grand Rapids, Mich.: Zondervan, 1992); Linda Kintz, *Between Jesus and the Market: The Emotions That Matter in Right-Wing America* (Durham, N.C.: Duke University Press, 1997), 84–87.

20. Kintz, *Between Jesus and the Market*, 87; Star Parker with Lorenzo Benet, *Pimps, Whores and Welfare Brats: From Welfare Cheat to Conservative Messenger* (New York: Pocket Books, 1997).

21. James, *Never Forget*, 84.

22. Along with the materials cited in n.6, see also Richard Delgado and Jean Stefancic, *No Mercy: How Conservative Think Tanks and Foundations Changed America's Social Agenda* (Philadelphia: Temple University Press, 1996).

23. More detailed information on Keyes can be found at his web site: www.keyes2000.org; copy in author's possession. For a less laudatory view, see Doug Ireland, "The 'Black Conservative' Con: Alan Keyes Does the Hustle," *Nation* 261 (October 30, 1995): 500–503.

24. Tafel, *Party Crasher*, 112.

25. Gunderson, along with his long-time companion, Bob Morris, has written an autobiography in which he describes his struggles with being both gay and conservative and the political turmoil surrounding his outing. Gunderson and Rob Morris with Bruce Bawer, *House and Home* (New York: E. P. Dutton, 1996). In a similar vein see Robert E. Bauman, *The Gentleman from Maryland: The Conscience of a Gay Conservative* (New York: Arbor House, 1986). A founder of the Young Americans for Freedom, Bauman was forced to come out in the early 1980s after being charged with criminal solicitation.

26. On this banner year for Republican women and its implications see Elinor Burkett, *The Right Women: A Journey through the Heart of Conservative America* (New York: Scribner, 1998), 15–17.

27. Sara Evans and Harry Boyte define "free spaces" as communally grounded and autonomous associations that permit people to work out alternative visions of society and to engage in social change. They configure free spaces as central to a developing movement culture that sustains protest on both the individual and the collective levels. While the Black Church during the civil rights movement is paradigmatic for Evans and Boyte, who focus primarily on leftist and liberal causes, this idea is equally useful for the study of the conservative movement: *Free Spaces: The Sources of Democratic Change in America* (New York: Harper & Row, 1986). See

also Aldon Morris and Carol McClurg Muller, eds., *Frontiers in Social Movement Theory* (New Haven:Yale University Press, 1992).

28. This multicultural strategy is on display in Ralph Reed's "Casting a Wider Net: Religious Conservatives Move Beyond Abortion and Homosexuality," *Policy Review* 65 (Summer 1993): 31–35.

29. Kintz, *Between Jesus and the Market*, chapter 1. The articulation of this shared language and how conservatives use various forms of popular culture to reinforce a "sacred intimacy" is the primary focus of Kintz's book.

30. Texts of the speeches given by Novak, Gingrich, Woodson, and Connerly are available through the Independent Women's Forum web site: www.iwf.org; copies in author's possession. See also "Dallas Puts Log Cabin on National Stage," as well as remarks by Andrew Sullivan, both on the LCR web site at www.lcr.org/news; copies in author's possession.

31. Cynthia D. Kinnard, ed., *Antifeminism in American Thought: An Annotated Bibliography* (Boston: G. K. Hall, 1986).

32. Peter Collier and David Horowitz, who were editors of *Ramparts* magazine in the late 1960s, have been consistent advocates of this view. See their *Destructive Generation: Second Thoughts about the Sixties* (New York: Summit Books, 1989). They have also organized conferences for "former radicals" with titles such as "Second Thoughts about the 1960s" (in 1987) and "Second Thoughts about Race" (in 1990).

33. Leeden quoted in Megan Rosenfeld, "Feminist Fatales," *Washington Post*, November 30, 1995.

34. This is perhaps the most popular and frequently used narrative about what has gone wrong with the movement. In addition to Clint Bolick, *In Whose Name? The Civil Rights Establishment Today* (Washington, D.C.: Capital Research Center, 1988), 7, see also Bolick, *The Affirmative Action Fraud* (Washington, D.C.: Cato Institute, 1996); Bolick, *Changing Course: Civil Rights at the Crossroads* (New Brunswick, N.J.: Transaction, 1988); Joseph Perkins, ed., *A Conservative Agenda for Black Americans* (Washington, D.C.: Heritage Foundation, 1987); and Martin Carnoy, *Faded Dreams: The Politics and Economics of Race in America* (Cambridge: Cambridge University Press, 1994).

35. Susan Faludi, *Backlash: The Undeclared War against American Women* (New York: Crown, 1991); Cornel West, "Assessing Black Neoconservatism," in his *Prophetic Fragments* (Trenton, N.J.: Africa World Press, 1988): 55–63.

36. Rosalind Pollack Petchesky, "Antiabortion, Antifeminism, and the Rise of the New Right," *Feminist Studies* 7:2 (Summer 1981), 207.

37. Reed, "Casting a Wider Net," 31. While Reed acknowledges the importance of these issues in the past, he urges that the Religious Right expand into other arenas such as crime, education, and other "profamily" causes.

38. A good representative sample of leftist and liberal opinion about Thomas and his "appropriation" of Malcolm X can be found in Toni Morrison, ed., *Race-*

ing Justice, En-gendering Power: Essays on Anita Hill, Clarence Thomas and the Construction of Social Reality (New York: Pantheon, 1992), and Robert Chrisman and Robert L. Allen, eds., *Court of Appeal: The Black Community Speaks Out on the Racial and Sexual Politics of Clarence Thomas vs. Anita Hill* (New York: Ballantine Books, 1992). See also Ronald Suresh Roberts, *Clarence Thomas and the Tough Love Crowd* (New York: New York University Press, 1995), which is presently one of the only book-length studies of black conservatism written by a nonconservative scholar, along with Amy Elizabeth Ansell, *New Right, New Racism: Race and Reaction in the United States and Britain* (New York: New York University Press, 1997), which is notable for its comparative approach.

39. Dinesh D'Souza, *The End of Racism: Principles for a Multiracial Society* (New York: Free Press, 1995), 235. See also Joseph Conti and Brad Stetson, *Challenging the Civil Rights Establishment: Profiles of a New Black Vanguard* (Westport, Conn.: Praeger, 1993).

40. Thomas Sowell, *A Conflict of Visions* (New York: William Morrow, 1987). He elaborates on this theme in *Civil Rights: Rhetoric or Reality?* (New York: Quill, 1984).

41. Linda Chavez, *Out of the Barrio: Toward a New Politics of Hispanic Assimilation* (New York: Basic Books, 1991), 4–5; Bruce Bawer, *A Place at the Table: The Gay Individual in American Society* (New York: Touchstone, 1993), 148.

42. Susan Au Allen quoted in Nguyen, "An Inconvenient Woman."

43. For an elaboration of these views see Charles Murray, *Losing Ground: American Social Policy, 1950–1980* (New York: Basic Books, 1984); Walter Williams, *The State against Blacks* (New York: McGraw-Hill, 1982) and *Do the Right Thing* (Stanford: Hoover Institute Press, 1995); Armstrong Williams, *Beyond Blame: How We Can Succeed by Breaking the Dependency Barrier* (New York: Free Press, 1995). Many of these ideas have roots in Milton Friedman's classic defense of the free market: *Capitalism and Freedom* (Chicago: University of Chicago Press, 1962).

44. Bawer, *A Place at the Table*, 10.

45. Chris Bull and John Gallagher, *Perfect Enemies: The Religious Right, the Gay Movement, and the Politics of the 1990s* (New York: Crown, 1996).

46. Adam Meyerson, "Manna 2 Society: The Growing Conservatism of Black America," *Policy Review* 68 (Spring 1994): 5. The possibilities of this emergent coalition are also discussed in detail in Urvashi Vaid, *Virtual Equality: The Mainstreaming of Gay and Lesbian Liberation* (New York: Anchor Books, 1995), especially chapter 5: "The Supremacist Right." See also Paul Weyrich, "Getting Serious about Blacks," *Conservative Digest* (July–August 1989): 11–14, and William Keyes, "Blacks and Republicans," *Conservative Digest* (July–August 1989): 47–49. On the strategic usefulness of this tactic, the longtime lesbian feminist activist Suzanne Pharr writes:

Community by community, the Religious Right works skillfully to divide us along fissures that already exist. It is as though they have a political seismograph to locate the racism and sexism in the lesbian and gay community, the

sexism and homophobia in communities of color. While the Right is united by their racism, sexism and homophobia in their goal to dominate all of us, we are divided by our own racism, sexism and homophobia.
Pharr quoted in Barbara Smith, "Blacks and Gays," in Chip Berlet, ed., *Eyes Right! Challenging the Right Wing Backlash* (Boston: South End Press, 1995), 275.

NOTES TO CHAPTER I

1. *Seneca Falls Declaration of Sentiments and Resolutions* (1848), reprinted in Diane Ravitch, ed., *The American Reader: Words That Moved a Nation* (New York: Harper/Collins, 1990), 83–85. Emphasis mine.

2. The concept of civil religion was first put forth by Robert Bellah in his "Civil Religion in America," *Daedalus* 96 (Winter 1976): 1–21. A good series of interpretations of this idea can be found in Donald G. Jones and E. Richey, eds., *American Civil Religion* (New York: Harper & Row, 1974).

3. Perry Miller, *The New England Mind: The Seventeenth Century* (New York: Macmillan, 1939), is widely credited with the "rediscovery" of scholarly interest in this phenomenon. See also Sacvan Bercovitch's more critical interpretation in *The American Jeremiad* (Madison: University of Wisconsin Press, 1978); and Conrad Cherry, ed., *God's New Israel: Religious Interpretations of American Destiny* (Englewood Cliffs, N.J.: Prentice-Hall, 1971).

4. Frederick Douglass, "What to a Slave Is the Fourth of July?" (1852), reprinted in David Hollinger, ed., *The American Intellectual Tradition*, Vol. 1 (New York: Oxford University Press, 1989), 362.

5. Ibid., 366.

6. Michael Walzer, "The Prophet as Social Critic," *Interpretation and Social Criticism* (Cambridge, Mass.: Harvard University Press, 1987), 75.

7. Douglass, "What to a Slave," 372. Wilson J. Moses defines messianism as the expectation of or identification with a personal savior in the form of a prophet, a messiah, or a Mahdi; as the concept of the redemptive mission of the black race; as the journalistic and artistic presentations of certain black individuals (i.e., Joe Louis) as symbolic messiahs; and as the guiding spirit of "prophetism" and prophetic movements, especially Ethiopianism. Douglass's use of the Old Testament passage "Princes shall come out of Egypt; Ethiopia shall soon stretch forth her hands unto God" (Psalms 68:31) is entirely consistent with the variants of Ethiopianism in the mid- to late nineteenth century. As a form of black messianism, Ethiopianism viewed the redemption of Africa via Christianity and freedom from foreign domination as both necessary and inevitable. Thus, it planted the seeds of African nationalism and Afro-American, Afro-British, and Afro-Caribbean pan-Africanism. Wilson Jeremiah Moses, *Black Messiahs and Uncle Toms: Social and Literary Manipulations of a Religious Myth*, rev. ed. (University Park: Pennsylvania State University Press, 1993), 1–16. Douglass's ability to speak in a double

voice, at once African American and American, is also consistent with what David Howard-Pitney calls "the Afro-American jeremiad" in *The Afro-American Jeremiad* (Philadelphia: Temple University Press, 1990).

8. On Thomas's connections to Lincoln and Douglass as well as Malcolm X, see Stephen Macedo, "Douglass to Thomas," *New Republic*, September 30, 1991, 23–24.

9. Patricia J. Williams, "Clarence X, Man of the People" in Joe Wood, ed., *Malcolm X: In Our Own Image* (New York: St. Martin's Press, 1992), 192; see also Williams, "A Rare Case Study of Muleheadedness and Men," in Toni Morrison, ed., *Race-ing Justice, En-gendering Power* (New York: Pantheon Books, 1992): 159–171.

10. Amiri Baraka, "Malcolm as Ideology," in Wood, ed., *Malcolm X*, 21.

11. Manning Marable, "Clarence Thomas and the Crisis of Black Political Culture," in Morrison, ed., *Race-ing Justice*, 61–85. Marable discusses "neoaccommodationist-conservative black spokespersons" on page 72.

12. Manning Marable, "Black Fundamentalism: Louis Farrakhan and the Politics of Conservative Black Nationalism," *Dissent* 45 (Spring 1998): 69–76. Adolph Reed, "The Descent of Black Conservatism," *Progressive* 61 (October 1997): 18–20. Both are especially strident on the question of patronage. As Reed put it, the "reproductive advantage driving the principle of selection" among black conservatives is "getting paid."

13. Elizabeth Wright, "Without Commerce and Industry, the People Perish: Marcus Garvey's Gospel of Prosperity," *Issues and Views* (Spring 1991): 16.

14. Alan Keyes, *Masters of the Dream: The Strength and Betrayal of Black America* (New York: William Morrow, 1995), 108–109.

15. We are confronted by the oddity of both leftists and conservatives "Uncle Tom-ing" each other. Keyes's charge of racial opportunism stands alongside the very same charges being made against Thomas and other black conservatives. Of course, the use of Uncle Tom in this manner forms something of a tradition in the intraracial debates that have structured African American political thought at least since the turn of the century. It reached something of an apex in the hands of Malcolm X, who drew the historically dubious but rhetorically useful distinction between "House Negroes" and "Field Negroes." See his "Message to the Grass-Roots" (1963), reprinted in George Breitman, ed., *Malcolm X Speaks: Selected Speeches and Statements* (New York: Grove Weidenfeld, 1965), 3–17. And on the political symbolism of Uncle Tom in general, see Moses, *Black Messiahs and Uncle Toms*.

16. There is, however, a collection of the writings of contemporary figures such as Thomas, Shelby Steele, Loury, Walter Williams, and Representative Gary Franks. Stan Faryna et al., eds., *Black and Right: The Bold New Voice of Black Conservatives in America* (Westport, Conn.: Praeger, 1997).

17. For a nice overview of how this tension between the universal and the particular has structured contemporary African American intellectual life see William Banks, *The Black Intellectual: Race and Responsibility in American Life* (New York: Norton, 1996), especially chapters 11 and 12.

18. Anne Wortham, "The New Ethnicity versus Individualist Pluralism," *Lincoln Review* 4:3 (Winter 1984): 19–30, and *The Other Side of Racism* (Columbus: Ohio State University Press, 1980). A similar argument can be found in works such as Allan C. Brownfeld and J. A. Parker, "Returning to the Goal of a 'Color Blind' American Society," *Lincoln Review* 2:1 (Summer 1981): 3–22; in Susan Love Brown, "Why Being Black Causes Confusion," *Lincoln Review* 2:4 (Winter–Spring 1982): 15–19; and in the works of Thomas Sowell, especially *Civil Rights: Rhetoric or Reality?* (New York: Quill, 1984).

19. Wortham, *The Other Side of Racism*, 13.

20. Stanley Crouch, "How Long? So Long," *The All-American Skin Game, or the Decoy of Race* (New York: Pantheon, 1995), 83. Emphasis in the original. Shelby Steele also appeals to the legacy of Ellison in his *The Content of Our Character* (New York: Harper Perennial, 1991):

> One of my favorite passages in Ralph Ellison's *Invisible Man* is his description of the problem of blacks as "not actually one of creating the uncreated conscience of [our] race, but of creating the *uncreated features of [our] face*. Our task is one of making ourselves individuals" (30). Emphasis in the original.

For similar expression of this idea, see Randall Kennedy, "My Race Problem—And Ours," *Atlantic Monthly* (May 1997): 55–66, as well as his *Race, Crime and the Law* (New York: Pantheon, 1997); and Orlando Patterson, *The Ordeal of Integration: Progress and Resentment in America's 'Racial' Crisis* (Washington, D.C.: Civitas/Counterpoint, 1997).

21. The text of Loury's speech to the "Second Thoughts about Race" conference is reprinted as "Second Thoughts and First Principles" in his *One by One from the Inside Out: Essays and Reviews on Race and Responsibility in America* (New York: Free Press, 1995): 195–203.

22. Loury's middle-of-the-road position on the relevance of race in American life may also help to explain the softening of his opposition to affirmative action and race set-asides in employment. See, for example, his "Unequalized," *New Republic*, April 6, 1998, 10–11. Nathan Glazer, who led the charge against affirmative action in the 1970s, has also had a change of heart in light of the persistence of racial inequality. See his "In Defense of Preference," also in *New Republic* (April 6, 1998), 18–21, 24–25.

23. Walter J. Bowie, "It's Not Racism, It's Us," *Lincoln Review* 9:1 (Fall 1988), 17.

24. Joseph Conti and Brad Stetson identify this position as one of the key fixtures of "New Black Vanguard Thought." *Challenging the Civil Rights Establishment: Profiles of a New Black Vanguard* (Westport, Conn.: Praeger, 1993): 33–41.

25. Thomas Sowell, *Ethnic America* (New York: Basic Books, 1981), 295.

26. *Destiny*, December 1990/January 1991, 2.

27. For a fuller treatment of these ideas and their implications, see especially Kevin K. Gaines, *Uplifting the Race: Black Leadership, Politics and Culture in the Twentieth Century* (Chapel Hill: University of North Carolina Press, 1996); Wilson J.

Moses, *The Golden Age of Black Nationalism, 1850–1920* (New York: Oxford University Press, 1988); and Paula Giddings, *When and Where I Enter: The Impact of Black Women on Race and Sex in America* (New York: Bantam Books, 1985), especially chapter 6.

28. A. Leon Higginbotham, "An Open Letter to Justice Clarence Thomas from a Federal Judicial Colleague," in Morrison, ed., *Race-ing Justice*, 17.

29. Kelly Miller, "Radicals and Conservatives," in *Radicals and Conservatives and Other Essays on the Negro in America* (1908; New York: Schocken Books, 1968), 25. This exchange between Booker T. Washington and a Prince Kropotkin is recounted by Eugene Genovese as a witticism that has plagued all southern conservatives since 1865. Genovese, *The Southern Tradition* (Cambridge, Mass.: Harvard University Press, 1994), 21.

30. Montgomery was of course denounced as a traitor to the race. On Montgomery and others who expressed similar views, see August Meier, *Negro Thought in America, 1880–1915: Racial Ideologies in the Age of Booker T. Washington* (Ann Arbor: University of Michigan Press, 1963), 38–41.

31. Glenn Loury, "Two Paths to Black Power," *First Things* 26 (October 1992), 19. Conti and Stetson give the matter of Loury's rhetorical style sustained attention in their *Challenging the Civil Rights Establishment*, 202–204.

32. Loury, "Two Paths to Black Power," 20. Also "Black Dignity and the Common Good," reprinted in Loury, *One by One from the Inside Out*, 13–31.

33. One of the best treatments of the Washington–Du Bois "debate" is still Meier, *Negro Thought in America*, especially Part Five.

34. D'Souza, *The End of Racism*, 184–189. See also Clint Bolick, *In Whose Name? The Civil Rights Establishment Today* (Washington, D.C.: Capital Research Center, 1988); and Ethelbert W. Haskins, *The Crisis in Afro-American Leadership* (Buffalo, N.Y.: Prometheus Books, 1988).

35. D'Souza, *The End of Racism*, 184.

36. W. E. B. Du Bois, "A Negro Nation within the Nation," [1935], reprinted in Philip S. Foner, ed., *W. E. B. Du Bois Speaks: Speeches and Addresses, 1920–1963* (New York: Pathfinder, 1970), 77–86.

37. Ibid., 81. Perhaps the more interesting historical question is whether Washington's strategies have ever been effective. On this matter, see Winston Charles McDowell, "The Ideology of Black Entrepreneurship and Its Impact on the Development of Black Harlem, 1930–1964," Ph.D. diss., University of Minnesota, 1996.

38. Du Bois, "A Negro Nation," 82. No summary suffices to capture the rich complexity of Du Bois's social thought as it developed over the course of his long lifetime. Among the best sources on Du Bois are Manning Marable, *W. E. B. Du Bois: Black Radical Democrat* (Boston: Twayne, 1986); David Levering Lewis, *W. E. B. Du Bois: Biography of a Race, 1868–1919* (New York: Holt, 1994); and Adolph Reed, *W. E. B. Du Bois and American Political Thought: Fabianism and the Color Line* (New York: Oxford University Press, 1999).

39. On this gradual transformation of American conservatism at the turn of the century, see Robert Green McCloskey, *American Conservatism in the Age of Enterprise, 1865–1910* (New York: Harper & Row, 1964).

40. Elizabeth Wright, "Booker T. Washington: Our Greatest Warrior," *Issues and Views* (Spring 1992): 1–4.

41. Ibid., 3.

42. Ibid., 2.

43. Wright quoted in D'Souza, *The End of Racism*, 184. See also Thomas W. Pauken, "Plantation Politics, White Liberal Style," *Lincoln Review* 3:1 (Summer 1982): 47–52. This theme has also been taken up in Clarence M. Weaver, *It's OK to Leave the Plantation: A Journey from Liberalism to Conservatism* (New York: Reeder Books, 1996).

44. The idea that civil rights leaders and organizations such as the NAACP and the Urban League form an industry designed for the enrichment of a middle-class elite at the expense of the black poor has become a hallmark of black conservatism. See Elizabeth Wright's "Cashing In on the 'Black Problem': Race and Poverty as an Industry," *Issues and Views* (Fall 1989): 1–5; Thomas Sowell, *Civil Rights: Rhetoric or Reality?;* Thomas W. Pauken, "Plantation Politics, White Liberal Style"; and D'Souza, *The End of Racism*, chapter 6.

45. Washington quoted in David Howard-Pitney, *The Afro-American Jeremiad*, 70.

46. Booker T. Washington, "Atlanta Exposition Address" (1895), reprinted in Howard Brotz, ed., *African-American Social and Political Thought, 1850–1920* (New Brunswick, N.J.: Transaction, 1993): 356–359.

47. Elizabeth Wright, "Never Again," *Issues and Views* (Summer 1991), 1.

48. Wright, "Without Commerce and Industry, the People Perish," 15.

49. See Wilson J. Moses, *The Golden Age of Black Nationalism;* and E. Francis White, "Africa on My Mind: Gender, Counter Discourse and African-American Nationalism," reprinted in Beverly Guy-Sheftall, ed., *Words of Fire: An Anthology of African-American Feminist Thought* (New York: Free Press, 1995): 504–524.

50. Garvey, "The True Solution of the Negro Problem," (1922), reprinted in Brotz, ed., *African-American Social and Political Thought*, 554–555. Also, "An Appeal to the Soul of White America," in Brotz, ed., *African-American Social and Political Thought*, 555–559.

51. Wright, "Without Commerce and Industry, the People Perish," 16. Along with Garvey (and like Clarence Thomas), the *Issues and Views* group has laid claim to Malcolm X. See "The True Legacy of Malcolm X: Are We Ready for His Message?" *Issues and Views* (Winter 1989): 1–4.

52. A number of black conservatives have gone out of their way to denounce afrocentrism, but none as forcefully as Shelby Steele. See Steele, *The Content of Our Character;* also Anne Wortham, *The Other Side of Racism;* and Stanley Crouch, *Notes from a Hanging Judge* (New York: Oxford University Press, 1990).

53. Garvey, "An Appeal to the Soul of White America" (1923), reprinted in Brotz, ed., *African-American Social and Political Thought*, 558.

54. Garvey, "An Appeal to the Conscience of the Black Race to See Itself" (1923), reprinted in Brotz, ed., *African-American Social and Political Thought*, 562–566.

55. Quoted in Amy Jacques Garvey, *Garvey and Garveyism* (New York: Octagon Books, 1986), 92.

56. Wright, "Never Again," 1. For more details on Fuller and the history of Fuller Products Company, see Juliet E. K. Walker, *The History of Black Business in America: Capitalism, Race and Entrepreneurship* (London: Prentice Hall International, 1998), 295–298.

57. "Remembering S. B. Fuller," *Lincoln Review* 9:1 (Fall 1988), 59–61, and "S. B. Fuller: Master of Enterprise," *Issues and Views* (Winter 1989): 1–3. Fuller (along with Washington and Garvey) is also praised by Tony Brown in "Prophets in Their Own Time," *New Pittsburgh Courier*, October 2, 1991.

58. Black conservatives have been supportive of attempts to "recover" the history of African American entrepreneurship, especially John Sibley Butler's *Entrepreneurship and Self-Help among Black Americans: A Reconsideration of Race and Economics* (New York: State University of New York Press, 1991).

59. The cultural dimension is a bit harder to get at. But unlike *Issues and Views*, which tends to focus almost exclusively on economic matters, the quarterly *Lincoln Review* takes a somewhat broader approach, running articles not only on McKay and Hurston but also on Joe Louis (Nick Thimmesch, "Joe Louis Had Class," *Lincoln Review* 2:2 (Summer 1981); Langston Hughes (Eugene Kraft, "Langston Hughes, Fictional Interracial Friendships, and Anger," *Lincoln Review* 10:4 (Fall 1991–Winter 1992); and other writers and cultural figures.

60. Bill Kaufman, "Zora Neale Hurston and Clarence Thomas," *Lincoln Review* 10: 4 (Fall 1991–Winter 1992): 11–15. Hurston is also mentioned with great approval for her stance against *Brown* in "The Issue Is Economics, Not Who Likes You: The Damage of *Brown v. Board of Education*," *Issues and Views* (Summer 1995): 1, 2, 4. For a broader perspective, see Andrew Delbanco, "The Political Incorrectness of Zora Neale Hurston," *Journal of Blacks in Higher Education* 18 (Winter 1997–1998): 103–107.

61. Mary Helen Washington, "Zora Neale Hurston: A Woman Half in Shadows," in Alice Walker, ed., *I Love Myself When I Am Laughing . . . and Then Again When I Am Looking Mean and Impressive: A Zora Neale Hurston Reader* (New York: Feminist Press, 1979), 22. See also Robert Hemenway, *Zora Neale Hurston: A Literary Biography* (Urbana: University of Illinois Press, 1977), chapter 12.

62. Zora Neale Hurston, "How It Feels," reprinted in Walker, ed., *I Love Myself*, pp. 152–155. To substantiate his claim that Hurston favored limited government, Kaufman also draws on Hurston's criticism of the *Brown* desegregation decision, which she felt reinforced the idea of black inferiority. Hemenway, *Zora Neale Hurston*, discusses Hurston's letter to the *Orlando Sentinel* (August 11, 1955) about *Brown* on pages 336–337.

63. Hurston, "Mourner's Bench, Communist Line: Why the Negro Won't Buy Communism," *American Legion Magazine* 50 (June 1951): 14–15, 55–60. Some of Hurston's criticisms of the CP appear to mirror her critique of the *Brown* decision, but her anticommunism went beyond the CP's "insulting" perspective on blacks and encompassed the idea that communists were an internal threat to the country. In "A Negro Voter Sizes Up Taft," *Saturday Evening Post*, December 8, 1951, she speculates that had Taft been in Congress during the New Deal era, the presence of communists and their sympathizers would have been rooted out that much earlier.

64. For a more detailed discussion of the connections between the Lincoln Institute and the World Anti-Communist League, see Deborah Toler, "Black Conservatives," in Chip Berlet, *Eyes Right!* (Boston: South End Press, 1995), 296–298. As Toler points out, during the 1980s black conservatives tended to focus their anticommunism in foreign policy toward African nations, especially Mozambique and South Africa. Also John S. Saloma, *Ominous Politics: The New Conservative Labyrinth* (New York: Hill & Wang, 1984), chapter 12, "Black Republicans."

65. Ralph de Toledano, "The Poet Who Loved His People," *Lincoln Review* 3:2 (Fall 1982): 17. Toledano was the associate editor of *The New Leader*, an anticommunist weekly, in the 1940s and handled McKay's copy when he submitted essays.

66. McKay did express very positive views of Booker T. Washington and Tuskegee, which he called "perhaps the greatest all-Negro institution in the world." See "For Group Survival," (1937), reprinted in Wayne F. Cooper, ed., *The Passion of Claude McKay* (New York: Schocken, 1973), 234–239. McKay was also generally supportive of Garvey and the UNIA. See for example "Garvey as a Negro Moses" (1922), reprinted in Cooper, *The Passion of Claude McKay*, 65–69.

67. Toledano, "The Poet Who Loved His People," 21. The quotation is taken from a letter from McKay to Max Eastman, October 16, 1944. A similar expression of faith and politics appears in another letter to Eastman, dated September 16, 1946, in which McKay writes: "I joined the Catholic church because structurally, traditionally and fundamentally it is the foe of Communism," and, tellingly, he concludes: "and please remember that there is a *formidable left wing* within the Catholic church because it can accommodate all, even you" (italics mine). Both letters in Cooper, *Passion of Claude McKay*. Toledano chooses to ignore McKay's expressions of fidelity to the Catholic Left.

68. See for example John Ehrman, *The Rise of Neoconservatism: Intellectuals and Foreign Affairs, 1945–1994* (New Haven: Yale University Press, 1995).

69. Glenn Loury's "Liberal Racism," *One by One from the Inside Out*, 225–235, is a nice representation of this view.

70. For details on Schuyler's life and conversion to conservative politics, see his autobiography, *Black and Conservative* (New York: Arlington House, 1966); William Ingersoll, "Reminiscences of George S. Schuyler," Oral History Research Office, Columbia University, 1962; his obituaries in the *National Review* (September 30,

1977) and the *New York Times* (September 7, 1977); and Harry McKinley Williams, Jr., "When Black Is Right: The Life and Writings of George S. Schuyler," Ph.D. diss., Brown University, 1988.

71. Conti and Stetson, *Challenging the Civil Rights Establishment*, 85. The mention is made in relation to Schuyler's rebuking the CP in his autobiography and incurring the "wrath" of the party in return.

72. Schuyler's personal and political journey from "Left" to "Right" does seem similar to the ones made by many contemporary neoconservatives, although he is never mentioned in studies of them. See, for example, Alan Wald, *The New York Intellectuals: The Rise and Decline of the Anti-Stalinist Left from the 1930s to the 1980s* (Chapel Hill: University of North Carolina, 1987), especially chapter 11, "The Bitter Fruits of Anticommunism"; and Peter Steinfels, *The Neoconservatives: The Men Who Are Changing America's Politics* (New York: Touchstone, 1979).

73. Schuyler, *Black and Conservative*, 341.

74. Jackson quoted in Taylor Branch, *Parting the Waters: America in the King Years, 1954–63* (New York: Simon & Schuster, 1988), 373.

75. King, "Letter from a Birmingham City Jail" (1963), reprinted in James Melvin Washington, ed., *A Testament of Hope: The Essential Writings of Martin Luther King, Jr.* (San Francisco: Harper & Row, 1986), 302.

76. On King's use of the jeremiad form see David Howard-Pitney, *The Afro-American Jeremiad*, chapter 6, as well as Robert Michael Franklin, *Liberating Visions: Human Fulfillment and Social Justice in African American Thought* (Minneapolis: Fortress Press, 1990), chapter 4.

77. The ACRI is the newest addition to the growing number of conservative "civil rights" advocacy groups. It was founded, incidentally, on the anniversary of King's birth, and King is constantly appealed to. For instance, ACRI News Release, "Connerly Commemorates Anniversary of 'I Have a Dream'" (September 1, 1998). Also, Connerly, *Creating Equal: My Fight against Race Preferences* (San Francisco: Encounter Books, 2000).

78. Connerly quoted in Barry Bearak, "Questions of Race Run Deep for Foe of Preferences," *New York Times*, July 27, 1997.

79. The "wages of whiteness" was a term originally used by W. E. B. Du Bois in his book *Black Reconstruction* (1935) and has been applied to broad stretches of American history and working-class culture by David Roediger, *The Wages of Whiteness: Race and the Making of the American Working Class* (London: Verso Press, 1991), and by Toni Morrison, *Playing in the Dark: Whiteness and the American Literary Imagination* (New York: Vintage, 1993).

80. Quoted in "A King Convert," Editorial, *Augusta Business Chronicle*, October 5, 1998.

81. King, "Keynote Address to the National Conference for New Politics" (August 31, 1967), quoted in Franklin, *Liberating Visions*, 127. Because conservatives and others have presented such a distorted version of King's political and social

philosophy, Michael Eric Dyson has recently called for a ten-year moratorium on the "I Have A Dream" speech so that King's other work might be granted the exposure it deserves. Dyson, *I Might Not Get There with You: The True Martin L. King, Jr.* (New York: Free Press, 2000).

82. This line appeared in a speech given on December 24, 1967. Quoted in James H. Cone, *Martin & Malcolm & America: A Dream or a Nightmare* (Maryknoll, N.Y.: Orbis Books, 1991), 213.

83. Wright, quoted in D'Souza, *End of Racism*, 167.

84. D'Souza, *End of Racism*, 199. But, as Robert Michael Franklin attempts to demonstrate by looking at King's pastoral writing in advice columns, this reading of King's ministry ignores his dedication to personal outreach and self-improvement. Moreover, it fails to acknowledge the integrated nature of King's ideas and practices as a political leader and a minister interested not only in securing equal rights but in uplifting the race as well. Franklin, *Liberating Visions*, chapter 4.

85. See, for example, Martin Kilson, "Anatomy of Black Conservatism," *Transition* 59 (1994): 4–19; and Robin D. G. Kelley, *Yo' Mama's Disfunktional! Fighting the Culture Wars in Urban America* (Boston: Beacon Press, 1997), especially chapter 3.

86. For a fascinating exchange on these issues see George Lipsitz, "The Possessive Investment in Whiteness: Racialized Social Democracy and the 'White' Problem in American Studies"; Walter Williams's response, "A Tragic Vision of the Black Problem"; and Lipsitz's reply to Williams, "Toxic Racism," all in *American Quarterly* 47:3 (September 1995). The best primer on the work of Crenshaw, Bell, and others is Kimberle Crenshaw et al., eds. *Critical Race Theory: The Key Writings That Formed the Movement* (New York: Free Press, 1995).

87. Cheryl Harris, "Whiteness as Property," *Harvard Law Review* 106:8 (June 1993): 1768.

88. See also Michael Omi and Howard Winart, *Racial Formation in the United States* (New York: Routlege, 1994).

89. Kelley, *Yo' Mama's Disfunktional!* 81.

90. Manning Marable, *Black Liberation in Conservative America* (Boston: South End Press, 1997), 12. Overall, the book is representative of the types of ideas and strategies being developed by leftists to meet the challenges posed not only by black conservatives but also by the conservative movement in general.

NOTES TO CHAPTER 2

1. Thomas Sowell, *Civil Rights: Rhetoric or Reality?* (New York: Quill, 1984), 37.

2. Daniel P. Moynihan, *The Negro Family: A Case for National Action* (Washington, D.C.: Office of Planning and Research, U.S. Department of Labor, 1965), 2–3.

3. Nathan Glazer, *Affirmative Discrimination: Ethnic Inequality and Public Policy* (New York: Basic Books, 1975).

4. Variants of this argument were developed in texts such as Irving Kristol, *Two*

Cheers for Capitalism (New York: Mentor Books, 1978); and George Gilder, *Wealth and Poverty* (New York: Basic Books, 1981). The idea of a "culture of poverty" was first presented by Oscar Lewis in his *Five Families* (New York: Basic Books, 1959), *The Children of Sanchez* (New York: Random House, 1961), and *La Vida* (New York: Random House, 1966). For a good overview of this literature and its political implications, see Stephen Steinberg, *Turning Back: The Retreat from Racial Justice in American Thought and Policy* (Boston: Beacon Press, 1995).

5. Daniel P. Moynihan, "The Politics of Stability," *New Leader* (October 9, 1967), 7.

6. Patrick Buchanan, *Right from the Beginning* (Boston: Little, Brown, 1988), 306.

7. Clint Bolick, *In Whose Name? The Civil Rights Establishment Today* (Washington, D.C.: Capital Research Center, 1988), 7–8.

8. Dinesh D'Souza, *The End of Racism* (New York: Free Press, 1995), 235.

9. The fact that "Eastern" was in some circles a code word for "Jewish" should not be overlooked.

10. Sidney Blumenthal, *The Rise of the Counter-Establishment: From Conservative Ideology to Political Power* (New York: Harper & Row, 1988).

11. M. Stanton Evans, *The Liberal Establishment* (New York: Devin-Adair, 1965), 18. See also William F. Buckley, Jr., *Up from Liberalism* (New Rochelle: Arlington House, 1968); and Jeffrey Hart, *The American Dissent: A Decade of Modern Conservatism* (Garden City, N.Y.: Doubleday, 1966), a survey of the views of contributors to the *National Review* in the 1950s and 1960s.

12. Buckley, *Up from Liberalism*, xv.

13. Tom Kahn, "The Problems of the New Left," *Commentary* 42:1 (July 1966): 30–38; Nathan Glazer, "The New Left and Its Limits," *Commentary* 46:1 (July 1968): 31–39; Diana Trilling, "On the Steps of Low Library: Liberalism and the Revolution," *Commentary* 46:5 (November 1968): 29–55; Bayard Rustin, "'Black Power' and Coalition Politics," *Commentary* 42:3 (September 1966): 35–40. For a fuller discussion of *Commentary*'s transformation and the resulting tensions it created, see Gary Dorrien, *The Neoconservative Mind: Politics, Culture, and the War of Ideology* (Philadelphia: Temple University Press, 1993), 162–168; Mark Gerson, *The Neoconservative Vision: From the Cold War to the Culture Wars* (Lanham, Md.: Madison Books, 1996), chapter 3.

14. "Come On In, The Water's Fine," Editorial, *National Review*, March 9, 1971. See also Louis Harap, "*Commentary* Moves to the Right," *Jewish Currents* 25:11 (December 1971).

15. Podhoretz quoted in Dorrien, *The Neoconservative Mind*, 165.

16. Dorrien, *The Neoconservative Mind*, 2–6, 13–18; Michael Harrington, *Toward a Democratic Left: A Radical Program for a New Majority* (New York: Macmillan, 1968); Michael Harrington, "The New Class and the Left," in B. Bruce-Briggs, ed., *The New Class?* (New Brunswick, N.J.: Transaction Books, 1979). Christopher Lasch summarizes the "New Class" debate in his book *The True and Only Heaven: Progress and Its Critics* (New York: Norton, 1991), 509–529.

17. Glenn Loury, *One by One from the Inside Out* (New York: Free Press, 1995).

18. Richard M. Nixon, "Inaugural Address," January 20, 1969, *Inaugural Addresses of the Presidents of the United States* (Washington, D.C.: GPO, 1969), 277.

19. For a nice discussion of this phenomenon see David Farber, "The Silent Majority and Talk about Revolution," in Farber, ed., *The Sixties: From Memory to History* (Chapel Hill: University of North Carolina Press, 1994): 291–316.

20. Robert Woodson, "Editorial," *Washington Times*, August 14, 1991.

21. Robert Woodson, "Saving the Poor from the Saviors," *Destiny* (June 1991), 35. See also Robert Woodson, *On the Road to Economic Freedom* (Washington, D.C.: Regnery-Gateway, 1987). Similar views have been expressed by Elizabeth Wright, editor of the black conservative newsletter *Issues and Views*, and by the economist Walter Williams. See for example Wright, "Cashing in on the 'Black Problem': Race and Poverty as an Industry," *Issues and Views* (Fall 1989): 9–13; and Williams, *The State against Blacks* (New York: McGraw-Hill, 1982).

22. Biographical information on Woodson can be found in Joseph Conti and Brad Stetson, *Challenging the Civil Rights Establishment: Profiles of a New Black Vanguard* (Westport, Conn.: Praeger, 1993), especially chapter 4.

23. Murray Friedman, "The New Black Intellectuals," *Commentary* 69:3 (June 1980): 46.

24. C. Mason Weaver, *It's Okay to Leave the Plantation* (Bonsell, Calif.: Reeder, 1996), i.

25. Ibid., 65.

26. Ezola Foster, *What's Right for All Americans: A Fearless Los Angeles Schoolteacher Challenges the Black Political Establishment* (Waco, Tex.: WRS, 1995).

27. Doggett quoted in Elinor Burkett, *The Right Woman: A Journey through the Heart of Conservative America* (New York: Scribner, 1998), 66–67.

28. Star Parker, *Pimps, Whores and Welfare Brats* (New York: Simon & Schuster, 1997). Similar views, especially on education, have been expressed by Foster, *What's Right for All Americans*. Foster characterizes the CRE as "socialist" and insists that promoting "family values does not mean building day-care centers and passing family leave laws. Family values demand love and marriage before baby and carriage" (12).

29. Linda Chavez, *Out of the Barrio: Toward a New Politics of Hispanic Assimilation* (New York: Basic Books, 1991), 4–5.

30. On the far-reaching implications of this decision see Guadalupe San Miguel, Jr., *"Let All of Them Take Heed": Mexican Americans and the Campaign for Educational Equality in Texas, 1910–1981* (Austin: University of Texas Press, 1987), 177–181.

31. Chavez, *Out of the Barrio*, 4.

32. Ibid., 77.

33. Thomas Sowell, *Ethnic America* (New York: Basic Books, 1981), 268.

34. Rodriguez, quoted in Robert Bryce, "Political Tug of War," *Hispanic Maga-*

zine (August 1995); online version: www.hispanicmagazine.com; copy in author's possession.

35. Chavez, *Out of the Barrio*, 38. See also "The End of Bilingual Education," *Weekly Standard*, August 11, 1997; Scott Baldauf, "GOP Increasingly Speaks the Language of Hispanics," *Christian Science Monitor*, February 19, 1998; and Dan Walters, "Bilingual Poll Changes Tenor," *Sacramento Bee*, October 16, 1997, which reports on a *Los Angeles Times* poll that found that 84 percent of Latino voters endorse the dismantling of bilingual education programs.

36. Hayakawa, the son of Japanese immigrants who settled in Canada, generated the English-only campaign with a 1982 bill to make English the official language of the United States. Although subcommittees of the Senate and House Judiciary Committees held hearings on the measure to amend the Constitution, it failed to pass. The ensuing movement, however, merely shifted its focus to the state level, where it has enjoyed more success. Richard Delgado and Jean Stefancic, *No Mercy: How Conservative Think Tanks and Foundations Changed America's Social Agenda* (Philadelphia: Temple University Press, 1996), chapter 1.

37. Yzaguirre quoted in James Crawford, *Hold Your Tongue: Bilingualism and the Politics of "English Only"* (Reading, Mass.: Addison-Wesley, 1992), 148.

38. John Tanton, WITAN IV Memo, October 10, 1986, quoted in Crawford, *Hold Your Tongue*, 151. Copies of the memo are also available from The People for a United Way. See also Delgado and Stefancic, *No Mercy*, chapter 1.

39. Linda Chavez, "Opening a Window of Opportunity," *Jewish World Review*, December 17, 1997; online version at www.jewishworldreview.com; copy in author's possession. Also, Chavez's "The End of Bilingual Education" on the ballot initiative in California (Proposition 227) to end bilingual education in the state's public schools. Chavez's advocacy organization, Center for Equal Opportunity, was involved in the campaign for Prop. 227, titled "English for Children." In a poll, the Center found that 81 percent of Hispanic parents supported the effort.

40. Arthur Hu, "Conservative Asian American Voters," *Asian Week*, January 3, 1992; Patrick Anderson, "Ups, Downs on Left, Right for San Francisco Asians in Elections," *Asian Week*, November 18, 1994.

41. Richard Rodriguez, *Hunger of Memory: The Education of Richard Rodriguez* (New York: Bantam Books, 1982), 26–27.

42. Richard Rodriguez, *Days of Obligation: An Argument with My Mexican Father* (New York: Penguin, 1992), 36.

43. Norah Vincent, "Beyond Lesbian," in Bruce Bawer, ed., *Beyond Queer: Challenging Gay Left Orthodoxy* (New York: Free Press, 1996), 185.

44. Bruce Bawer, *A Place at the Table: The Gay Individual in American Society* (New York: Touchstone, 1993), 147–148. Apparently, Bawer is attempting to create something of a gay conservative consciousness, linking members of the Log Cabin Republicans and other political commentators. See for example his edited volume, *Beyond Queer*.

45. "About LCR: Who We Are," Log Cabin Republican Home Page, www.lcr.org/about; copy in author's possession.

46. Dorr Legg, "I Am Glad I Am a Homosexual," *One,* quoted in Richard Tafel, *Party Crasher: A Gay Republican Challenges Politics as Usual* (New York: Simon & Schuster, 1999), 51.

47. Mel White, *Stranger at the Gate: To Be Gay and Christian in America* (New York: Simon & Schuster, 1994); Tafel, *Party Crasher;* Bruce Bawer, "Lecture at St. John's Cathedral," in Bawer, ed., *Beyond Queer,* 226–248; and Andrew Sullivan, *Virtually Normal: An Argument About Homosexuality* (New York: Knopf, 1995).

48. Jonathan Rauch, "Beyond Oppression," *New Republic,* May 10, 1993. Reprinted in Bawer, ed., *Beyond Queer,* 125–126.

49. Rebecca E. Klatch, *Women of the New Right* (Philadelphia: Temple University Press, 1987), 6. Klatch's schema does not account for the existence of conservative women who are also lesbians, however. In my research I have not encountered a large number of lesbian conservatives who have published materials; the exceptions are Norah Vincent and Carolyn Lochhead, the only women authors included in Bawer, ed., *Beyond Queer.*

50. Burkett, *The Right Women,* 211.

51. Sylvia Ann Hewlett, *A Lesser Life: The Myth of Women's Liberation in America* (New York: William Morrow, 1986), 208, 216.

52. Burkett, *The Right Women,* 162–163; Megan Rosenfeld, "Not NOW, Dear: The Conservative Alternative of Concerned Women for America," *Washington Post,* September 26, 1992.

53. Grace Paine Terzian quoted in Joyce Price, "No 'Angry Agenda,' No Feminists at New Women's Quarterly," *Washington Times,* September 13, 1995. The article profiles the Independent Women's Forum, one of the newest conservative women's organizations, and its new quarterly, *Women's Quarterly.*

54. Megan Rosenfeld, "Feminist Fatales," *Washington Post,* March 26, 1994.

55. Eliza Newlin Carney, "A New Breed of 'Feminists,'" *National Journal,* March 26, 1994, 728. Not all conservative women reject the label "feminism." See, for example, Katherine Kersten, "What Do Women Want? A Conservative Feminist Manifesto," *Policy Review* 53 (Spring 1991): 4–15; also Judith Stacey, "The New Conservative Feminism," *Feminist Studies* 9:3 (Fall 1983): 559–583.

56. Thanks to Barbara Spindel for suggesting the connections between Thomas's defense and the IWF in a wonderful paper done in my graduate seminar on conservatism, women, and gender at the University of Minnesota.

57. Bruce Bawer, "Notes on Stonewall," in Bawer, ed., *Beyond Queer,* 5.

58. On the history of Mattachine, see John D'Emilio, *Sexual Politics, Sexual Communities: The Making of a Homosexual Minority in the United States, 1940–1970* (Chicago: University of Chicago Press, 1983), chapter 4. See also Harry Hay, *Radically Gay: Gay Liberation in the Words of Its Founder,* ed. Will Roscoe (Boston: Beacon Press, 1996).

59. Mattachine documents and statements quoted in Urvashi Vaid, *Virtual Equality: The Mainstreaming of Gay and Lesbian Liberation* (New York: Anchor, 1995), 53. On Mattachine's adoption of assimilation, see also Jonathan Katz, *Gay American History: Lesbians and Gay Men in the U.S.A.* (New York: Avon, 1976), 627–631.

60. Carl Wittman, "Refugees from Amerika," *San Francisco Free Press*, December 22–January 7, 1970.

61. Chris Bull and John Gallagher, *Perfect Enemies: The Religious Right, the Gay Movement and the Politics of the 1990s* (New York: Crown, 1996), 16–17.

62. Sullivan quoted in Barbara Smith, "Blacks and Gays: Healing the Great Divide," in Chip Berlet, ed., *Eyes Right! Challenging the Right Wing Backlash* (Boston: South End Press, 1995), 274.

63. This argument has been most forcefully developed by Urvashi Vaid in her *Virtual Equality*, especially chapter 8.

64. For a fascinating insider's perspective on Reagan's use of American mythology see Peggy Noonan, *What I Saw at the Revolution: A Political Life in the Reagan Era* (New York: Random House, 1990). Noonan was Reagan's chief speech writer.

65. Henry Bonilla, "CAMBIO! The Rising Tide of Republican Hispanic Voters," *Rising Tide* (May–June 1994).

66. David Gutierrez, *Walls and Mirrors: Mexican Americans, Mexican Immigrants and the Politics of Ethnicity* (Berkeley: University of California Press, 1995), 76.

67. Neil Foley, "Becoming Hispanic: Mexican Americans and the Faustian Pact with Whiteness," *Reflexiones* (1997): 53–54.

68. Foley, "Becoming Hispanic," 61. The quotation is from Gary A. Greenfield and Don B. Kates, Jr., "Mexican Americans, Racial Discrimination and the Civil Rights Act of 1866," *California Law Review* 63 (January 1975): 700.

69. The conference was held in Washington, D.C., October 17–18, 1987. Glazer, Podhoretz, and Kristol, along with Martin Perez, Hilton Kramer, and William Philips, participated on the panel "Second Thoughts: A Generational Perspective." Conference papers and presentations were subsequently published as Collier and Horowitz, eds. *Second Thoughts: Former Radicals Look Back at the Sixties* (Lanham, Md.: Madison Books, 1989).

70. The second conference took place, again in Washington, D.C., in the spring of 1990. Its proceedings have been published as Peter Collier and David Horowitz, eds. *Second Thoughts about Race in America* (Lanham, Md.: Madison Books, 1991).

71. Stanley Crouch, "Role Models," in Collier and Horowitz, eds., *Second Thoughts about Race*, 54. See also his *Notes of a Hanging Judge: Essays and Reviews, 1979–1989* (New York: Oxford University Press, 1990), and, more recent, *The All-American Skin Game, or the Decoy of Race* (New York: Pantheon, 1995).

72. Steele, *The Content of Our Character*, 65, and "The Recoloring of Campus Life," in Collier and Horowitz, eds., *Second Thoughts about Race*, 83–96.

73. Walter Williams, "After Civil Rights," in Collier and Horowitz, eds., *Second Thoughts about Race*, 30.

74. Julius Lester, "What Ever Happened to the Civil Rights Movement," in Collier and Horowitz, eds., *Second Thoughts about Race*, 9.

75. Jane Mansbridge, *Why We Lost the ERA* (Chicago: University of Chicago Press, 1986).

76. Kersten, "What Do Women Want? A Conservative Feminist Manifesto," 5.

77. Fuller quoted in Kersten, "What Do Women Want?" 7.

78. Ibid., 14.

79. Roiphe, *The Morning After: Sex, Fear, and Feminism* (Boston: Little, Brown, 1993), 5.

80. Leedan quoted in Paul M. Barrett, "A New Wave of Counterfeminists Is Providing Conservatism with a Sophisticated Female Face," *Wall Street Journal*, October 13, 1995; Laura Ingraham, "Enter, Women," *New York Times*, April 16, 1995.

81. See for example Bawer, *A Place at the Table*, especially chapter 3, which confronts queer studies; Paul Varnell, "The Limits of Gay Identity," *Windy City Times*, August 31, 1995; Christina Hoff Sommers, *Who Stole Feminism? How Women Have Betrayed Women* (New York: Touchstone 1994); and Crouch, *The All-American Skin Game*.

82. What became known as the "southern strategy" was articulated by Kevin Phillips in his *The Emerging Republican Majority* (Garden City, N.Y.: Anchor, 1970). In this book, written after the 1968 election season, Phillips argues: "The Democratic Party fell victim to the ideological impetus of a liberalism which had carried it beyond programs taxing the few for the benefit of the many (the New Deal) to programs taxing the many on behalf of the few (the Good Society)" (37). Phillips suggested that the Republican Party could establish a majority by bypassing the traditional base of the Democratic Party—big labor, northern urban centers, and minorities—and appealing to the frustrations of the white working class, to whites in the Sunbelt states and to the older Democratic base in the South. The success of this strategy is detailed in Thomas Byrne Edsall with Mary D. Edsall, *Chain Reaction: The Impact of Race, Rights and Taxes on American Politics* (New York: Norton, 1991).

83. Allan Bloom, *The Closing of the American Mind* (New York: Simon & Schuster, 1987); Roger Kimbal, *Tenured Radicals: How Politics Has Corrupted Higher Education* (New York: Harper & Row, 1990); and Dinesh D'Souza, *Illiberal Education: The Politics of Race and Sex on Campus* (New York: Free Press, 1991), are the best representatives of this argument.

84. NAS, "The Way to Reduce Campus Tensions," in Patricia Aufderheide, ed., *Beyond PC: Towards a Politics of Understanding* (St. Paul, Minn.: Graywolf Press, 1992), 7–10.

85. Stefancic and Delgado, *No Mercy*, chapter 7. London quoted on page 125.

86. Manning Marable, "Along the Color Line: Why Conservatives Fear Multiculturalism," *Collegian* (University of Massachusetts at Amherst), November 10, 1993, 11.

87. Dinesh D'Souza, *The End of Racism: Principles for a Multiracial Society* (New York: Free Press, 1995), 556.

88. Ibid., 499.

89. The AEI Project on Mediating Structures was begun in 1975. Its initial conclusions were published two years later as *To Empower People: The Role of Mediating Structures* (Washington, D.C.: AEI, 1977).

90. Peter Berger, "Ideologies, Myths and Moralities," in Irving Kristol and Paul Weaver, eds., *The Americans: 1976* (Lexington, Ky.: Lexington Books, 1976), 346.

91. On the transitions in Berger's perspective of the value of capitalism see Dorrien, *The Neoconservative Mind*, chapter 6.

92. For Woodson's adoption of the idea of mediating structures, see Conti and Stetson, *Challenging the Civil Rights Establishment*, 168–174.

93. See for example Bill E. Lawson, ed., *The Underclass Question* (Philadelphia: Temple University Press, 1992); Robin D. G. Kelley, *Yo Mama's Disfunktional! Fighting the Culture Wars in Urban America* (Boston: Beacon Press, 1997); and Stephen Steinberg, *Turning Back: The Retreat from Racial Justice in American Thought* (Boston: Beacon, 1995), especially Part II.

94. Dorrien, *The Neoconservative Mind*, 383.

95. Cheryl Harris, "Whiteness as Property," *Harvard Law Review* 106:8 (June 1993), 1788. Emphasis in original.

96. Nathan Glazer, "In Defense of Preference," *New Republic*, April 6, 1998, 24.

97. Part of the problem with the debates on affirmative action has been the inattention to the point of exit (what graduates go on to do) as opposed to the point of entry. In this regard, William G. Bowen and Derek Curtis Bok's *The Shape of the River: Long-Term Consequences of Considering Race in College and University Admissions* (Princeton: Princeton University Press, 1998), is a welcome addition.

98. Glenn Loury, "Conservatives Isolate Black Intellectuals," *New York Times*, op-ed page, November 30, 1997.

99. Michael Novak, *The Rise of the Unmeltable Ethnic: Politics and Culture in the Seventies* (New York: Macmillan, 1973), 74.

100. Charles A. Taylor, "The Politics of Recognition," in Amy Gutman, ed., *Multiculturalism* (Princeton: Princeton University Press, 1994), 43.

101. K. Anthony Appiah, "Identity, Authenticity, Survival: Multicultural Societies and Social Reproduction," in Gutman, ed., *Multiculturalism*, 153.

NOTES TO CHAPTER 3

1. Christine Stansell, "White Feminists and Black Realities: The Politics of Authenticity," in Toni Morrison, ed., *Race-ing Justice, En-gender-ing Power: Essays on Anita Hill, Clarence Thomas, and the Construction of Social Reality* (New York: Pantheon, 1992), 258.

2. Henry Louis Gates, "Introduction: On Bearing Witness," in Henry Louis

Gates, ed., *Bearing Witness: Selections from African American Autobiography in the Twentieth Century* (New York: Pantheon, 1991), 7.

3. See, for example, Arnold Krupat, *For Those Who Come After: A Study of Native American Autobiography* (Berkeley: University of California Press, 1985); Sidonie Smith, *A Poetics of Women's Autobiography: Marginality and the Fictions of Self-Representation* (Bloomington: Indiana University Press, 1987); Joanne M. Braxton, *Black Women Writing Autobiography: A Tradition within a Tradition* (Philadelphia: Temple University Press, 1991); and Paul Robinson, *Gay Lives: Homosexual Autobiography from John Addington Symonds to Paul Monette* (Chicago: University of Chicago Press, 1999).

4. For example, Patricia J. Williams, *The Alchemy of Race and Rights: Diary of a Law Professor* (Cambridge, Mass.: Harvard University Press, 1991); and Richard Delgado, "When a Story Is Just a Story: Does Voice Really Matter?" *Virginia Law Review* 95 (1990): 2413–2415.

5. Stansell, "White Feminists and Black Realities," 261. The details of his sister's life were included in a *Los Angeles Times* article (July 5, 1991) by Karen Tumulty. On a related note, see Julianne Malveaux, "Why Are the Black Conservatives All Men?" *MS* (March–April 1991): 60–61.

6. George Schuyler, *Black and Conservative: The Autobiography of George S. Schuyler* (New Rochelle, N.Y.: Arlington House, 1966), 1. This is in fact the first line of the first chapter of the text.

7. Ibid., 2.

8. Richard Rodriguez, *Hunger of Memory: The Education of Richard Rodriguez, an Autobiography* (New York: Bantam Books, 1983), 1. My reading of Rodriguez's autobiography has been very influenced by Ramon A. Gutierrez's "Richard Rodriguez and the Political Language of White Men," in Renate von Bardeleben, ed., *Gender, Self, and Society* (Frankfurt, Germany: Peter Lang, 1993): 383–394.

9. Rodriguez, *Hunger of Memory*, 7.

10. Marvin Liebman, *Coming Out Conservative: An Autobiography* (San Francisco: Chronicle Books, 1992), 12–13.

11. Ibid., 13.

12. Bruce Bawer, *A Place at the Table: The Gay Individual in American Society* (New York: Touchstone, 1993), 13.

13. Zora Neale Hurston, "How It Feels to Be a Colored Me," reprinted in Alice Walker, ed., *I Love Myself When I Am Laughing . . . and Then Again When I Am Looking Mean and Impressive: A Zora Neale Hurston Reader* (New York: Feminist Press, 1979), 152–155.

14. Schuyler, *Black and Conservative*, 3–4.

15. Ibid., 10.

16. Booker T. Washington, *Up from Slavery* (1901; New York: Dover Press, 1995), 2–3.

17. Houston A. Baker, *Modernism and the Harlem Renaissance* (Chicago: University of Chicago Press, 1987), chapters 3 and 4.

18. Schuyler, *Black and Conservative*, 48.

19. Rodriguez, *Hunger of Memory*, 22.

20. Ibid., 46.

21. Ibid., 48.

22. Liebman, *Coming Out Conservative*, 25.

23. Ibid., 46.

24. Ibid., 87.

25. Schuyler, *Black and Conservative*, 28.

26. Rodriguez, *Hunger of Memory*, 147.

27. Stephen Carter, *Reflections of an Affirmative Action Baby* (New York: Basic Books, 1992), 12.

28. Rodriguez, *Hunger of Memory*, 151.

29. One of the most interesting books on the role of communism in the conversion to conservatism is John P. Diggs, *Up from Communism: Conservative Odysseys in American Intellectual Development* (New York: Harper & Row, 1975). Also Alan Wald, *New York Intellectuals: The Rise and Decline of the Anti-Stalinist Left from the 1930s to the 1960s* (Chapel Hill: University of North Carolina Press, 1987).

30. Michael W. Peplow's *George S. Schuyler* (Boston: Twayne, 1980) has a good overview of Schuyler's life and literary and journalistic writings during the 1930s and 1940s. See chapter 1.

31. Schuyler, *Black and Conservative*, 150.

32. George S. Schuyler, "The Negro-Art Hokum," *Nation* (June 26, 1926), reprinted in Gerald Early, ed., *Speech and Power: The African American Essay and Its Cultural Content from Polemics to Pulpit* (Hopewell, N.J.: Ecco Press, 1993), 85–87.

33. On this point Schuyler is vague, writing: "I joined the JBS sometime in the early 1960s." See also Hollie I. West, "A Black, Biting John Bircher," *Washington Post*, September 6, 1973.

34. Schuyler, *Black and Conservative*, 350.

35. Editorial, "George S. Schuyler, Iconoclast," *Crisis* 72 (October 1965): 484–485. The prevailing view of Schuyler was that he was an iconoclastic thinker, and the black historian John Henrick Clarke has had something of the final word on the subject. He wrote: "I used to tell people that George got up in the morning, waited to see which way the world was turning, then struck out in the opposite direction. He was a rebel who enjoyed playing the role" (Clarke quoted in Ishmael Reed, "Introduction," to George S. Schuyler, *Black No More* [1931; New York: Modern Library, 1999], vii.) While this may be in part accurate, it also tends to relegate Schuyler's political stances to mere role playing and contrariness. Hence, Schuyler's critique and his political conservatism are rendered safe and harmless. See also Carleton L. Lee's unfavorable review of *Black and Conservative* in the *Negro History Bulletin* 30 (June 1967): 22–23 and Ann Rayson, "George Schuyler, Paradox among 'Assimilationist' Writers," *Black American Literature Forum* 12 (1978): 102–106.

36. Schuyler to Loeb, May 5, 1969, quoted in Kathryn Talalay, *Composition in Black and White: The Life of Philippa Schuyler* (New York: Oxford University Press, 1995), 278. This book is a wonderful source for information on Schuyler's personal life during his career, and the life of his daughter Philippa is extraordinary in its own right. The product of an interracial marriage, she was used by the Schuylers as an example of the potential of such unions. By all accounts she was something of a genius and a musical prodigy. Driven by her parents to succeed, she did become a concert pianist. Yet she was haunted by her racial identity and spent years trying to deny her African heritage. At one point she begged her father not to publicly acknowledge that she was his daughter. The effects of this on Schuyler's political views remains an interesting point of speculation.

37. Liebman, *Coming Out Conservative*, 143.

38. In addition to *Coming Out Conservative*, see also Gregory L. Schneider, *Cadres for Conservatism: Young Americans for Freedom and the Rise of the Contemporary Right* (New York: New York University Press, 1999), chapters 2 and 3, as well as William Rusher, *The Rise of the Right* (New York: William Morrow, 1984).

39. Liebman, *Coming Out Conservative*, 154–156.

40. Ibid., 155.

41. Bawer, *A Place at the Table*, 75.

42. Ibid., 78.

43. Glenn Loury, *One by One from the Inside Out* (New York: Free Press, 1995), 7.

44. Ibid., 7.

45. Ibid., 3.

46. Ibid., 314.

47. "Hannah Arendt on Hannah Arendt," in Melvyn A. Hill, ed., *Hannah Arendt: The Recovery of the Public World* (New York: St. Martin's Press), 333.

48. Hannah Arendt, *The Human Condition* (Chicago: University of Chicago Press, 1973), 45.

49. Arendt, *On Revolution* (New York: Penguin Books, 1990), 60.

50. Ibid., 92.

51. Lisa Disch, *Hannah Arendt and the Limits of Philosophy* (Ithaca: Cornell University Press, 1994), especially chapter 1, "Storytelling and the Archimedean Ideal."

52. Hannah Arendt, Letter to Gershom Scholem, quoted in Richard J. Bernstein, *Hannah Arendt and the Jewish Question* (Cambridge, Mass.: MIT Press, 1996), 1.

53. Hannah Arendt, *Rahel Varnhagen: The Life of a Jewish Woman*, rev. ed., trans. Richard and Clara Winston (New York: Harcourt Brace Jovanovich, 1974), 224.

54. Hannah Arendt, *Essays on Understanding, 1930–1945* (New York: Brace, Harcourt, 1994), 11–12.

55. Hannah Arendt, quoted in Richard A. Bernstein, *Hannah Arendt and the Jewish Question* (Cambridge, Mass.: MIT Press, 1996), 2.

56. I will note but not speculate too much on why Parker's autobiography as well as Ezola Foster's polemic are both introduced by male conservatives—Limbaugh in

Parker's case and Walter Williams in Foster's. It does, however, recall the traditional practice of authenticating women's voices by having men legitimate them.

57. Star Parker, *Pimps, Whores, and Welfare Brats: From Welfare Cheat to Conservative Messenger, the Autobiography of Star Parker* (New York: Pocket Books, 1997), 4.

58. Ibid., 52.

59. Ibid., 54.

60. Ibid., 56.

61. Ibid., 37.

62. Ibid., 50.

63. Ibid., 119.

64. Ibid., 150.

65. On the implications of these ideas in the past see Paula Giddings, *When and Where I Enter: The Impact of Black Women on Race and Sex in America* (New York: Bantam Books, 1984), especially chapters 5 and 6.

66. Stuart Hall, "The Toad in the Garden: Thatcherism among the Theorists," in Cary Nelson and Lawrence Grossberg, eds., *Marxism and the Interpretation of Culture* (Urbana: University of Illinois Press, 1988), 44.

67. Toni Morrison, *Playing in the Dark: Whiteness and the Literary Imagination* (New York: Vintage, 1992), 64. See also her "On the Backs of Blacks," *Time* 142 (Fall 1993), 57.

68. Toni Morrison, "Introduction: Friday on the Potomac," in Morrison, ed., *Race-ing Justice*, xxix.

69. Bruce Robbins, "Introduction," in Bruce Robbins, ed., *The Phantom Public Sphere* (Minneapolis: University of Minnesota Press, 1993), vii–xxvi.

70. Liebman, *Coming Out Conservative*, 258.

NOTES TO CHAPTER 4

1. Kevin Phillips, *Post-Conservative America: People, Politics and Ideology in a Time of Crisis* (New York: Vintage, 1983), 30; Dan T. Carter, *From George Wallace to Newt Gingrich* (Baton Rouge: Louisiana State University Press, 1996); David Horowitz, *Beyond Left and Right* (Urbana: University of Illinois Press, 1997); and Mary G. Brennan, *Turning Right in the Sixties: The Conservative Capture of the GOP* (Chapel Hill: University of North Carolina Press, 1995).

2. Jerome L. Himmelstein, *To the Right: The Transformation of American Conservatism* (Berkeley: University of California Press, 1990), 89.

3. Liebman's open letter and Buckley's response both appeared in the *National Review* (July 9, 1990). Both are reproduced in Appendix A of Liebman's autobiography, *Coming Out Conservative* (San Francisco: Chronicle Books, 1992), 257–261.

4. A thorough study of the Communist Party's attitudes toward homosexuals has yet to be written. The Party was generally silent on the matter but did oust members, such as Harry Hay, who publicly proclaimed themselves to be gay. See

John D'Emilio, *Sexual Politics, Sexual Communities: The Making of a Homosexual Minority in the United States, 1940–1970* (Chicago: University of Chicago Press, 1983), 58–63; and Stuart Timmons, *The Trouble with Harry Hay: Founder of the Modern Gay Movement* (Boston: Alyson Publications, 1990).

5. Ralph Reed, Jr., "Casting a Wider Net: Religious Conservatives Move beyond Abortion and Homosexuality," *Policy Review* 65(Summer 1993), 24. Reed's positions also appeared to have been inspired by the call for greater ecumenism and a softening of the fire-and-brimstone approach to politics recommended in Thomas C. Atwood's "Through a Glass Darkly: Is the Christian Right Overconfident It Knows God's Will?" *Policy Review* 54 (Fall 1990): 44–52.

6. Steve Bruce, *Pay TV: Televangelism in America* (London: Routledge, 1990).

7. Steve Bruce, *The Rise and Fall of the New Christian Right* (Oxford: Clarendon Press, 1990), 86–89. Regionalism also played a dramatic role in the rise of evangelical movements in the 1970s and 1980s. The Moral Majority may have had chapters in all fifty states by 1986, but the earliest and strongest by far were in the South and Southwest. The classic text of fundamentalism remains George Marsden's *Fundamentalism and American Culture* (New York: Oxford University Press, 1980). On patterns of voting behavior, see also Lyman Kellstedt and Corwin Smidt, "Measuring Fundamentalism: An Analysis of Different Operational Strategies," and Lyman Kellstedt et al., "The Puzzle of Evangelical Protestantism: Core, Periphery and Political Behavior," both in John C. Green et al., eds., *Religion and the Culture Wars* (Lanham, Md.: Rowman, Littlefield, 1996).

8. Richard Hofstadter, *The Paranoid Style in American Politics and Other Essays* (New York: Vintage, 1967).

9. Seymour Martin Lipset, "The Sources of the Radical Right," in Daniel Bell, ed., *The Radical Right: The New American Right*, expanded and updated (New York: Anchor Books, 1964), 309.

10. Seymour Martin Lipset, *Revolution and Counter-Revolution* (London: Heinemann, 1969), 165.

11. Cornel West, "Religion and the Left," *Monthly Review* 36:3 (July–August 1984): 14. Status theory and the stress on irrationality have come under fire from other quarters as well. In *The Intellectuals and McCarthy* (Cambridge, Mass.: MIT Press, 1967), Michael Paul Rogin critiques the application of these ideas to followers of McCarthyism, and Steve Bruce takes on the assumption of irrationality within the Religious Right in his *Rise and Fall of the New Christian Right*. See also Charles L. Harper and Kevin Leicht, "Explaining the New Religious Right: Status Politics and Beyond," in David Bromley and Anson Shupe, eds., *New Christian Politics* (Macon: Mercer University Press, 1984), 101–112, which defines "status" more broadly and without the association with irrationality.

12. Garry Wills, *Under God: Religion and American Politics* (New York: Simon & Schuster, 1990), 17.

13. Falwell quoted in David Bollier, *Liberty and Justice for Some: Defending a Free*

Society from the Religious Right's Holy War on Democracy (Washington, D.C.: People for the American Way, 1982), 71. Falwell also discusses his former beliefs in his autobiography, *Strength for the Journey: An Autobiography* (New York: Simon & Schuster, 1987), chapter 11.

14. Paul Weyrich, "Building a Moral Majority," *Conservative Digest* 5 (August 1979): 18–19. Two of the best studies on the abortion debates as well as the prolife and prochoice movements and their participants are Kristin Luker's *Abortion and the Politics of Motherhood* (Berkeley: University of California Press, 1984) and Faye Ginsburg's *Contested Lives: The Abortion Debate in an American Community* (Berkeley: University of California Press, 1989). Also, Rosalind Pollack Petchesky, "Antiabortion, Antifeminism, and the Rise of the New Right," *Feminist Studies* 7:2 (Summer 1981): 213–215.

15. Wills, *Under God*, 19.

16. Bruce, *Rise and Fall of the New Christian Right*, 47–49; James D. Hunter, *Evangelicalism: The Coming Generation* (Chicago: University of Chicago, 1987); Stuart Rothenberg and Frank Newport, *The Evangelical Voter in American Politics* (Washington, D.C.: Free Congress Research and Education Fund, 1984).

17. Phyllis Schlafly, "ERA Means Unisex Society," *Conservative Digest* 4 (July 1978): 14–16; Carol Felsenthal, *The Sweetheart of the Silent Majority: The Biography of Phyllis Schlafly* (New York: Doubleday, 1981); Phyllis Schlafly, *The Positive Woman* (New Rochelle, N.Y.: Arlington House, 1977).

18. Beverly LaHaye, *The Spirit-Controlled Woman* (Eugene, Ore.: Harvest House, 1976), 71. In a similar vein see Connaught C. Marshner, *The New Traditional Women* (Washington, D.C.: Free Congress Research and Education Foundation, 1982), and Midge Decter, *The New Chastity and Other Arguments against Women's Liberation* (New York: Coward, McCann & Geoghegan, 1972). For a good overview of these ideas see Susan Faludi, *Backlash: The Undeclared War against American Women* (New York: Crown, 1981).

19. Jerry Falwell, *Listen, America!* (Garden City, N.Y.: Doubleday-Galilee, 1980), 151.

20. George Gilder, *Men and Marriage* (Gretna, La.: Pelican, 1986) and *Naked Nomads: Unmarried Men in America* (New York: Quadrangle/New York Times Press, 1974); Michael Levin, *Feminism and Freedom* (New Brunswick, N.J.: Transaction, 1987).

21. Andrea Dworkin, *Right Wing Women* (New York: Perigee, 1983), 21–23.

22. Pamela Johnston Conover and Virginia Gray, *Feminism and the New Right* (New York: Praeger, 1983); Ira E. Deutchman and Sandra Prince-Embury, "Political Ideology of Pro- and Anti-ERA Women," *Women and Politics* 2 (1982): 39–55; Rebecca Klatch, *Women of the New Right* (Philadelphia: Temple University Press, 1987). Building on this earlier work, a set of more recent studies has attempted to go inside the worlds of conservative women and antifeminists. See, for example, Christel J. Manning, *God Gave Us the Right: Conservative Catholic, Evangelical Protestant, and Orthodox*

Jewish Women Grapple with Feminism (New Brunswick, N.J.: Rutgers University Press, 1999); Elinor Burkett, *The Right Women* (New York: Scribner, 1998); and Linda Kintz, *Between Jesus and the Market: The Emotions That Matter in Right-Wing America* (Durham, N.C.: Duke University Press, 1997).

23. Janet K. Boles, *The Politics of the Equal Rights Amendment: Conflict and the Decision Process* (New York: Longman, 1979), 4.

24. Ibid., 27.

25. Quoted in Chris Bull and John Gallagher, *Perfect Enemies* (New York: Crown, 1996), 16.

26. Diane Ehrensaft and Ruth Milkman, "Sexuality and the State: The Defeat of the Briggs Initiative and Beyond," *Socialist Review* 9:3 (May–June 1979), 55–72.

27. Cliff John, "Anita Bryant's Starling Reversal," *Ladies' Home Journal* 97:12 (December 1980): 62–68.

28. James Davidson Hunter, *Evangelicalism: The Coming Generation* (Chicago: University of Chicago Press, 1987), 6–7.

29. The attack at the hands of the IRS also led Robert Billings to organize Christian School Action, one of the first religious-political groups within the emergent New Christian Right, in 1977. Peter Skerry, "Christian Schools versus the I.R.S.," *Public Interest* 61 (Fall 1980): 18–41; Bruce, *Rise and Fall of the New Christian Right*, 41–43; Robert Zwier, *Born-Again Politics: The New Christian Right in America* (Downers Grove, Ill.: InterVarsity Press, 1982), 25–26.

30. On Viguerie's efforts see Sidney Blumenthal, "Mail-Order Politics," *In These Times*, July 18–24, 1979, 12–13, as well as his *The Rise of the Counter-Establishment* (New York: Harper & Row, 1988). Also, Himmelstein, *To the Right*, chapter 4; and Alan Crawford, *Thunder on the Right* (New York: Pantheon, 1980), 42–77.

31. Sara Diamond, *Spiritual Warfare* (Boston: South End Press, 1989), 63–66.

32. Skerry, "Christian Schools versus the I.R.S," 31–33.

33. Lou Cannon, *President Reagan: The Role of a Lifetime* (New York: Simon & Schuster, 1991), 812–813. Marvin Liebman tells a particularly poignant story about Reagan's fears that his son, Ron, might be gay because he decided to pursue a career as a dancer. Liebman, *Coming Out Conservative*, 16–17.

34. Steven Bruce locates this moment as the fall of the Religious Right and argues, in fact, that it was doomed to fail; *Rise and Fall of the New Christian Right*, chapter 7. A more accurate portrayal, given the reorganization of the Religious Right in the early 1990s, suggests that the late 1980s presented more of a temporary setback. On the different phases of the Religious Right, see Justin Watson, *The Christian Coalition: Dreams of Restoration, Demands for Recognition* (New York: St. Martin's Press, 1997), 26–27, and Matthew C. Moen, "The Evolving Politics of the Christian Right," *PS: Political Science and Politics* 39 (September 1996): 461–464.

35. Joe Canason, "The Religious Right's Quiet Revival," *Nation* 254 (April 27, 1992), 554.

36. Dinesh D'Souza, "Jerry Falwell Is Reaching Millions and Drawing Fire," *Conservative Digest* (December 1986): 5–12.

37. On Robertson see David Edwin Harrell, *Pat Robertson: A Personal, Political, and Religious Portrait* (New York: Harper & Row, 1987); Alec Foege, *The Empire God Built: Inside Pat Robertson's Media Machine* (New York: Wiley, 1996); and Robert Boston, *The Most Dangerous Man in America? Pat Robertson and the Rise of the Christian Coalition* (Amherst, N.Y.: Prometheus Books, 1996).

38. Bob Sector, "Pat Robertson Shuns Taint of TV Ministries," *Los Angeles Times*, July 6, 1987.

39. Marlee Schwartz and Charles R. Babcock, "Anti-Christian Bashing," *Washington Post*, February 2, 1988.

40. Pat Robertson, "700 Club" (October 13, 1986). Quoted in Jim Castelli, *A Plea for Common Sense: Resolving the Clash between Religion and Politics* (San Francisco: Harper & Row, 1988), 142. All of chapter 6 of the book deals with the disjuncture between Robertson's statements to the national media and his views as expressed on the "700 Club" and to the religious press.

41. Russell Chandler, "Robertson Moves to Fill Christian Right Vacuum," *Los Angeles Times*, May 5, 1990.

42. Brooks quoted in Larry Lipman, "Jewish Vote Not Just for Democrats Anymore," *Washington Post*, September 9, 1996. In an op-ed piece, Frank Rich points to Reed's role in softening (and peddling) the views of the Christian Right: "Jews and the Post-Reed Religious Right," *New York Times*, January 14, 1998. Also, David Twersky, "Jewish Politics Group Seeks to 'Interface' between Congress, Jews," *Metro West Jewish Times*, June 12, 1995; Rick Hellman, "Jewish GOP," *Jewish Chronicle*, May 30, 1997.

43. Brooks quoted in Joseph A. D'Agostino, "Conservative Spotlight: National Jewish Coalition," *Human Events* (August 7, 1998). The NJC also typically maintains that the Republicans have a superior policy toward Israel. See, for example, Seth Gitell, "Gingrich, GOP See Gains in 1998 from Clinton's Squeeze of Israel," *Forward*, July 3, 1998.

44. Ralph Reed, Jr., *Politically Incorrect* (Dallas: Word Books, 1994), 219.

45. Gustav Niebuhr, "Christian Coalition Sees Recruiting Possibilities among Catholics," *New York Times*, October 7, 1995; Carolyn Curtis, "The Crucial Catholic Vote," *Washington Post*, September 2, 1996; Heidi Schlumpf, "How Catholic Is the Catholic Alliance?" *Christianity Today*, May 20, 1997; and Justin Watson, *The Christian Coalition*, 67–68.

46. John Persinos, "Has the Christian Coalition Taken Over the Republican Party?" *Campaigns and Elections* 15 (September 1994): 20–24.

47. Buchanan quoted in Dan T. Carter, *From George Wallace to Newt Gingrich*, 95.

48. Michael Rogin, *Ronald Reagan: The Movie* (Berkeley: University of California Press, 1987), xiii–xiv.

49. Reed quoted in Watson, *The Christian Coalition*, 65.

50. See also Thomas B. Edsall, "Gay Rights and the Christian Right," *Washington Post*, August 10, 1992.

51. Matthew Dorf, "GOP Jews Oppose Cutting Off Funds for Abortion Stance," *Jewish Chronicle*, January 15, 1998.

52. James Pinkerton, "A Conservative Argument for Gay Marriage," *Los Angeles Times*, op-ed page, June 3, 1993.

53. Steven Seidman, "Transfiguring Sexual Identity: AIDS and the Contemporary Construction of Homosexuality," *Social Text* 7:1–2 (Fall 1988), 188.

54. Sheldon quoted at http://ftp.qrd.org/qrd/religion/anti/TVC, posted November 1, 1994; copy in author's possession.

55. Quoted in Jean Hardisty, "Constructing Homophobia: Colorado's Right-Wing Attack on Homosexuals," in Chip Berlet, ed., *Eyes Right! Challenging the Right Wing Backlash* (Boston: South End Press, 1995), 87.

56. Norman Podhoretz, "The Culture of Appeasement," *Harper's* 255:1529 (October 1977), 29–31.

57. Elizabeth Wright, "In the Name of 'Civil Rights' Homosexuals Remake Society," *Issues and Views* (Spring 1996): 3–4.

58. Thomas B. Edsall, "Powell Proving Divisive among Conservatives," *Washington Post*, October 23, 1995.

59. Joseph E. Broadus, "Family Values vs. Homosexual Rights: Tradition Collides with an Elite Social Tide," in Stan Farnya et al., eds., *Black and Right* (Westport, Conn.: Praeger, 1997), 19.

60. Peter Kirsanow, "A Black Conservative Looks at Abortion," in Faryna, ed., *Black and Right*, 115–116.

61. Earl Jackson, "To Assure That the Republican Party Is Open and Accessible to All" (February 1999), online at www.nationalcenter.inter.net/P21NVJackson-CCC299; copy in author's possession.

62. John E. Young, "Christian Coalition Revamps Agenda to Reach Out to Inner Cities," *Washington Post*, April 24, 1997.

63. Kevin Phillips, *Post-Conservative America*, 55–57.

64. Robert Novak, *The Agony of the GOP 1964* (New York: Macmillan, 1965), 63–64.

65. Republican Mainstream Committee, "Our Action Agenda," online at www.mainstream.org; copy in author's possession.

66. Chris Roseburg, "Moderate Republicans Seek to Rip the Heart Out of the Party," *The Voice of Free Americans*, 1998; online version at www.acclaimedmedia .com/vofa/politics; copy in author's possession.

67. Rowland quoted in "Some Just Want to Focus on 2000," *Capital Hill Blue*, August 6, 1999, online journal at www.capitalhillblue.com; copy in author's possession.

68. Andrew Sullivan, *Virtually Normal: An Argument about Homosexuality* (New York: Knopf, 1995), 171. Emphasis in the original.

69. Ibid., 182.

70. Ibid., 137.

71. Paul Weyrich, "Open Letter to Conservatives" (February 16, 1999). A copy of this letter is available from the Free Congress Foundation web site at www.freecongress.org; copy in author's possession.

72. James Dobson, "Symposium," *Insight on the News*, March 29, 1999; Carmen Pate, "Symposium," *Insight on the News*, March 29, 1999.

73. The current thinking among Dobson, Thomas, and others, as well as interviews with Robertson, Falwell, and various leaders of the Religious Right, can be found in Thomas and Dobson, *Blinded by Might: Can the Religious Right Save America?* (Grand Rapids, Mich.: Zondervan, 1999). See also Ramesh Ponnuru's review of the book and the debate: "Public Judgement: Is It Time to Give Up on the American People?" *National Review*, March 22, 1999.

NOTES TO THE CONCLUSION

1. On earlier efforts by the party to attract blacks, see Hanes Walton, Jr., *Black Republicans: The Politics of the Black and Tan* (New York: Scarecrow Press, 1975); Pearl Robinson, "Whither the Future of Blacks in the Republican Party," *Political Science Quarterly* 97:2 (Summer 1982): 207–231, and Hanes Walton, Jr., "Defending the Indefensible: The African American Conservative Client Spokespersons of the Reagan-Bush Era," *Black Scholar* (Fall 1994): 46–50. For more details about Atwater's efforts, see Thomas Byrne Edsall with Mary D. Edsall, *Chain Reaction: The Impact of Race, Rights and Taxes on American Politics* (New York: Norton, 1991): 220–230.

2. Matthew Ress, "Black and Right," *New Republic*, September 30, 1991, 21.

3. Scott Shepard, "GOP Stretches Out Its Reach to Minorities," *Austin American Statesman*, July 22, 1998.

4. The position of many black conservatives toward the party is summarized in Alan Keyes, "My Race for the Senate," *Policy Review* (Spring 1989): 2–8. Along with a good deal of discontent about the unwillingness of black voters to support him, Keyes is also exercised over the Republican Party's failure to provide financial and moral backing.

5. Sam Fulwood III, "Black GOP Women Rip the Party in Letter," *Los Angeles Times*, April 24, 1998.

6. Quoted in Carla Marinacci, "At S.F. Meeting, Pro-Choice Women Lament Their Bitter Dilemma," *San Francisco Chronicle*, March 11, 2000.

7. Falwell quoted in Frank Rich, "Has Jerry Falwell Seen the Light?" *New York Times*, November 6, 1999; Waveney Ann Moore, "Falwell's Forum Called Positive Sign by Gays," *Seminole Times*, November 13, 1999; Deb Price, "Rev. White Becomes Gay Gandhi," *Detroit News*, December 6, 1999; Sally Macdonald, "Striving for Peace between Gays and the Christian Right," *Seattle Times*, January 15, 2000.

8. Tafel quoted in Katherine Q. Seelye, "Gay Voters Finding G.O.P. Newly Receptive to Support," *New York Times*, August 11, 1999. Throughout the 1999–2000

primary season, the LCR and other gay Republicans continued to press the front-runner, George W. Bush, as well as his challenger, John McCain, for a meeting. McCain did eventually meet with the group, although Bush refused to do so. As a result, the LCR backed McCain. Recently, the long-awaited meeting between Bush and the LCR did take place. What effect, if any, this will have on the general election in November 2000 is still unclear. Alison Mitchell, "Bush Talks to Gays and Calls It Beneficial," *New York Times*, April 13, 2000.

9. LCR, "GOP Gets 33% of Gay Vote in House Races," December 10, 1998, available at LCR web site, www.lcr.org; copy in author's possession. Also Richard Tafel, "Big Tent or Small Minds?" op-ed page, *Baltimore Sun*, June 21, 1998; and Seelye, "Gay Votes Finding G.O.P. Newly Receptive to Support."

10. Antonio Olivojoseph Trevino, "Foes Find Common Cause against Gay Rights Activism," *Los Angeles Times*, August 17, 1999.

11. Tony Perry, "Blood Thicker Than Politics for Fongs," *Los Angeles Times*, October 21, 1998; William Booth, "California Race Could Signal New Cohesion for Asian Voters," *Washington Post*, November 3, 1998; Joel Kotkin, "GOP Wiped Out in the Land of Reagan," *Wall Street Journal*, November 6, 1998; Lee Clifford, "Immigration, the Recession and the Nativist Temptation," *Asian Week*, October 2, 1992; Gregory Rodriguez, "Latino Clout Depends on GOP Remake," *Los Angeles Times*, November 15, 1998.

12. In "The End of the Rainbow: The Poverty of Racial Politics and the Future of Liberalism," *Mother Jones* 22 (September–October 1997), Michael Lind notes "the high number of blacks who supported Proposition 187" as well as polls have found that non-Hispanic blacks favored cuts in immigration "by a ratio of 11-to-1." Similarly, Marable notes the tensions between Latinos and African Americans over political power, affirmative action, and immigration policy in his *Black Liberation in Conservative America* (Boston: South End Press, 1997): 225–227.

13. Quoted in Rene Sanchez, "Both Parties Courting Latinos Vigorously," *Washington Post*, October 26, 1998.

14. Matt Fong, "APA Roundtable: The Case for George W. Bush," *Asian Week*, July 7, 1999. Fong hopes, of course, that Bush will be equally appealing to Asian-Americans.

15. David Segal, "D.C. Public Interest Law Firm Puts Affirmative Action on Trial," *Washington Post*, February 20, 1998; Kate Zernike, "Campus Affirmative Action Embattled; Handbooks Encourage Student Suits," *Boston Globe*, January 27, 1999; Ethan Bronner, "Conservatives Open Drive against Affirmative Action," *New York Times*, January 26, 1999. For an alternative view of efforts to end affirmative action see Robin M. Bennefield, "Running for Cover: Fear and Paranoia Surrounding Affirmative Action Lawsuits Unjustified, Experts Say," *Journal of Blacks in Higher Education* 16 (October 14, 1999): 22–24; and Warren Richey, "Ending Affirmative Action Proves Harder Than It Looks," *Christian Science Monitor*, March 10, 2000.

16. Julius Lester, "Missing the Point: A Dissent," *Los Angeles Times*, October 4, 1998.

17. For a good overview of these issues see Donald G. Nieman, *Promises to Keep: African Americans and the Constitutional Order, 1776 to the Present* (New York: Oxford University Press, 1991), and Derrick Bell, *Faces at the Bottom of the Well: The Permanence of Racism* (New York: Basic Books, 1992).

18. Glenn Loury, "Conservatives Isolate Black Intellectuals," *New York Times*, November 30, 1997.

19. Patterson, "The Paradoxes of Integration," *New Republic*, November 6, 1995, 24–27. He elaborates on these themes in *The Ordeal of Integration: Progress and Resentment in America's 'Racial' Crisis* (Washington, D.C.: Civitas Counterpoint, 1997).

20. Peter Brimelow, *Alien Nation: Common Sense about America's Immigration Disaster* (New York: Random House, 1996), 69–70. Brimelow also expresses anxiety about the future of his blonde, blue-eyed son. This is about as far from the vision of interracial unions depicted in *Guess Who's Coming to Dinner* as one can get.

Bibliography

Ansell, Amy Elizabeth. *New Right, New Racism: Race and Reaction in the United States and Britain* (New York: New York University Press, 1997).

Arendt, Hannah. *The Human Condition* (Chicago: University of Chicago Press, 1973).

———. *Rahel Varnhagen: The Life of a Jewish Woman*. Rev. edition, trans. Richard and Clara Winston (New York: Harcourt Brace Jovanovich, 1974).

———. "Hannah Arendt on Hannah Arendt," in Melvyn A. Hill, ed., *Hannah Arendt: The Recovery of the Public World* (New York: St. Martin's Press, 1979).

———. *On Revolution* (New York: Penguin Books, 1990).

Argestinger, Amy. "Christian Coalition Courts Black Churches," *Washington Post*, May 11, 1997.

Atwood, Thomas C. "Through the Gall Darkly: Is the Christian Right Overconfident It Knows God's Will?" *Policy Review* 54 (Fall 1990): 44–52.

Au Allen, Susan. "Women and the Affirmative Action Revolution," *Vital Speeches of the Day* (New York: City News Publishing Company, April 1, 1997).

Aufderheide, Patricia. ed. *Beyond PC: Toward a Politics of Understanding* (St. Paul, Minn.: Graywolf Press, 1992).

Baldauf, Scott. "GOP Increasingly Speaks the Language of Hispanics," *Christian Science Monitor*, February 19, 1998.

Banks, William M. *The Black Intellectuals: Race and Responsibility in American Life* (New York: Norton, 1996).

Baraka, Amiri. "Malcolm as Ideology," in Joe Wood, ed., *Malcolm X: In Our Own Image* (New York: St. Martin's Press, 1992), 18–35.

Barnes, Fred. "The Minority Minority: Black Conservatives and White Republicans," *New Republic*, September 30, 1991, 22–23.

Barrett, Paul M. "A New Wave of Counterfeminist Is Providing Conservatism with a Sophisticated Female Face," *Wall Street Journal*, October 13, 1995.

Bauman, Robert E. *The Gentleman from Maryland: The Conscience of a Gay Conservative* (New York: Arbor House, 1986).

Bawer, Bruce. *A Place at the Table: The Gay Individual in American Society* (New York: Touchstone, 1993).

———, ed. *Beyond Queer: Challenging the Gay Left Orthodoxy* (New York: Free Press, 1996).

Bell, Daniel, ed. *The Radical Right: The New American Right.* Expanded and updated (New York: Anchor Books, 1964).

Bercovitch, Scavan. *The American Jeremiad* (Madison: University of Wisconsin Press, 1978).

Berlet, Chip, ed. *Eyes Right! Challenging the Right Wing Backlash* (Boston: South End Press, 1995).

Bernstein, Richard A. *Hannah Arendt and the Jewish Question* (Cambridge, Mass.: MIT Press, 1996).

Blumenthal, Sidney. *The Rise of the Counter-Establishment: From Conservative Ideology to Political Power* (New York: Harper & Row, 1988).

Bobbio, Norberto. *Left and Right: The Significance of a Political Distinction.* Trans. Allan Cameron (Chicago: University of Chicago Press, 1996).

Boles, Janet K. *The Politics of the Equal Rights Amendment: Conflict and the Decision Process* (New York: Longman, 1979).

Bolick, Clint. *Changing Course: Civil Rights at the Crossroads* (New Brunswick, N.J.: Transaction, 1988).

———. *In Whose Name? The Civil Rights Establishment Today* (Washington, D.C.: Capital Research Center, 1988).

———. *The Affirmative Action Fraud: Can We Restore the American Civil Rights Vision?* (Washington, D.C.: Cato Institute, 1996).

Bowen, William G., and Derek Curtis Bok. *The Shape of the River: Long-Term Consequences of Considering Race in College and University Admissions* (Princeton: Princeton University Press, 1998).

Bowie, Walter Jr. "It's Not Racism, It's Us." *Lincoln Review* 9:1 (Fall 1988): 39–48.

Branch, Taylor. *Parting the Waters: America in the King Years, 1954–63* (New York: Simon & Schuster, 1988).

Brennan, Mary G. *Turning Right in the Sixties: The Conservative Capture of the GOP* (Chapel Hill: University of North Carolina Press, 1995).

Brimelow, Peter. *Alien Nation: Common Sense about America's Immigration Disaster* (New York: Random House, 1996).

Brinkley, Alan. "The Problem of American Conservatism." *American Historical Review* 99 (April 1994): 409–429.

Brown, Susan Love. "Why Being Black Causes Confusion." *Lincoln Review* 2:4 (Winter–Spring 1982): 15–19.

Brownfeld, Allan C., and J. A. Parker. "Returning to the Goal of a 'Color Blind' American Society." *Lincoln Review* 2:2 (Summer 1981): 3–22.

Bruce, Steve. *The Rise and Fall of the New Christian Right: Conservative Protestant Politics in America, 1978–1988* (Oxford: Clarendon Press, 1990).

Buchanan, Patrick. *Right from the Beginning* (Boston: Little, Brown, 1988).

Buckley, William F. *Up from Liberalism* (New Rochelle, N.Y.: Arlington House, 1968).

———, ed. *Did You Ever See a Dream Walking?: American Conservative Thought in the Twentieth Century* (Indianapolis: Bobbs-Merrill, 1970).

Bull, Chris, and John Gallagher, *Perfect Enemies: The Religious Right, the Gay Movement, and the Politics of the 1990s* (New York: Crown, 1996).

Burkett, Elinor. *The Right Women: A Journey through the Heart of Conservative America* (New York: Scribner, 1998).

Canason, Joe, et al. "The Promise Keepers Are Coming: The Third Wave of the Religious Right." *Nation* 263 (October 7, 1996): 12–19.

Carnoy, Martin. *Faded Dreams: The Politics and Economics of Race in America* (Cambridge: Cambridge University Press, 1994).

Carter, Dan T. *From George Wallace to Newt Gingrich: Race in the Conservative Counterrevolution, 1963–1994* (Baton Rouge: Louisiana State University Press, 1996).

Carter, Stephen. *Reflections of an Affirmative Action Baby* (New York: Basic Books, 1992).

Chavez, Linda. *Out of the Barrio: Toward a New Politics of Hispanic Assimilation* (New York: Basic Books, 1991).

———. "The End of Bilingual Education," *Weekly Standard*, August 11, 1997.

Crawford, James. *Hold Your Tongue: Bilingualism and the Politics of "English Only"* (Reading, Mass.: Addison-Wesley, 1992).

Chrisman, Robert, and Robert L. Allen, eds. *Court of Appeal: The Black Community Speaks Out on the Racial and Sexual Politics of Clarence Thomas vs. Anita Hill* (New York: Ballantine, 1992).

"Christian Coalition Hires Black Liaison," *Christian Century*, April 24, 1996, 448.

Connerly, Ward. *Creating Equal: My Fight against Race Preferences* (San Francisco: Encounter Books, 2000).

Conover, Pamela Johnston, and Virginia Gary. *Feminism and the New Right: Conflict over the American Family* (New York: Praeger, 1983).

Conti, Joseph, and Brad Stetson. *Challenging the Civil Rights Establishment: Profiles of a New Black Vanguard* (Westport, Conn.: Praeger, 1993).

Cooper, Wayne F., ed. *The Passion of Claude McKay: Selected Poetry and Prose, 1912–1948* (New York: Schocken Books, 1973).

Crawford, Alan. *Thunder on the Right: The "New Right" and the Politics of Resentment* (New York: Pantheon, 1980).

Crouch, Stanley. *Notes from a Hanging Judge: Essays and Review, 1979–1989* (New York: Oxford University Press, 1990).

———. *The All-American Skin Game, or the Decoy of Race: The Long and Short of It, 1990–1994* (New York: Pantheon, 1995).

D'Agostino, Joseph A. "Conservative Spotlight: National Jewish Coalition," *Human Events* (August 7, 1998).

Decter, Midge. *The New Chastity and Other Arguments against Women's Liberation* (New York: Coward, McCann & Geoghegan, 1972).

Delbanco, Andrew. "The Political Incorrectness of Zora Neale Hurston." *Journal of Blacks in Higher Education* 18 (Winter 1997–1998): 103–107.

Delgado, Richard, and Jean Stefancic. *No Mercy: How Conservative Think Tanks and Foundations Changed America's Social Agenda* (Philadelphia: Temple University Press, 1996).

D'Emilio, John. *Sexual Politics, Sexual Communities: The Making of a Homosexual Minority in the United States, 1940–1970* (Chicago: University of Chicago Press, 1983).

de Toledano, Ralph. "The Poet Who Loved His People." *Lincoln Review* 3:2 (Fall 1982): 17–22.

———. "Claude McKay Revisited." *Lincoln Review* 7:4 (Spring 1987): 35–37.

Diamond, Sara. *Spiritual Warfare: The Politics of the Christian Right* (Boston: South End Press, 1989).

Diggins, John P. *Up from Communism: Conservative Odysseys in American Thought* (New York: Harper & Row, 1975).

Disch, Lisa. *Hannah Arendt and the Limits of Philosophy* (Ithaca, N.Y.: Cornell University Press, 1994).

Dorrien, Gary J. *The Neoconservative Mind: Politics, Culture, and the War of Ideology* (Philadelphia: Temple University Press, 1993).

D'Souza, Dinesh. *The End of Racism: Principles for a Multiracial Society* (New York: Free Press, 1995).

Dworkin, Andrea. *Right Wing Women* (New York: Perigee Books, 1983).

Edsall, Thomas Byrne, with Mary D. Edsall. *Chain Reaction: The Impact of Race, Rights and Taxes on American Politics* (New York: Norton, 1991).

———. "Gay Rights and the Christian Right," *Washington Post*, August 10, 1992.

Ehrman, John. *The Rise of Neoconservatism: Intellectuals and Foreign Affairs, 1945–1994* (New Haven: Yale University Press, 1995.

Evans, Sara, and Harry Boyte. *Free Spaces: The Sources of Democratic Change in America* (New York: Harper & Row, 1986).

Faludi, Susan. *Backlash: The Undeclared War against Women* (New York: Crown, 1991).

Farber, David. "The Silent Majority and Talk about Revolution," in Farber, ed.,

The Sixties: From Memory to History (Chapel Hill: University of North Carolina Press, 1994), 291–316.

Falwell, Jerry. *Strength for the Journey: An Autobiography* (New York: Simon & Schuster, 1987).

Faryna, Stan, et al., eds. *Black and Right: The Bold New Voice of Black Conservatives in America* (Westport, Conn.: Praeger, 1997).

Felsenthal, Carol. *The Sweetheart of the Silent Majority: The Biography of Phyllis Schlafly* (Garden City, N.Y.: Doubleday, 1981).

Foege, Alec. *The Empire God Built: Inside Pat Robertson's Media Machine* (New York: Wiley, 1996).

Foley, Neil. "Becoming Hispanic: Mexican Americans and the Faustian Pact with Whiteness." *Reflexiones* (1997): 53–70.

Fong, Matt. "APA Roundtable: The Case for George W. Bush," *Asian Week*, July 21, 1999.

Foster, Ezola. *What's Right for All Americans: A Fearless Los Angeles Schoolteacher Challenges the Black Political Establishment* (Waco, Tex.: WRS, 1995).

Franklin, Robert Michael. *Liberating Visions: Human Fulfillment and Social Justice in African American Thought* (Minneapolis: Fortress Press, 1990).

Friedman, Murray. "The New Black Intellectuals." *Commentary* 69:6 (June 1980): 46–52.

Gaines, Kevin K. *Uplifting the Race: Black Leadership, Politics and Culture in the Twentieth Century* (Chapel Hill: University of North Carolina Press, 1996).

Gardiner, Steve L. "Promises to Keep: The Christian Men's Movement." *Dignity Report* 3:4 (Fall 1996): 1–9.

Garvey, Amy Jacques. *Garvey and Garveyism* (New York: Octagon Books, 1986).

Genovese, Eugene D. *The Southern Tradition: The Achievement and Limitations of an American Conservatism* (Cambridge, Mass.: Harvard University Press, 1994).

Giddings, Paula. *When and Where I Enter: The Impact of Black Women on Race and Sex in America* (New York: Bantam Books, 1985).

Gilder, George. *Wealth and Poverty* (New York: Basic Books, 1981).

———. *Men and Marriage* (Gretna, La.: Pelican, 1986).

Glazer, Nathan. *Affirmative Discrimination: Ethnic Inequality and Public Policy* (New York: Basic Books, 1975).

———. "In Defense of Preference," *New Republic*, April 6, 1998, 18–21, 24–25.

Greider, William, and Harold Logan. "Why Blacks Are Turning Conservative." *Conservative Digest* (October 1978): 28–34.

Green, John C., et al., eds. *Religion and the Culture Wars: Dispatches from the Front* (Lanham, Md.: Rowman & Littlefield, 1996).

Grossberg, Lawrence. *We Gotta Get Out of This Place: Popular Conservatism and Postmodern Culture* (Berkeley: University of California Press, 1994).

Gunderson, Steven, and Rob Morris, with Bruce Bawer. *House and Home* (New York: Dutton, 1996).

Gutierrez, David G. *Walls and Mirrors: Mexican Americans, Mexican Immigrants, and the Politics of Ethnicity* (Berkeley: University of California Press, 1995).

Gutierrez, Ramon A. "Lusting for Power: Richard Rodriguez and the Political Language of White Men," in Renate von Bardeleben, ed., *Gender, Self, and Society*. Proceedings of the Fourth International Conference on Hispanic Cultures of the United States (Frankfurt, Germany: Peter Lang, 1993), 383–393.

Gutman, Amy, ed. *Multiculturalism* (Princeton: Princeton University Press, 1994).

Hall, Stuart. "The Toad in the Garden: Thatcherism among the Theorists," in Cary Nelson and Lawrence Grossberg, eds., *Marxism and the Interpretation of Culture* (Urbana: University of Illinois Press, 1988), 35–57.

Harrington, Michael. *Toward a Democratic Left: A Radical Program for a New Majority* (New York: Macmillan, 1968).

———. "The New Class and the Left," in B. Bruce-Briggs, ed., *The New Class?* (New Brunswick, N.J.: Transaction, 1979).

Harris, Cheryl. "Whiteness as Property." *Harvard Law Review* 106:8 (June 1993): 1709–1771.

Hartz, Louis. *The Liberal Tradition in America: An Interpretation of American Political Thought Since the Revolution* (New York: Harcourt, Brace & World, 1955).

Haskins, Ethelbert W. *The Crisis in Afro-American Leadership* (Buffalo, N.Y.: Prometheus Books, 1988).

Hay, Harry. *Radically Gay: Gay Liberation in the Words of Its Founder*, ed. Will Roscoe (Boston: Beacon Press, 1996).

Hellman, Rick. "Jewish GOP." *Jewish Chronicle*, May 30, 1997.

Hemenway, Robert. *Zora Neale Hurston: A Literary Biography* (Urbana: University of Illinois Press, 1977).

Hewlett, Sylvia Ann. *A Lesser Life: The Myth of Women's Liberation in America* (New York: William Morrow, 1986).

Himmelstein, Jerome L. *To the Right: The Transformation of American Conservatism* (Berkeley: University of California Press, 1990).

Horowitz, David A. *Beyond Left and Right: Insurgency and the Establishment* (Urbana: University of Illinois Press, 1997).

——— and Peter Collier. *Destructive Generation: Second Thoughts about the Sixties* (New York: Summit Books, 1989).

——— and Peter Collier, eds. *Second Thoughts: Former Radicals Look Back at the Sixties* (Lanham, Md.: Madison Books, 1989).

———. *Second Thoughts about Race in America* (Lanham, Md.: Madison Books, 1991).

Howard-Pitney, David. *The Afro-American Jeremiad: Appeals for Justice in America* (Philadelphia: Temple University Press, 1990).

Hu, Arthur. "Conservative Asian Voters," *Asian Week*, January 3, 1992.

Hurston, Zora Neale. "Mourner's Bench, Communist Line: Why the Negro Won't Buy Communism." *American Legion Magazine* 50 (June 1951): 14–15, 55–60.

―――. "A Negro Voter Sizes Up Taft," *Saturday Evening Post*, December 8, 1951.

―――. "How It Feels to Be a Colored Me," reprinted in Alice Walker, ed., *I Love Myself When I Am Laughing . . . and Then Again When I Am Looking Mean and Impressive: A Zora Neale Hurston Reader* (New York: Feminist Press, 1979), 152–155.

Ingersoll, William. "Reminiscences of George S. Schuyler." Oral History Research Office, Columbia University, 1962.

Ingraham, Laura. "Enter, Women," *New York Times*, April 16, 1995.

Ireland, Doug. "The 'Black Conservative' Con: Alan Keyes Does the Hustle." *Nation* 261 (October 30, 1995): 500–503.

James, Kay Coles. *Never Forget* (Grand Rapids, Mich.: Zondervan, 1992).

Kauffman, Bill. "Zora Neale Hurston and Clarence Thomas." *Lincoln Review* 10:4 (Fall 1991–Winter 1992): 11–14.

Kazin. Michael. "The Grass-Roots Right: New Histories of U.S. Conservatism." *American Historical Review* 97 (February 1992): 136–155.

Kelley, Robin D. G. *Yo' Mama's Disfunktional! Fighting the Culture Wars in Urban America* (Boston: Beacon Press, 1997).

Kennedy, Randall. "My Race Problem—And Ours." *Atlantic Monthly* (May 1997): 55–66.

―――. *Race, Crime, and the Law* (New York: Pantheon, 1997).

Kersten, Katherine. "What Do Women Want? A Conservative Feminist Manifesto." *Policy Review* 56 (Spring 1991): 4–15.

Keyes, Alan. "My Race for the Senate." *Policy Review* 48 (Spring 1989): 2–8.

―――. *Masters of the Dream: The Strength and Betrayal of Black America* (New York: William Morrow, 1995).

Keyes, William. "ANC: African Terrorists." *Lincoln Review* 6:2 (Fall 1985): 31–35.

―――. "Blacks and Republicans." *Conservative Digest* (July–August 1989): 47–49.

Kilson, Martin. "Anatomy of Black Conservatism." *Transition* 59 (1994): 4–19.

Kinnard, Cynthia D., ed. *Antifeminism in American Thought: An Annotated Bibliography* (Boston: G. K. Hall, 1986).

Kintz, Linda. *Between Jesus and the Market: The Emotions That Matter in Right-Wing America* (Durham, N.C.: Duke University Press, 1997).

Kirk, Russell, ed. *The Portable Conservative Reader* (New York: Penguin, 1982).

Klatch, Rebecca. *Women of the New Right* (Philadelphia: Temple University Press, 1987).

LaHaye, Beverly. *The Spirit-Controlled Woman* (Eugene, Ore.: Harvest House, 1976).

Lasch, Christopher. *The True and Only Heaven: Progress and Its Critics* (New York: Norton, 1991).

Lawson, Bill E. *The Underclass Question* (Philadelphia: Temple University Press, 1992).

Levin, Michael. *Feminism and Freedom* (New Brunswick, N.J.: Transaction, 1987).

Lewis, David Levering. *W. E. B. Du Bois: Biography of a Race, 1868–1919* (New York: Holt, 1994).

Liebman, Marvin. *Coming Out Conservative, An Autobiography: A Founder of the Modern Conservative Movement Speaks Out on Personal Freedom, Homophobia, and Hate Politics* (San Francisco: Chronicle Books, 1992).

Lind, Michael S. *Up from Conservatism: Why the Right Is Wrong for America* (New York: Free Press, 1996).

———. "The End of the Rainbow: The Poverty of Racial Politics and the Future of Liberalism." *Mother Jones* 22 (September/October 1997): 39–43.

Lipsitz, George. "The Possessive Investment in Whiteness: Racialized Social Democracy and the 'White' Problem in American Studies." *American Quarterly* 47:3 (September 1995): 369–387.

Logan, Harold. "Why Blacks Are Turning Conservative." *Conservative Digest* (October 1978): 28–34.

Loury, Glenn. *One by One from the Inside Out: Essays and Reviews on Race and Responsibility in American Life* (New York: Free Press, 1995).

———. "Conservative Isolate Black Intellectuals," *New York Times*, November 30, 1997.

———. "Unequalized," *New Republic*, April 6, 1998, 10–11.

Luker, Kristin. *Abortion and the Politics of Motherhood* (Berkeley: University of California Press, 1984).

Macedo, Stephen. "Douglass to Thomas," *New Republic*, September 30, 1991, 23–24.

Malveaux, Julianne. "Why Are the Black Conservatives All Men?" *MS* (March–April 1991): 60–61.

Manning, Christel J. *God Gave Us the Right: Conservative Catholic, Evangelical Protestant, and Orthodox Jewish Women Grapple with Feminism* (New Brunswick, N.J.: Rutgers University Press, 1999).

Marable, Manning. "Black Reaganism: A Rogue's Gallery," *Washington DC Afro-American*, April 24, 1982.

———. *W. E. B. Du Bois: Black Radical Democrat* (Boston: Twayne, 1986).

———. "Black Fundamentalism: Louis Farrakhan and the Politics of Conservative Black Nationalism." *Dissent* 45 (Spring 1998): 69–76.

Marshner, Connaught C. *The New Traditional Women* (Washington, D.C.: Free Congress Research and Education Foundation, 1982).

McCloskey, Robert Green. *American Conservatism in the Age of Enterprise, 1865–1910* (New York: Harper & Row, 1964).

McDowell, Winston Charles. "Ideology of Black Entrepreneurship and Its Impact on the Development of Black Harlem, 1930–1964," Ph.D. diss., University of Minnesota, 1996.

McLean, Nancy. "White Women and Klan Violence in the 1920s: Agency, Complicity, and the Politics of Women's History." *Gender & History* 3 (Autumn 1991): 285–303.

Meier, August. *Negro Thought in America, 1880–1915: Racial Ideologies in the Age of Booker T. Washington* (Ann Arbor: University of Michigan Press, 1963).

Meyerson, Adam. "Manna 2 Society: The Growing Conservatism of Black America." *Policy Review* 68 (Spring 1994): 4–6.

Miller, Kelly. *Radicals and Conservatives and Other Essays on the Negro in America* (1908; New York: Schocken Books, 1968).

Morris, Aldon, and Carol McClurg Mueller, eds. *Frontiers in Social Movement Theory* (New Haven: Yale University Press, 1992).

Morrison, Toni, ed. *Race-ing Justice, En-gendering Power: Essays on Anita Hill, Clarence Thomas and the Construction of Social Reality* (New York: Pantheon, 1992).

———. *Playing in the Dark: Whiteness and the American Literary Imagination* (New York: Vintage, 1993).

———. "On the Backs of Blacks," *Time* (Fall 1993): 57.

Moses, Wilson Jeremiah. *Black Messiahs and Uncle Toms: Social and Literary Manipulations of a Religious Myth.* Revised edition (University Park: Pennsylvania State University Press, 1993).

Nguyen, Lan. "An Inconvenient Woman," *A Magazine*, March 31, 1998.

Niebuhr, Gustav. "Christian Coalition Sees Recruiting Possibilities among Catholics," *New York Times*, October 7, 1995.

Novak, Michael. *The Rise of the Unmeltable Ethnic: Politics and Culture in the Seventies* (New York: Macmillan, 1972).

Omi, Michael, and Howard Winart. *Racial Formation in the United States from the 1960s to the 1980s.* Second edition (New York: Routlege, 1994).

Parker, Star, with Lorenzo Benet. *Pimps, Whores, and Welfare Brats: From Welfare Cheat to Conservative Messenger, The Autobiography of Star Parker* (New York: Pocket Books, 1997).

Patterson, Orlando. *The Ordeal of Integration: Progress and Resentment in America's "Racial" Crisis* (Washington, D.C.: Civitas/Counterpoint, 1997).

Pauken, Thomas W. "Plantation Politics, White Liberal Style." *Lincoln Review* 3:1 (Summer 1982): 47–50.

Peplow, Michael W. *George S. Schuyler* (Boston: Twayne, 1980).

Persinos, John. "Has the Christian Coalition Taken Over the Republican Party?" *Campaigns and Elections* 15 (September 1994): 20–24.

Petchesky, Rosalind Pollack. "Antiabortion, Antifeminism, and the Rise of the New Right." *Feminist Studies* 7:2 (Summer 1981): 207–246.

Phillips, Kevin. *The Emerging Republican Majority* (Garden City, N.Y.: Anchor, 1970).

———. *Post-Conservative America: People, Politics and Ideology in a Time of Crisis* (New York: Vintage 1983).

Pinkerton, James. "A Conservative Argument for Gay Marriage," *Los Angeles Times*, June 3, 1993.

Powers, Richard H. "An American Tragedy: The Transformation of Booker T. Washington from Hero to Whipping Boy." *Lincoln Review* 11:1 (Winter–Spring 1993): 19–40.

Price, Joyce. "No 'Angry Agenda,' No Feminists at New Women's Quarterly," *Washington Times*, September 13, 1995.

Reed, Adolph, Jr. "The Descent of Black Conservatism." *Progressive* 61 (October 1997): 18–20.

Reed, Ralph, Jr. "Casting a Wider Net: Religious Conservative Move beyond Abortion and Homosexuality." *Policy Review* 65 (Summer 1993): 31–35.

———. *Politically Incorrect: The Emerging Faith Factor in American Politics* (Dallas: Word Books, 1994).

"Remembering S. B. Fuller." *Lincoln Review* 9:1 (Fall 1988): 59–62.

Rich, Frank. "Jews and the Post-Reed Religious Right," *New York Times*, January 14, 1998.

Robbins, Bruce, ed. *The Phantom Public Sphere* (Minneapolis: University of Minnesota Press, 1993).

Roberts, Ronald Suresh. *Clarence Thomas and the Tough Love Crowd: Counterfeit Heroes and Unhappy Truths* (New York: New York University Press, 1995).

Robinson, Pearl. "Whither the Future of Blacks in the Republican Party?" *Political Science Quarterly* 97:2 (Summer 1982): 207–231.

Rodriguez, Richard. *The Hunger of Memory: The Education of Richard Rodriguez, An Autobiography* (New York: Bantam Books, 1983).

———. *Days of Obligation: An Argument with My Mexican Father* (New York: Penguin, 1992).

Roediger, David. *The Wages of Whiteness: Race and the Making of the American Working Class* (London: Verso Press, 1991).

Rogin, Michael P. *Ronald Reagan, The Movie: And Other Episodes in Political Demonology* (Berkeley: University of California Press, 1987).

Roiphe, Katie. *The Morning After: Sex, Fear, and Feminism* (Boston: Little, Brown, 1993).

Rosenfeld, Megan. "Not NOW Dear: The Conservative Alternative of Concerned Women for America," *Washington Post*, September 26, 1992.

———. "Feminist Fatales," *Washington Post*, March 26, 1994.

Rossiter, Clinton. *Conservatism in America: The Thankless Persuasion.* Second edition (New York: Knopf, 1962).

Saloma, John S. *Ominous Politics: The New Conservative Labyrinth* (New York: Hill & Wang, 1984).

San Miguel, Guadalupe. *"Let All of Them Take Heed": Mexican Americans and the Campaign for Educational Equality in Texas, 1910–1981* (Austin: University of Texas Press, 1987).

Schneider, Gregory L. *Cadres for Conservatives: Young Americans for Freedom and the Rise of the Contemporary Right* (New York: New York University Press, 1999).

Schlafly, Phyllis. *The Positive Woman* (New Rochelle, N.Y.: Arlington House, 1977).

———. "ERA Means Unisex Society." *Conservative Digest* 4 (July 1978): 14–16.

Schuyler, George S. *Black and Conservative: The Autobiography of George S. Schuyler* (New York: Arlington House, 1966).

Seelye, Katherine Q. "Gay Voters Finding G.O.P. Newly Receptive to Support," *New York Times*, August 11, 1999.

Skerry, Peter. "Christian Schools versus the IRS." *Public Interest* 61 (Fall 1980): 18–41.

Smith, John David. *Black Judas: William Hannibal Thomas and Political History* (Atlanta: University of Georgia Press, 2000).

Sommers, Christina Hoff. *Who Stole Feminism? How Women Have Betrayed Women* (New York: Touchstone, 1994).

Sowell, Thomas. *Ethnic America: A History* (New York: Basic Books, 1981).

———. *Civil Rights: Rhetoric or Reality?* (New York: Quill, 1984).

———. *A Conflict of Visions* (New York: William Morrow, 1987).

Stacey, Judith. "The New Conservative Feminism." *Feminist Studies* 9:3 (Fall 1983): 559–583.

Steele, Shelby. *The Content of Our Character: A New Vision of Race in America* (New York: Harper Perennial, 1991).

———. *A Dream Deferred: The Second Betrayal of Black Freedom in America* (New York: Harper/Collins, 1998).

Steinberg, Stephen. *Turning Back: The Retreat from Racial Justice in American Thought* (Boston: Beacon, 1995).

Steinfels, Peter. *The Neoconservatives: The Men Who Are Changing America's Politics* (New York: Touchstone, 1979).

Sugrue, Thomas J. "Crabgrass-Roots Politics: Race, Rights, and the Reaction against Liberalism in the Urban North, 1940–1964." *Journal of American History* 82 (September 1995): 551–578.

Sullivan, Andrew. *Virtually Normal: An Argument about Homosexuality* (New York: Knopf, 1995).

Tafel, Richard. *Party Crasher: A Gay Republican Challenges Politics as Usual* (New York: Simon & Schuster, 1999).

Talalay, Kathryn. *Composition in Black and White: The Life of Philippa Schuyler* (New York: Oxford University Press, 1995).

Thomas, Carl, and Ed Dobson. *Blinded by Might: Can the Religious Right Save America?* (Grand Rapids, Mich.: Zondervan, 1999).

Thomas, Clarence. "Thomas Sowell and the Heritage of Lincoln: Ethnicity and the Individual." *Lincoln Review* 8:2 (Winter 1988): 7–20.

———. "No Room at the Inn." *Policy Review* 58 (Fall 1991): 72–78.

Vaid, Urvashi. *Virtual Equality: The Mainstreaming of Gay and Lesbian Liberation* (New York: Anchor Books, 1995).

Van Den Haag, Ernest. "The War between Paleos and Neos." *National Review* 41:3 (February 24, 1989): 21–23.

Viguerie, Richard A. *The New Right: We're Ready to Lead* (Falls Church, Va.: Viguerie Company, 1980).

Wald, Alan. *The New York Intellectuals: The Rise and Decline of the Anti-Stalinist Left from the 1930s to the 1980s* (Chapel Hill: University of North Carolina Press, 1987).

Walker, Juliet E. K. *The History of Black Business in America: Capitalism, Race and Entrepreneurship* (London: Prentice Hall International, 1998).

Walton, Hanes, Jr. *Black Republicans: The Politics of the Black and Tan* (New York: Scarecrow Press, 1975).

———. "Defending the Indefensible: The African American Conservative Client Spokespersons of the Reagan-Bush Era," *Black Scholar* (Fall 1994): 46–50.

Walzer, Michael. *Interpretation and Social Criticism* (Cambridge, Mass.: Harvard University Press, 1987).

Washington, Booker T. *Up from Slavery* (1901; New York: Dover Press, 1995).

Washington, James Melvin, ed. *A Testament of Hope: The Essential Writings of Martin Luther King, Jr.* (San Francisco: Harper & Row, 1986).

Watson, Justin. *The Christian Coalition: Dreams of Restoration, Demands for Recognition* (New York: St. Martin's Press, 1997).

Weaver, Clarence Mason. *It's OK to Leave the Plantation: A Journey from Liberalism to Conservatism* (New York: Reeder Books, 1996).

West, Cornel. "Assessing Black Neoconservatism." In Cornel West, *Prophetic Fragments* (Trenton, N.J.: Africa World Press, 1988), 55–63.

West, Hollie I. "A Black Biting Bircher." *Washington Post*, September 6, 1973.

Weyrich, Paul. "Getting Serious about Blacks." *Conservative Digest* (July–August 1989): 11–14.

———. "Building a Moral Majority." *Conservative Digest* 5 (August 1979): 18–19.

White, E. Frances. "Africa on My Mind: Gender, Counter Discourse and African American Nationalism," reprinted in Beverly Guy-Sheftall, ed. *Words of Fire: An Anthology of African American Feminist Thought* (New York: Free Press, 1995), 504–524.

White, Mel. *Stranger at the Gate: To Be Gay and Christian in America* (New York: Simon & Schuster, 1994).

———. "The Rhetoric of Intolerance: An Open Letter to Pat Robertson." Video recording. (Newport Beach: Justice Report, 1996).

Williams, Armstrong. *Beyond Blame: How We Can Succeed by Breaking the Dependency Barrier* (New York: Free Press, 1995).

Williams, Harry McKinley, Jr. "When Black Is Right: The Life and Writings of George S. Schuyler," Ph.D. diss., Brown University, 1988.

Williams, Walter E. *The State against Blacks* (New York: McGraw-Hill, 1982).

———. *Do the Right Thing: The People's Economist Speaks* (Stanford: Hoover Institute Press, 1995).

———. "A Tragic Vision of the Black Problem." *American Quarterly* 47:3 (September 1995): 409–415.

Wills, Garry. *Under God: Religion and American Politics* (New York: Simon & Schuster, 1990).

Wittman, Carl. "Refugees from Amerika," *San Francisco Free Press*, December 22–January 7, 1970.

Woodson, Robert. *On the Road to Economic Freedom: An Agenda for Black Progress* (Washington, D.C.: Regnery-Gateway, 1987).

Wortham, Anne. "The New Ethnicity versus Individualist Pluralism," *Lincoln Review* 4:3 (Winter 1984): 19–30.

———. *The Other Side of Racism* (Columbus: Ohio State University Press, 1980).

Wright, Elizabeth. "American Blacks and the Cultural Facts of Life," *Lincoln Review* 3:2 (Fall 1982): 39–42.

———. "Cashing In on the 'Black Problem,' or Race and Poverty as an Industry." *Issues and Views* (Fall 1989): 9–13.

———. "The True Legacy of Malcolm X: Are We Ready for His Message?" *Issues and Views* (Winter 1989): 1–4.

———. "Our Cunning Talented Tenth: A Self-Interested Middle Class Hinders Black Economic Progress." *Issues and Views* (Spring 1990): 20–22.

———. "The Race and Poverty Industry: The Next Generation." *Issues and Views* (Fall 1990): 13–16.

———. "Without Commerce and Industry, The People Perish: Marcus Garvey's Gospel of Prosperity." *Issues and Views* (Spring 1991): 16–18.

———. "Booker T. Washington: Our Greatest Warrior." *Issues and Views* (Spring 1992): 1–4.

———. "In the Name of Civil Rights: Homosexuals Remake Society." *Issues and Views* (Spring 1996): 3–4, 10, 12–14.

Young, John E. "Christian Coalition Revamps Agenda to Reach Out to Inner Cities," *Washington Post*, April 24, 1997.

Index

Index

Index

Civil Rights Act (1991), 79
civil rights establishment, 18–19; black conservatives on, 64–67, 90; Dinesh D'Souza, definition of, 59–60; enforcement of ideological orthodoxy, 18; and liberal establishment, 60–61
civil rights movement, 12; 1954–1965 phase of versus post–1965 phase of, 48–49, 56, 59; increasing irrelevance of, 56
Clinton, Bill, 157, 169; and homosexuals in the military, 162
Clinton, Hillary, 157
Collier, Peter, 81
Colorado anti-homosexual ballot initiative, 160–161
Colorado Black Republican Forum, 173
Colorado for Family Values, 161
color blindness, 3, 50, 51, 53, 174; criticism of, 53–54; John Harlan on, 179; Martin L. King, used to justify, 49; Julius Lester on, 179; and liberals, rejection of, 56; Glenn Loury on, 178–180; and "whiteness," 54
Commentary, 11, 84; and National Review, 61; and New Left, war on, 61–62
Communist Party, 45, 110, 111, 117
Concerned Americans for Individual Rights, 10
Concerned Women for America (CWA), 5, 8, 74, 143, 147, 160, 170; as grass-roots organization, 75; and National Organization for Women, opposition to, 74–75
Congress of Racial Equality, 9, 142
Connerly, Ward: and CCRI, 50; and homosexual conservatives, 12, 142; on Martin L. King, 50–51
conservatism: and American conservative tradition, 15; and ethnocentrism, 13; foundations of, 10; and gender, xii; Louis Hartz on, x; and homophobia, 13; Russell Kirk, definition of, x–xi; and race, xi-xii, 13; and States' Rights, xi-xii; transformation of, 138; and xenophobia, xii
Council of Conservative Citizens, 163
Crenshaw, Kimberle, 53
Crittenden, Danielle, 5
Crouch, Stanley, 13, 115; and "blackness," critique of, 82; on Ralph Ellison, 30; as fellow traveler, 13; on Martin L. King, 82
Crummell, Alexander, 41
Crusade for Justice, 68

culture of poverty, 90, 92; culture of virtue, versus, 94
culture wars, 87, 127, 157

Dartmouth Review, 87
Daughters of the American Revolution, 149
Decter, Midge, xiii, 4; and Committee for the Free World, 10; on feminism, 84; and Heritage Foundation, 10
Defense of Marriage Act, 164
Delany, Martin, 41
Destiny Magazine, 33
Disch, Lisa, 124
Dobson, Ed, 170
Dobson, James, 160, 170
Doggett, John, and Anita Hill-Thomas controversy, 66
Doggett, Teresa: on civil rights establishment, 66–67; and Republican Party, 66
Dorrien, Gary, critique of neoconservatism, 94–95
Dos Passos, John, 118
Douglass, Frederick, 30, 40, 49, 54, 109n. 7
Douglass Policy Institute, 173
D'Souza, Dinesh, 18, 181; on "acting white," 91, 97; on black cultural pathology, 91, 92, 93; on civil rights establishment, 18, 59–60; criticisms of, 91; on Zora Neale Hurston, 43; Illiberal Education, 88; on Washington-DuBois debate, 36
DuBois, W. E. B.: and Booker T. Washington, 35–38; and organic conservatism, 37
Dworkin, Andrea, 148
Dworkin, Ronald, 122

Eagle Forum, 74, 143, 161
Eisenman, Athena, 173
Ellison, Ralph, 30; and Crouch, used by, 30; and Shelby Steele, used by, 192n. 20
Emerson, Ralph Waldo, 99
Epstein, Joseph, 76
Equal Employment Opportunities Commission, 6, 18
equality of opportunity versus equality of results, 56–57; Thomas Sowell on, 57
Equal Rights Amendment (ERA), 16, 74, 147–149, 152; and Religious Right, 84; and Republican Party, 84; and Phyllis Schlafly, 78, 147, 149; and George Wallace, 148–149
ethnocentrism, 13, 158

Index

Wright, Richard, and *Black Boy*, 108

Young Americans for Freedom, 6, 45, 87, 111, 118, 152, 185n. 10

Yzaguirre, Raul, and criticism of U.S. English, 69

Zapanta, Al, 4

About the Author

Angela D. Dillard is Assistant Professor of History and Politics at the Gallatin School of Individualized Study at New York University.